"I am obsessed with this book! The prose is riveting. The blend of disparate methods is spectacular. The sheer adventure of student organizers fanning out across the country in a manner reminiscent of Freedom Summer will keep you turning the pages. Taken together, the portrait wrought is simply devastating. Walmart not only demands your labor and your loyalty, it claims your pride and strips you of dignity."

—KATHRYN EDIN, COAUTHOR OF *$2 A DAY: THE ART OF LIVING ON VIRTUALLY NOTHING IN AMERICA*

"Walmart—the largest U.S. employer—is a symbol for high inequality in America. Its many shop-floor employees are paid as little as possible and have never shared in the huge success and profits of the company. Why can't Walmart workers get a bigger share of the pie they helped create? This book, based on extensive interviews with Walmart workers, helps us understand why a job at Walmart might be the least bad option for many, how workers make sense of their jobs, and the challenges of organizing work at Walmart. *Working for Respect* is essential reading for a rich sociological understanding of the struggles of low-paid workers pitted against all-powerful corporations in America today."

—EMMANUEL SAEZ, UNIVERSITY OF CALIFORNIA, BERKELEY

"How do people find and flex their own power to improve their workplaces? What lessons can all of us learn from dogged and creative efforts to organize workers at Walmart, the biggest private employer in the world? What kinds of relationships between organizers and their communities are most likely to lead to organizing breakthroughs? *Working for Respect* is a gripping read—a thoughtful, perceptive, and accessible work that takes a multilayered approach, from in-depth interviews with Walmart workers to brain scans to a crash course in front-line organizing and beyond. This is a book for students of organizing, for academics interested in helping to counter rampant economic inequality, and for anyone who cares about winning material gains and respect for all workers in the age of Trump."

—ANNA GALLAND, EXECUTIVE DIRECTOR, MOVEON.ORG

"Working for Respect is an extraordinary book, both in its deft and original intertwining of multiple research methods and in the insights it generates."

—ERIK OLIN WRIGHT, AUTHOR OF *ENVISIONING REAL UTOPIAS*

"Working for Respect is at once a brilliant analysis of the lives of Walmart workers and an original effort to bridge the tension between scholarly work and activism. Along the way, Reich and Bearman raise the bar for mixed-method research in the social sciences."

—MITCHELL DUNEIER, MAURICE P. DURING PROFESSOR OF SOCIOLOGY, PRINCETON UNIVERSITY

"Working for Respect is an engaging read that bristles with fresh insights into both the experience of low-wage service sector work and the dilemmas facing the labor movement. It offers an ethnography of what the authors dub 'Walmartism,' as well as an argument about the ways in which social ties centered on trust have the potential to jumpstart social change. A must-read for any sociologist of labor."

—RUTH MILKMAN, CUNY GRADUATE CENTER

"With *Working for Respect*, Reich and Bearman issue a rare invitation: to go with them to Walmart, to listen with them to the workers and to the managers who roam the stores, to take in the culture of low-wage work in America, and also to listen to the students who participated in what became the Summer for Respect. This is a gripping book about the relationship between social ties and social change, remarkable for its intelligence and the subtlety of its distinctions. We learn that in the end it is trust rather than good feeling that inspires collective action for social change."

—CAROL GILLIGAN, AUTHOR OF *IN A DIFFERENT VOICE*

WORKING
FOR RESPECT

THE MIDDLE RANGE

EDITED BY PETER S. BEARMAN AND SHAMUS R. KHAN

The Middle Range, coined and represented by Columbia sociologist Robert Merton, is a style of work that treats theory and observation as a single endeavor. This approach has yielded the most significant advances in the social sciences over the last half century; it is a defining feature of Columbia's department. This book series seeks to capitalize on the impact of approaches of the middle range and to solidify the association between Columbia University and its Press.

The Conversational Firm: Rethinking Bureaucracy in the Age of Social Media, Catherine J. Turco

WORKING FOR RESPECT

COMMUNITY
AND CONFLICT
AT WALMART

ADAM REICH
AND PETER BEARMAN

Columbia University Press
New York

Columbia University Press gratefully acknowledges the generous support for this book provided by Publisher's Circle member Harriet Zuckerman.

Columbia University Press
Publishers Since 1893
New York   Chichester, West Sussex
cup.columbia.edu

Copyright © 2018 Columbia University Press
Paperback edition, 2021
All rights reserved

Library of Congress Cataloging-in-Publication Data
Names: Reich, Adam D. (Adam Dalton), 1981- author. |
Bearman, Peter S.,1956– author.
Title: Working for respect : community and conflict at Walmart /
Adam Reich and Peter Bearman.
Description: New York : Columbia University Press, [2018] |
Includes bibliographical references and index.
Identifiers: LCCN 2018003817| ISBN 9780231188425 (cloth) |
ISBN 9780231188432 (pbk.) | ISBN 9780231547826 (e-book)
Subjects: LCSH: Wal-Mart (Firm)—Employees. | Discount houses (Retail trade)—
United States—Management—Case studies. | Retail trade—Moral
and ethical aspects—United States. | Corporations—Moral
and ethical aspects—United States.
Classification: LCC HF5429.215.U6 R45 2018 | DDC 331.7/613811490973—dc23
LC record available at https://lccn.loc.gov/2018003817

Cover design: Milenda Nan Ok Lee
Cover photo: Chris Hondros / © Getty Images

Peter dedicates this book to Sophie,
Adam to his parents.

CONTENTS

FIGURES

ACKNOWLEDGMENTS

Our debts to others on this project start sometime around the end of January 2014. At the time, Adam had been collaborating with Audra Makuch, then working for the United Food and Commercial Workers International Union (UFCW) as the executive assistant to the regional director, on a project designed to study the structure of social change activism in New York City. One afternoon, as Audra and Adam were driving to an interview on the East Side of New York, they got to talking about how that summer would be the fiftieth anniversary of the Freedom Summer campaign. It occurred to both of them that a project that got college students into the field, organizing on behalf of people working in low-wage jobs, might be able to make an impact.

Walmart seemed the obvious target, and although Audra wasn't working on Walmart, she knew Andrea Dehlendorf, then the field director of the Organization United for Respect at Walmart (OUR Walmart), a voluntary association of current and former Walmart associates. OUR Walmart is not a labor union, in that it is not seeking to have Walmart recognize or bargain with the organization as a representative of Walmart's employees. As its codirector Dan

Schlademan put it, "Labor has given up lots of its power by living inside the idea that the only way workers could have a union is if the employer permits it or the government blesses it. . . . We weren't going to wait for the government or Walmart. The goal now is a worker-supported, sustainable organization of and for workers." At the time we came into contact with OUR Walmart, it received funding and staff support from the UFCW. It is now an independent project of the New World Foundation.

Andrea began working with OUR Walmart after having spent years organizing hotel workers in Las Vegas, janitors in Los Angeles, and airport, security and other service workers across California. She was a good choice to lead OUR Walmart's organizing effort, as she had been a key figure in the some of the most successful organizing efforts of the previous two decades.

Sometime in February, Audra and Adam were able to get on Andrea's schedule. They made the pitch for a student engagement program modeled after Freedom Summer. Andrea was already planning a summer organizing program and had already come up with a catchy phrase: the Summer for Respect. It seemed like an easy fit. Andrea, and the other leaders of the OUR Walmart campaign, had long realized that new strategies were critical to building a base of people willing to challenge the country's largest corporate employer. A program modeled after Freedom Summer—also a new strategy for the time—fit the bill.

Throughout the summer project and since, Audra, Andrea, and a whole host of OUR Walmart staff and worker-leaders—Dan Schlademan, Eric Schlein, Eddie Iny, Angela Williamson, Girshriela Green, Cindy Murray, Colby Harris, to name only a few—have been tremendously supportive of the work we have been doing. It is rare for a labor organization to be as open and interested in academic work as we have found OUR Walmart to be, which we think is a testament to these leaders' creativity and commitment. We are grateful for their help and for their trust.

Back at Columbia in the spring of 2014, Adam worked with INCITE, a research center that Peter directs and with which Adam is affiliated, to figure out what we could reasonably do, and how much it would cost, and who would run the program, and whether it was going to be okay with Columbia University. Michael Falco, associate director of INCITE, did the heavy lifting here. If Falco didn't already know all the answers, he quickly figured out how to know them. Terrell Frazier, then the communications director at INCITE, helped to design the training we would offer to students. By early March, legal counsel at Columbia provided the framework for ensuring that we had a strong firewall between our intellectual products and the UFCW and OUR Walmart, which protected us from having to obtain the union's consent for papers and books (like this book) that we thought we might write. Around the same time, a budget had been created and forwarded to Andrea, who sent it through the UCFW budgetary process as a grant to INCITE.

While the UFCW was doing its thing, INCITE recruited students. Adam met with a student group at Columbia, Student-Worker Solidarity, thanks to a tip from our colleague Shamus Khan. Adam also wrote to friends at other universities who were connected to the labor movement. INCITE advertised the program on Idealist. com. By the middle of April, after reviewing résumés and interviewing candidates, Adam had found 20 students willing to give over their summer to the project. The work was important, interesting, and challenging. It didn't hurt that the UFCW was paying them the weekly equivalent of the $15 per hour for which OUR Walmart and others had been advocating as a just wage.

Meanwhile, back at INCITE, Peter had just finished a paper on the neural bases of popularity that came from a new kind of group-based fMRI research design put into place by Noam Zerubavel. Once the students were enrolled, we realized we could replicate and extend our first fMRI study by getting longitudinal scans. At the time, we thought we could learn whether participation in change organizations changed people. That turned out to be more difficult to measure, and maybe less interesting, than what we ultimately discovered about the neural bases of solidarity—discussed in chapter 5. In less than a month, Zerubavel and Bearman designed a study, navigated the IRB process, and secured fMRI space and time at the hospital. Falco came up with the $40,000 we needed for the scans somewhere in the recesses of the INCITE budget. The whole project—from the conversation in the car with Audra to the first night of the program in May—took less than four months to put together. We thank Michael Falco, Noam Zerubavel, and Terrell Frazier for all their help in those early months.

Our biggest debt, of course, is to the associates at Walmart and the students and organizers whose experiences make up the bulk of this book. Given our abbreviated time frame and lack of experience with this sort of organizational collaboration, students faced a lot of uncertainty—about their jobs and when their first checks would arrive, about where they would be staying, about how to respond to situations that arose in the field—that demanded patience, creativity, and open-mindedness. The fact that the summer went as smoothly as it did, which as we shall see was not *entirely* smoothly, is a testament to the students' hard work and commitment and good humor. And many of the students have continued to be involved in the project since they returned from the field, reflecting on their experiences in ways that have greatly enriched the final product.

From start to finish, Suresh Naidu, an economist at Columbia, has been a key collaborator in the broader project of which this book is a part. The first week of the Summer for Respect, he gave the students a primer on the economics of the retail industry and the challenges and opportunities facing the labor movement. In the years since the students returned from the field, Suresh and Adam have together been working with OUR Walmart and other worker organizations to figure out how social science might contribute to strengthening movements among those working in low-wage jobs. Many of the analyses included here were conducted with Suresh's intellectual and technical support.

Several graduate students and colleagues have contributed in ways large and small to this project. Adam Storer, now a doctoral student in sociology at Berkeley, helped us obtain and analyze the

Glassdoor and Yelp data. Mark Hoffman distinguished the neural signatures of instrumental versus affective relations. As noted earlier, Noam Zerubavel ran the fMRI and network components of the study that figure prominently in our understanding of the development of community among students discussed in chapter 5, and Terrell Frazier ran the oral history components of the project from start to end. Michael Jaron helped us obtain the data from the discussion board, and Jean-Philippe Cointet generated the maps of the conversation structure of the board.

Other friends and relatives contributed in many ways that they may not precisely recognize, but that shaped the unfolding of the manuscript. For Peter, these include Alessandra Nicifero, Ben Bearman, and Mike Eigen. For Adam, they include Teresa Sharpe, Umberto Crenca, Marshall Ganz, and Michael Burawoy.

We also thank all of the people who helped provide the intensive training to students at the beginning of the summer. Mary Marshall Clark, the director of Columbia's Center for Oral History Research, offered students a crash course in oral history interviewing. Amy Castenell, then with Color of Change and now at Fission Strategy, gave a training in social media. Melissa Goldman and Vincent Peone gave the students a lesson in videography. Hilary Klein, then at Make the Road New York and now with the Center for Popular Democracy, discussed the history of U.S. social movements. Andrea Dehlendorf, Colby Harris, and Cindy Murray taught students about Walmart and organizing at Walmart.

In terms of our own process, one of us took the lead on some chapters, the other on other chapters. We would each rewrite what the other wrote. At a certain point we couldn't remember who wrote what, and that is the version you are reading. We owe an institutional debt to INCITE for providing research space and a community with whom to explore and develop new ideas. Bearman acknowledges a fellowship from the Guggenheim Foundation that facilitated the completion of this work.

Teresa Sharpe, Mitch Duneier, Christopher Muller, Cat Turco, and Yinon Cohen helped move our thinking in very important ways and we are greatly indebted to them. We have also benefited from comments provided by Robert Reich, Benjamin Rohr, Rebecca Breslaw, Audrey Augenbraum, Charlotte Wang, Michael Falco, Sam Lutzker, and Bill McAllister. Finally, we thank Eric Schwartz at Columbia University Press for his grace and goodwill.

WORKING
FOR RESPECT

INTRODUCTION

The Real, Real Walmart

The camera focuses on a young African American man with close-cropped hair and a cherubic smile, standing in the middle of a brightly lit shopping aisle. He is wearing a short-sleeved, blue, collared shirt and a name tag with only his first name: "Anthony." As upbeat, folksy music swells in the background, Anthony speaks directly and confidently into the camera: "I am the next American success story."[1]

We watch as Anthony moves boxes of frying pans on a dolly in the back of the store. His voice continues: "Working for a store where 75 percent of store management started as hourly associates. There's opportunity here!" Now Anthony is at a home in an unbuttoned plaid shirt and t-shirt, studying microeconomics at the kitchen table. A woman—his mother?—walks across the sight line of the camera on her way to the stove, where two pots are boiling. "I can use Walmart's education benefits to get a degree!" Back in work clothes, Anthony is at a computer console in the middle of some sort of situation room: "Maybe work in IT!" Next he stands on the roof of a Walmart Supercenter, surrounded by hundreds of solar panels as the sun begins to set over rolling hills in the background: "Or be an engineer, helping Walmart conserve energy!" Then Anthony is restocking paper towels in the aisles. "Even today, when our store does well, I earn quarterly bonuses!" The spot finishes the way it began, with Anthony in the middle of the aisle looking earnestly into the camera: "When people look at me, I hope they see someone working their way up." The Walmart logo appears as a woman's voice says, "Opportunity: That's the real Walmart."

Anthony Thompson, 19 years old in the video, really does, or did, work at Walmart, one of many employees at the massive company who have appeared in its advertisements. In *The Walmart Way*, Don Soderquist—a former vice chairman and COO of the company—describes the "ingenious idea" of the company's marketing department to "use our own associates instead of professional models in our TV ads and monthly circulars." It was a hit:

> We tried it. Our associates did a great job, and it was a huge success. The associates who appeared in TV spots and circulars became celebrities in their communities, and Wal-Mart associates from all over the country wanted to be in the commercials.[2]

Watching the advertisement, it is hard not to wonder what the "fake Walmart" is against which the company feels compelled to offer the "real." And it is only a short step from here to an appreciation of the fact that the advertisement, more than anything, indicates the success that an earlier generation of social change advocates have had connecting the Walmart brand with low wages and unjust working conditions. From this perspective, Anthony's advertisement is just one more battle in a decades-long war for the marginal customer's heart and mind and dollar.[3]

A different sort of insight is possible, though, if we get to know people like Anthony and come to understand the somewhat complicated, sometimes conflicted feelings that they have about places like Walmart. At the time of the commercial, Anthony believed everything he said. He really was enthusiastic about the work that he was doing, the community of people he worked with, and the mission of the store. He really did feel that there were opportunities. Just a year later, though, Anthony felt differently about the 30-second spot: "You know, since Walmart has gotten what they wanted from me, it's like I've just been tossed to the curb." The original commercial was part of an advertising campaign called The Real Walmart. Anthony thinks that he and the other workers featured in the commercials should put together a follow-up campaign: "The Real, Real Walmart." Then, he says, "If we were to put the commercials side by side, the then and the now, there are, like, a lot of people in this world that would be, like, really? So is this what happens?"

From where he sat at the time we interviewed him, Anthony felt like Walmart had deliberately misled him—given him a false sense of hope so that he would parrot the company line in the commercial before being tossed to the curb. He felt tricked into being an enthusiastic employee. But his reinterpretation of his earlier enthusiasm is somewhat misleading, in that it presents too neat a dichotomy between the Walmart he loved and the Walmart from which he came to feel estranged. Walmart was the same place before and after the commercial. Anthony really did see opportunity there, before he had a set of experiences that made him retrospectively understand himself as having been used.

And Anthony's understanding of Walmart would continue to change. Two years after our first interview with him, when he visited us in New York, the metaphor he used to describe the company was that of an abusive spouse that you know you need to leave but "you can't find a way to get out." He said that he would "never recommend Walmart to anyone" except for those who do not have any other options, which is why he recommended it to his cousin who had never finished high school, and his ex-girlfriend, and the friend of his who had a criminal record.

To understand low-wage jobs like those at Walmart, we have to make sense of the real enthusiasm that people express for them as well as the abuse they experience within them. To *change* places like Walmart, impacting the brand—the central idea of earlier generations of change activists and hence the motivation for framing Walmart as unjust and low-wage—is insufficient without also impacting the social relations between these companies and those who work for them: that is, the people whose work generates the staggering profits on their balance sheets. And to alter these relations, we have to get inside them; we have to know who these workers are, where they come from, what they get out of their work, and what they want from it. In short, we have to engage with the company and the people who work there. This book is a result of our and our students' engagement. One of our ambitions is that it changes the ways you engage with these kinds of companies as well.

THE SUMMER FOR RESPECT

A young white woman, with dark brown hair pulled back in a ponytail, silver leaf earrings dangling from her ears, stands at the front of a classroom in Knox Hall at Columbia University in New York City. She introduces herself as Beth. Like Anthony, Beth is also 19 years old. She has just finished her freshman year at Barnard College. Rather than go back home to San Francisco for the summer, she has signed up to spend nine weeks organizing and conducting oral history interviews with Walmart workers in Chicago. The other 19 participants in the room, undergraduates or recent graduates from Columbia and a smattering of other schools across the country, are there for the same reason: a program called the Summer for Respect, which we have jointly organized with a labor organization called the Organization United for Respect at Walmart, or OUR Walmart, an independent organization of, by, and for people working at Walmart that, at the time, had staffing support and resources from the United Food and Commercial Workers International Union (UFCW). Teams of four students will head to five different parts of the United States: Chicago, southwest Ohio, central Florida, Dallas, and Los Angeles. Beth and the others are looking for the same things that Anthony hoped to find at Walmart: a community, a place to grow, an experience that might be translated into an opportunity down the line. For the students, tonight, May 26, 2014, is the first night of the project.

Knox Hall, where the students convene for three days of training, occupies the northern wing of the Union Theological Seminary in the Morningside Heights neighborhood of Manhattan. The rooms and halls are furnished in dark wood: dark wooden floors, dark wooden tables; misted glass windows and stolid, dark, wooden doors separate the faculty offices from the halls. The doors are usually shut; the halls are unusually quiet. The old stone exterior and quaint interior courtyard of the quadrangle are so stereotypical of the elite university that they are a favorite set for the city's burgeoning TV and film industry. When Serena van der Woodsen of *Gossip Girl* attends Yale University, it is filmed here at Union Theological Seminary. When Philip and Elizabeth Jennings, the Cold War Russian spies on *The Americans*, lurk outside a prestigious university in the District of Columbia, it is filmed here as well.

One by one, the participants stand up to introduce themselves to one another. The prompt: in five minutes or less, explain what motivated you to join this summer program. "San Francisco is a very liberal place in a lot of ways," Beth begins, "and so I grew up steeped in a lot of lefty, progressive, ideas. But at the same time, San Francisco just surpassed Manhattan in terms of income inequality, which is not something that I saw for a long time growing up." Despite the students' different backgrounds, this tension—between a commitment to egalitarianism and a social position that benefits immensely from inequality—is one with which they are all familiar by virtue of being a part of the project. The students are staying nearby in the Aloft Hotel in a quickly gentrifying neighborhood in Harlem. They're eating Thai food and barbecue ribs in an Ivy League seminar room. At the equivalent of $15 per hour, their pay matches

OUR Walmart's ambitions for Walmart wages, but not the reality of what most Walmart jobs pay.

Students negotiate this tension differently. Some draw on the similarities they imagine they share with Walmart workers, implicitly distancing themselves from the other students and the cultural capital they all share. Max, a black transgender person and rising junior at Barnard, was in and out of shelters in New Haven as a child: "I grew up in a lot of poverty and sickness. Poverty not like the romanticized type that you read in books . . . and more [like we] can't put food on the table." Max's mother and grandmother are currently unemployed, living on disability, and facing eviction: "And so this summer is going to be very personal to me, and very political." Others connect with the project by drawing on histories of social justice struggle in their families: Wendy's Salvadoran grandfather had directed a school that organized against that country's military government; Michelle's Puerto Rican grandparents had fought for the island's self-determination. While the particular plights of those working at Walmart were outside their immediate experience, for these students, social justice struggle had been the family business and helped them make sense of their own participation. And still others understand their participation in the project as a reaction against their own privilege and myopia. Alexis, who grew up in Westchester County amid "enormous privilege," said that she had been taught to see injustice as something "really, really far away" and that this project signified her recognition of its proximity. Kevin, from Walnut Creek, California, felt as though his whole life "has been about me," and he just "want[ed] to focus on others for a bit." Arthur, a white, recent college graduate who grew up in Connecticut and wore an Industrial Workers of the World t-shirt to this first night, said he was most excited about the project because "we're all workers" and "workers, as a class of people, are the ones who hold the power." By this account, the differences between Walmart workers and privileged college students and recent graduates were far less than what united them all against the forces of international capital.

FREEDOM SUMMER

On the eve of the hottest part of the summer of 1964, hundreds of young activists had gathered for training in Oxford, Ohio, as part of a project known as Freedom Summer. They too had decided to forgo whatever plans they had for their summers. Instead, they would spend time in Mississippi organizing African Americans to register to vote.

The Freedom Summer project was led by Robert "Bob" Moses. Born and raised in Harlem, Moses had received a master's degree in philosophy from Harvard University in 1957 before leading the Student Nonviolent Coordinating Committee's (SNCC) voter registration efforts in Mississippi.[4] Moses was essential in helping to convince the more skeptical members of SNCC that the benefits of a large-scale infusion of white volunteers in Mississippi would outweigh its costs.[5] On the first night of that training, it was left to Moses to inform the assembled group of volunteers that three of their compatriots—James Chaney, Andrew Goodman, and Michael Schwerner—had gone missing in Nashoba County. Later, the whole world would know that the three had been murdered. The dangers of participation in the summer program were real. Moses said he would understand if students chose not to participate. And yet he could not in good conscience *not* ask them to go. They went.

In 1964, the Freedom Summer project was designed to exploit—and thereby amplify into the consciousness of northern elites—the racism that the program intended to combat.[6] Organizers of the project like Moses and James Forman recognized that sending white students, children of the elite, to the epicenter of the struggle for racial justice would focus the nation's attention in a way that SNCC, a majority black organization, had been unable to do since it began work in Mississippi in 1961.[7] By this measure, the strategy proved remarkably successful. The kidnapping and murder of the three volunteers—two white and one black—was a grim proof of concept. The deaths of these volunteers sparked public outrage, whereas the murders of other black organizers—Reverend George Lee, Herbert Lee, and Medgar Evers—had been met with relative silence. The Freedom Summer project, and especially the brutalization of students at the hands of police and state-sanctioned mobs, was one of the summer's top news stories[8] and helped to relegitimize social protest for a public still emerging out of the shadows of McCarthyism.[9] Longer term, Freedom Summer helped give rise to a generation of student activists—those who were energized by their own participation in the program, and those influenced by those participants.[10] It was some of the children of those activist cohorts who gathered for the Summer for Respect, 50 years later.

For all the incredible achievements of the Freedom Summer project, it was, by conventional outcome measures, a failure. While some African Americans were successfully registered to vote, many more were not. The project's Mississippi Freedom Democratic Party delegation, established in response to black exclusion from Mississippi's Democratic Party, was turned away from the Democratic National Convention in Atlantic City in August of 1964. The murders of Chaney, Goodman, and Schwerner, as well as other acts of violence against participants in the program, belied the notion that the presence of Northern whites would reduce violence against the young activists. And the strategic tensions within SNCC, exacerbated by Freedom Summer, would lead to internal fissures from which the organization never fully recovered.[11] If there was creative potential in the dissonance of Freedom Summer[12]—in the encounters between elite, white students from the North and Southern blacks—there were dangers on both sides of the encounter as well.

The Summer for Respect was not Freedom Summer. We had 20 students, not 1,000. The dangers that confronted our students were not even remotely similar to the dangers that the Freedom Summer volunteers knew they faced. Our students were getting paid. Freedom Summer volunteers were not. In contrast to the 1964 Freedom Summer participants, our students were always connected to us, their parents, and their friends through email, cell phones, and Facebook.

We were also not the first to try to rekindle the spirit of 1964 on behalf of the contemporary labor movement. Since 1995, when the reformer John Sweeney won the presidency of the AFL-CIO as a result of the first contested election in the organization's history, a new cohort of labor leaders had gained prominence, many of whom had been involved in the student movements of the 1960s and 1970s.[13] They knew from personal experience that students could bring energy, idealism, resources, and time to an aging, bureaucratic set of organizations.[14] And since their rise to power they had sought to bring labor into even closer contact with academia through student programs like Union Summer—itself an allusion to Freedom Summer. The relationship between these new leaders and existing labor organizations was never entirely without tension. As Rick Fantasia and Kim Voss write, the backgrounds and dispositions of the new union leaders "would tend to make for a closer resemblance to Silicon Valley entrepreneurs than to veteran staffers of the trade union movement."[15] If they were not careful, they might seem just as out of touch to the workers they now represented as the organization men they had swept aside.[16] Moreover, the track record of the university engagement for which these leaders advocated has been mixed. On the one hand, Union Summer was responsible for a rise in student-labor alliances and labor-related protest on college campuses.[17] It likely contributed to the wave of attention to the sweatshop conditions in which university-branded clothing was produced; to the Battle for Seattle and antiglobalization protests that emerged in the late 1990s and early 2000s; and to an upsurge in unionization drives among graduate students across the country. On the other hand, Union Summer did not lead in any clear way to a rise in union membership or bargaining power, leading some reformers to call it "union bummer," a drain of resources, money spent on privileged college kids who are just about the last people in the world in need of help from organized labor.[18]

Even though we knew that we were not organizing Freedom Summer, we were aware of the risks and problems with sending elite college students to engage in labor organizing at Walmart.

We didn't think it likely that there was any physical danger, but we knew that students' time in the field would be tense and difficult, both because of management's antagonism toward labor organizing and because of the differences between the students and the workers with whom they would be working. Nevertheless, like Freedom Summer, the Summer for Respect was premised on a belief in the possibility of understanding, community, and solidarity across difference; and even more optimistically, on the creative potential of worlds colliding, on the idea that new understandings and practices could emerge out of new kinds of relationships. Like Freedom Summer, it seemed to us at the time that the students' privilege could be a double-edged sword.

FREEDOM IS MORE THAN MONEY FOR A HAMBURGER AND CUP OF COFFEE

The politics of 2014, and today, are different in important ways from the politics of 1964. The lines between the advantaged and the disadvantaged, between oppressors and oppressed, have blurred slightly. In 1964, the white student volunteers from the North were considered by many to be "race traitors." At best they were allies, members of an oppressive white power structure hoping to use their unfairly acquired advantages to positive effect. Their motivations—voluntarism, idealism, guilt—were relatively straightforward. In 2014, the participants in the Summer for Respect were still undoubtedly elite: three-quarters of them came from Ivy League schools. But many related to the project in terms that highlighted their personal proximity to the struggles they thought they would be addressing. Many were the children of immigrants or had grown up poor. Half were students of color.

And so the students' relationship to the summer project was complicated. After all, weren't these students living advertisements for the expanding promise of the American Dream? Wasn't their upward mobility made possible by the victories of the civil rights pioneers before them, who had fought to give them the opportunity to attend the elite schools from which they previously had been excluded? Wendy, a Latina from Brentwood, New York, was a first-generation college student and a rising senior at Brown. Valerie was an African American rising junior at Vanderbilt, a school that had admitted its first black undergraduates in 1964, the same year as Freedom Summer.[19] The fact that these students had been able to make it to such elite institutions was surely evidence that their doors had opened, at least a crack.

In 1964, the racial structure of domination was clear as day; Freedom Summer could easily point to unfreedom in the denial of the vote for black Americans; in the exclusion of blacks from lunch counters and buses; in rampant employment discrimination and redlining; in a long and ongoing history of state and state-sanctioned violence. In turn, the freedoms that Freedom Summer and the civil rights movement sought to win were largely negative ones—the freedom from state-supported racial domination and discrimination.

By the late 1960s, civil rights leaders had begun to shift their sites from negative conceptions of freedom to positive ones. Martin Luther King Jr. was supporting striking sanitation workers in Memphis, Tennessee, when he was assassinated on April 4, 1968. Speaking in Memphis that March, he referred to the limits of civil rights in the absence of economic rights:

> With Selma and the voting rights bill one era of our struggle came to a close and a new era came into being. Now our struggle is for genuine equality, which means economic equality. For we know that it isn't enough to integrate lunch counters. What does it profit a man to be able to eat at an integrated lunch counter if he doesn't have enough money to buy a hamburger and a cup of coffee?[20]

In building a bridge between racial justice and economic justice, King made the argument that negative freedom, freedom from interference, was incomplete without something more—in this case, the provision of material well-being.

We were expecting to hear echoes of King's call for positive freedom, for material well-being, in the field in 2014. Instead, we found that people who work in low-wage jobs today are not only, or even primarily, striving for material well-being, the money for a burger and cup of coffee. They are, more basically, working for respect.

The struggle for respect is a struggle for nondominating relationships. Where classical liberal theory defines freedom as freedom from interference by others, the workers we encountered at Walmart are not trying to free themselves from their relationships so much as to equalize them. The things they want depend on the constraint of social relations, on membership in a community of relative equals.[21] They inchoately understand that freedom is not an individual attribute (even if individuals experience it), but neither is it a feature of the macrostructure (even if structures make it more or less possible); it is something found, won, and lost at the level of interaction, in the relationships one has within the workplace and outside it.

Simply put, our goal in this book is to better understand how people pursue freedom in the contemporary American workplace, and how they might go about doing so more effectively. We look specifically at the way in which people's social ties both inhibit and make possible its achievement. Under what conditions do people's reciprocal obligations to one another create an opportunity for expanded freedom, and when do they shut it down?

The communities that we are in and the social ties we have with others often act as tethers, anchoring us to the world as it is, and reproducing our positions within it. Symbolically, those with whom we are closest serve as points of reference, models for what is possible in our own lives and standards for what constitutes fair treatment. Often our closest ties blind our imaginations to what might be possible. Occasionally, though, the material and symbolic relations we have with others can become bonds of solidarity, catalyzing a new sense of self and new conception of self-interest, leading people to act collectively in pursuit of a perhaps more uncertain but also more hopeful future.

Because the relationships that we have with others at work are not free, because they are saturated with hierarchy and domination, work settings rarely spontaneously give rise to the recognition of collective interests and the practice of collective action. And so this book consequently examines the importance of *organizers* as the actors who help both to build new ties and facilitate the reinterpretation of existing ties to create communities that can contest the world as it is. That such a process rarely occurs without confict is well known.

Our focus is, first, on Walmart and Walmart workers, and by association the millions of Americans working low-wage jobs at places like Walmart. Walmart is the largest private employer in the world. Over 1.4 million people work for the company in the United States alone, which is nearly a full percentage point of the country's employed civilian labor force.[22] But if every Walmart looks pretty much the same, the experience of working at Walmart varies considerably. Each store has its own culture, its own compositions of workers and customers, its own networks of relationships. And this variation exists in spite of the fact that Walmart's home office in Bentonville, Arkansas, micromanages its sprawling bureaucracy— Bentonville sets the store temperatures; Bentonville manages inventory; Bentonville allocates work hours to regional managers, who in turn allocate them to store managers, who in turn schedule employees, all on the basis of algorithms based on sales data and foot traffic from previous weeks, months, and years. Understanding these microclimates—the range of experiences that workers and managers and customers have at Walmart, as well as the range of experiences to which they are *comparing* their experiences at Walmart—can help us understand how Walmart reproduces its power and the circumstances in which it might be challenged.

Our second focus is on the experiences of our students during the Summer for Respect, the program they participated in for nine weeks of one summer. Here we examine the interactions between a group of relatively advantaged students and relatively disadvantaged workers; of the possibilities of and challenges to building understanding and solidarity across social difference. We explore what these students learned about Walmart, about organizing, about teamwork, and about themselves.

Finally, and most generally, the book is about public sociology, about our efforts as scholars simultaneously to understand the world and intervene in it. At this level it explores the relationship between scholars and activists, about the relationship between theory and practice. The Summer for Respect, a demonstration project, was unsettling—unsettling for our students, unsettling for OUR Walmart, and unsettling for Walmart workers. Following Michael Burawoy, we consider such discomfort "not noise to be expurgated but music to be appreciated."[23] By unsettling existing relations we can see them better, as tectonic plates are revealed during an earthquake or the norms of a social order become clearest when they are violated.

Substantively, then, this book is something like a Russian doll—it is a story about Walmart workers and OUR Walmart, couched within a story about a summer project involving 20 college students and recent college graduates, couched within a story about scholarship and social change. One theme runs through the book—the relationship between social ties and social change, between community and conflict, at Walmart and beyond. The ties we examine are of different sorts: ties among Walmart workers and their families; among Walmart workers and their coworkers, supervisors, and customers; among organizers and students and workers; among academics and activists. Throughout we focus on how and when the complex relations we have with others make possible (and constrain) opportunities for collective action.

Social relations don't exist in a vacuum. To understand the ties we have with others, we need to situate them in context. To understand the experience of low-wage work and the failure of past organizing efforts, we have to know something about the rise of the big-box store, the hollowing out of American communities, the decline of the American labor movement. To understand how we might help to change a place like Walmart, we have to learn something about processes of building community and trust, and the role that students and academics have played in the labor movements of the past. But most of all, to understand the experience of low-wage work and how to change it, we have to learn something about places like Walmart, the people who work there, what happens on the shop floor, the nature of control in the service sector, and how all of those processes and dynamics interact.

And so we come back, in different ways and from different angles, to the shop floor.

WALMART IS EVERYWHERE AND NOWHERE

It is the Sunday afternoon before the presidential election of 2016 and we are at the Walmart in Wilkes-Barre, Pennsylvania [#1623]. We have been working on the book for more than two years when we realize that we still haven't spent enough time in the stores. So we rent an RV off I-95 near the Massachusetts–Rhode Island border and head west. At most Walmarts, RVs are allowed to park overnight. As Bethany Moreton explains, "Taking an astute look at the 30 million recreational vehicle enthusiasts around the country and the potential for growth among retiring baby-boomers, the company . . . welcomed overnight RV parking at stores nationwide." Welcoming RVs was also a statement about the type of person to whom Walmart was meant to appeal, Moreton continues: the company "mapped a specific American culture within the larger one, and people knew when they were home."[24]

Our plan is to camp out with all the other RVs. It's quite a surprise for us to discover that there aren't any others out on the road. It turns out that RVing is mainly a summer activity in this neck of the woods, and it's no fun at all when it's freezing outside and you can't plug in. When we visit a Walmart, we wander, sometimes asking for help locating difficult-to-find items like essential oils or a car power inverter and hoping that such interactions can segue into conversations about workers' jobs. We often overhear conversations between workers and customers, between workers and managers, among workers.

The sporting counter here in Wilkes-Barre is buzzing. William, the older white man who works there, is talking to a customer about the recent rush on guns and ammunition, the boxes and boxes of bullets he has been selling all day. He compares the run to the days that Supplemental Security Income (SSI) checks are cut and wonders aloud whether they came early this month. The customer, standing next to his wife and young daughter, has another hypothesis: that others, like him, are buying ammunition in case they need it for Wednesday morning. There is a feeling of shared fate here. They don't expect that their man Donald Trump will win, and are stocking up in advance of a Clinton presidency.[25]

You have probably been inside a Walmart like the one in Wilkes-Barre, or driven past one. They are difficult to miss. Outside of cities small and large, Wilkes-Barre to Los Angeles, sit huge parcels of land dominated by big-box stores. Walmart anchors many of these tracts, drawing smaller outfits like pizza parlors and video game stores into its broader orbit. Walmart is not alone: Lowe's, Target, Best Buy, Staples, Bed Bath & Beyond. The list goes on and on. These stores often have their own dedicated parking lots, so distant from other stores that one has to drive to adjacent lots. The big-box movement has strip-malled America; like strip mining, it has so fundamentally transformed the countryside that even many locals seem to find the landscape alien.[26]

The box stores have also hollowed out small towns like Wilkes-Barre. The places where people met, shopped, talked, and thought about their communities have been sucked out of the center and deposited on the periphery. The action that remains is here in the aisles, where in order to arrive one has to drive, park, walk through the cavernous doors into a space that declares itself to be universal—a space so large that one cannot see its boundaries, a space where every shelf is packed with product, where every bin is full.

Walking into Walmart feels to us like entering a land without identity, without any markers. Nothing about the store tells us that we are in Wilkes-Barre, Mississippi or Ohio, California or New York. We cannot find any local displays. There are no signs telling us that we are somewhere. While there are products specific to the local demographic—the store in a black neighborhood features books with African American protagonists, which take the place of the romance novels elsewhere; there are plantains in the store where the Latinos come to shop—these differences are subtle. What jumps out is a sterile sameness. Even the giant TVs that blanket the entire back wall of the electronics department are on a loop of Walmart advertisements. There is no news, no immediate present. The biggest hint that we are somewhere at some specific time—aside from the people who buy there and the people who work there—are (and only in some stores) small boards where Walmart records its staggeringly small yearly donations to local causes: charter schools, clubs, teams. Walmart is everywhere and nowhere. Many are open 24 hours a day.

Once we walk into a Walmart Supercenter it is as though time ceases to have any meaning beyond seasons keyed to products keyed to holidays: Halloween, Christmas, Easter. Weirdly, on this early November day in northern Pennsylvania, there are almost no Thanksgiving products. The Christmas music starts right after Halloween, the Christmas displays appear in the first week of November. Inexplicably, the one American holiday about community, about sharing, is completely missing.

The sheer enormity of Walmart makes us feel small. The structure of the store suggests there is no time for conversation. The only seats in sight upon entering are two small wire benches, each barely large enough for two people, located in front of the rest rooms, which are in the front of the store—close to the exits, before and after one passes the cashiers, far from the products that might be stolen.

And yet, like plants in a hothouse, the people buying at Walmart and the people working at Walmart do get intertwined, they do find time to say hello, to pass the time. People try to build and preserve their connections with others, even in such deserts. When workers become attached to their customers and coworkers, these attachments let Walmart push them harder. And yet these ties are also the raw material through which new senses of collective identity can emerge and through which new forms of resistance become possible. The way in which relationships on the shop floor tend to tie people to the status quo, but can also occasionally unsettle it, is one of the puzzles we take up in this book.

It's 10 p.m. on a Saturday night at the Walmart in Vestal, New York [#1835], just outside Binghamton: People have been streaming into the store all day. We have been sitting in our RV in the parking lot watching the flow for what seems like forever. It is difficult to count the people coming in; every second, it seems, someone enters and someone leaves. We see people leave who we think we saw enter just a few minutes before. And many of them have huge carts full of stuff.

People don't seem to come to Walmart to shop. They come to buy. Walmart understands the distinction. Shopping in America involves making distinctions, highlighting aspects of who we are or who we want to become while separating ourselves from others. This is what branding is all about, and why companies spend so many millions of dollars nursing their brands. Shopping for a product connects us to a group identity of which we want to be a part. Coca-Cola—Taste the Feeling; Nike—Just Do It; Apple—Think Different. We're willing to pay more for the product because we're getting more than the product. We're getting the community associated with it. When we walk into an Apple Store we feel what it's like to be someone who uses Apple products—the smooth edges; all that glass; the helpful and hip but nerdy staff. The store helps us experience the brand.

Buying is about getting things. It is about the stuff rather than the signal. Walmart's genius is that it has branded buying—Always the Low Price. Always. Or, more recently—Save Money. Live Better. The person you are when you shop at Walmart is the person who is looking for the lowest price possible. Of course, Walmart hopes that you will see something that you didn't know you had to have and that you will buy it because it is absurdly cheap. Twelve-cup coffeemakers sell for under $15. Sweatshirts with hoods sell for $7.84. Inverters that can power small TVs from the cigarette lighter in your car sell for $8.74. But Walmart can and does survive on sales of things people need. And those things more often than not really do sell for less than anywhere else. Sometimes the difference is in pennies. The 100 generic coffee filters for your new coffeemaker that sell for $1.29 at Target around the corner sell for $1.28 at Walmart. The New England Coffee that sells for $4.98 at Walmart is $4.99 at Target.

On Saturday night the Vestal store teeters on the edge of chaos. Products on pallets occupy the centers of most aisles, and associates are furiously trying to manage the influx of stuff. One is on her knees working to get a special conditioner and shampoo display set up. Each column of bottles is 15 deep; there are eight rows for each of the five display levels. She has a shopping cart of over 600 items. Her idea appears to be to alternate columns of shampoo and conditioner to build green and white stripes. The aesthetic choice is hers, but her time isn't. Just as she settles in a customer asks for directions; she gets up and points her off toward the pet department, past the pallets stacked precariously with unpacked boxes of different sizes that block the view. As soon as she is back down, it happens again. Each line of product she puts up she carefully aligns. The front of each column is absolutely straight.

It's 9:30 a.m. at the Walmart in Pittston, Pennsylvania [#2543]: An older white woman is also on her knees, this time stocking hand soap. She is wearing kneepads. A middle-aged man stands next to her, and they chat about the local high school football team. The Pittston High Patriots just finished their season at 2–8; the only reason they won any games at all, she says, is that they had dropped down to a lower league. She is stocking as they talk; he leans over her conspiratorially. They compare notes on players before separating, and as he walks away he asks her to say hello to her husband for him.

Her fingers are cracked; she tells us, almost proudly, that she has *literally* worked them to the bone. Many of the hand soaps are shipped in packages of eight, which helps her back—since they're lighter that way—but destroys her fingers as she opens them. She slathers her hands with Vaseline that she leaves on overnight while she sleeps, but the damage is done. Nevertheless, she loves her job, she says, unprovoked, and then suggests we buy the new Christmas soap, which is flying off the shelves. Several shelves are half-empty, though she just stocked them last night. She picks out one she really likes, holds it open for one of us, laughs when it smudges on our nose. There's no time to ask her how she reconciles these things— the frenetic pace, the wounds on her hands, the low pay, and her love for her job—before another customer walks up with a cart and asks for help finding something.

In the grocery section at the Walmart in Hudson, New York [#2097], a young man says that he has been working at Walmart for only three months and so has "not yet been crushed into a fine powder." He tells us that he gets to decide how to get his stock up on the shelf, how he thinks about aligning the product to get more up there, how he has latitude about where he can put things, although they have to be right above the product label affixed to the shelf. In response to a question about essential oils, another associate tells us "I have some, by the candles"; others tell us, as we look for a particular kind of sweat-shirt, "Sure, we have that." We spent several days wandering around Walmart stores, pretending to be customers. We heard "they" only a handful of times. It was all "we, me, my."

Monday morning we find the store manager of the Walmart in Taylor, Pennsylvania [#4276] on a ladder, moving overstock cereal from the top of the shelf to the lower levels. He is a white man, in his thirties, with a hipster haircut—one side of his head is buzzed short, covered by hair combed over from the top. A store of this size has only one store manager. This is the guy here. He supervises the comanagers, the assistant managers, the support managers, the department managers, the associates—hundreds of people. What he is doing in grocery? "An experiment," he says. He is trying to count the number of additional cereal boxes he can move down from the top shelf where overstock is held, to figure out how much work was left undone by the night shift. The Walmart executives know that product sells more if the shelves are full. The store managers and the assistant managers want their product to flow out of the store as well—they are incentivized to want that. But it is the associates who experience directly how making full, attractively full, shelves serve as a barricade against the daily descent into chaos that each Walmart faces.

People try to find meaning in their work. They carve out spaces in which they are able to feel autonomous and creative, they search for distinction and respect. People are often proud of their jobs when they do them well, and frustrated when they are not given the space or tools to get their jobs done right. Walmart makes use of these inclinations to maximize the work they can get out of their employees, creating games through which workers can win recognition as they maximize their productivity, or allowing workers to take "ownership" over a display or product.[27] When workers become disillusioned, it is rarely because of meager pay or inconsistent hours; it is because they come to see the narrow boundaries of the freedoms they've been given; the inanity of the games they have been playing; the disrespect to which they are subjected. When and how people build community at work—even at places like Walmart— and when and how these sentiments give way to a sense of alienation and injustice, are central themes we engage in this book.

BLIND DATE

Three and a half weeks after the orientation at Columbia, on June 20, 2014, Beth sits in a Ford Fusion in the massive parking lot of the Pullman Walmart Supercenter [#5965], waiting for Anthony to call her back so she can conduct an interview with him. We thought that these kinds of interviews might do several things at once: they might deepen relationships between students and workers and between workers and OUR Walmart; they might help students, and the organization, arrive at a richer understanding of the lives, frustrations, and hopes of those working at Walmart; and they might give workers, through the process of the interview, access to what C. Wright Mills called the "sociological imagination," a capacity to connect one's private troubles to public issues, to see how one's life—however idiosyncratic it seems—is shaped by forces outside one's control and in turn reproduces the existing social order.[28]

The Pullman Walmart, on the far South Side of Chicago, is just a stone's throw from the historic company town of Pullman and the former headquarters of the Pullman Palace Car Company, which manufactured railcars back when most of the country's goods traveled by train. Pullman has long since folded. Today, Walmart merchandise doesn't arrive via the nearby rails, but rather by way of thousands of large tractor trailers owned and operated by Walmart that make their way up and down I-94.

Anthony calls. He has already caught the bus to head home, but he is still interested in doing the interview, and tells Beth he will get off the bus at a nearby intersection. In retrospect, Beth says, the whole thing felt "a bit like a blind date." She drives to the intersection and waits. Finally, she sees him—a *tall, gangly* man *in a Walmart-blue polo and khakis* crossing the street ahead. She calls him and tells him, *feeling only mildly creepy*, that she can see him and that he should keep walking down the sidewalk until he runs into her. As he walks up she realizes just how tall he is—at least six foot six. He has to *bend his legs and hunch over to squeeze into the car*. Once he is inside, Beth writes, *I introduced myself and told him I was glad to meet him. He returned the pleasantries, maintaining the smile that seemed to be a permanent fixture of his face.*

The next question is where they will conduct the interview. Anthony thinks that there will be too many people making noise at his home, and so Beth suggests that they drive to the hotel where she and her three teammates are staying. They are both quiet. Beth remembers, *We drove down Cicero Avenue, past miles of strip malls and planes flying just a little too close for comfort, until we got to the airport hotel complex.* They walk through the lobby, past the free scones and juice, and up to the second floor to Beth's room.

As they approach the hotel room door, Beth feels a pang of uncertainty. Her hotel room is the logical place to do the interview: *it was just mine so no one was going to interrupt and I could be quite confident it would be quiet and comfortable.* On the other hand, she continued, *it was my bedroom, and inviting a stranger into the place I kept all my most personal items, the place where I slept and, especially in the case of men, a place that immediately brought up ideas of sexuality made me uncomfortable and anxious to say the least. . . . I tried not to dwell on my discomfort.*

Beth does not know it at the time, but Anthony is feeling more anxious than she is. After all, it was Beth who had invited Anthony to do an "oral history interview," whatever that was; it was her hotel and her hotel room. It might be a setup. Anthony recalls thinking, "She could kidnap me! She could ambush me! Even though I'm a big dude, what if she just attacks me? What would I do in this situation?" Before they arrived at the hotel he texted his cousin, *I'm going to this random hotel, I don't know what might happen there.* At least there would be a textual trace if something were to happen.

The awkwardness dissipates for both of them soon after they begin recording. An interview defines roles in ways that a car ride doesn't, gives them a common understanding of what this interaction *is* and what its boundaries are.

As the interview reveals, the most accurate part of the Walmart commercial was its portrayal of Anthony—ebullient and relentlessly optimistic. Anthony grew up in the heart of the South Side of Chicago. His mother died when he was two years old; the woman in the commercial was an actress, the "wife of a sportscaster" Anthony thinks.

The youngest of four brothers, Anthony was raised under the strong disciplinary regime of a single father who wanted to protect his boys from the dangers of the surrounding neighborhood:

> We never really did anything. We went outside every now and then during the summer, but I always had to make sure I was with my brothers. We never went off the block or we never left either the porch or the backyard. . . . I think it was a little of him being scared for

us and him trying to protect us, as well as him not wanting us to kind of get into the life that was going on around us with the violence and the drama and stuff of the streets.

Social isolation was a parenting strategy, and one that Anthony credits with keeping him out of trouble. "I just really went to school, you know, came home every day, did my homework. I got pretty okay grades in school and did my homework, ate dinner, went to sleep. You know, we watched TV for fun. We never really did anything." But Anthony was also lonely, without many friends and not really knowing how to make them. Making friends is "still something that's hard," he says. The kinds of communities around him were ones that might do him harm, so he made do with being alone.

As we will see, the loneliness to which Anthony grew accustomed—the loneliness that his dad thought necessary for keeping him safe as a kid, but which transitioned into a deeper sort of isolation—would later make the network of coworkers he found at Walmart feel that much more like a beloved community. The ties we have, or don't have, outside the workplace shape how we make sense of things inside.

Despite his father's attempts to isolate Anthony from his surroundings, his surroundings would repeatedly break through the shield. When Anthony was in kindergarten, a kid across the street was shot. In the fifth grade, his family became homeless, and they all had to move into a shelter in a different part of town. That meant Anthony had to switch elementary schools: "The new school that I went to . . . it was slower. It was slower than my previous school, so, like, there were things that in fifth grade that I had learned in third grade in my old school, so I kind of felt like it held back my education a bit." The family's housing would be precarious in the years that followed too.

Beth, back in New York, had narrated her own oral history with Rebecca, a Chinese American Harvard student also on the Chicago team.[29] Beth was born and raised in the Noe Valley neighborhood of San Francisco. She remembers it as a "nice, small neighborhood" that "feels suburban, almost." She figured it was basically middle class. In America, nearly everyone except for the poorest poor and richest rich seems to consider themselves middle class.[30] In truth, Noe Valley then and now is one of the most expensive neighborhoods in one of the most expensive cities in the country—the average price per square foot of a home there was $1,318 in December of 2015, ten times the median price nationwide (and comparable to the price per square foot in Manhattan).[31] Small, two-bedroom, one-bath houses routinely sell for over $1 million today. Larger homes cost millions more.

There was no need for Beth's parents to quarantine her: "It was safe," she says, "and so my parents gave me a lot of freedom early, just to walk around by myself . . . There's the local bookstore, and the chocolate store, and you could get to know the people, and that was nice." Her favorite haunt was a nearby pottery studio, Terra Mia, where her mom and her nanny began taking her and her little sister when she was just four and a half. "It's one of those places where they have all sorts of pottery that you can paint yourself, and then they fire it, and it comes back and it's all nice." By the time she was in fifth grade, she was spending most of her summers there, where over time she transitioned from a customer to a member of the staff. Beth was able to move freely around the neighborhoods in which she lived; she was given the time, space, confidence, and money to create things that she could call her own.

Beth's mom, also a San Francisco native, had grown up in the San Francisco of the 1970s—a different place entirely. Beth and her mom each attended the same private high school, the Urban School of San Francisco. The school had been founded in 1966, footsteps from the intersection of Haight and Ashbury Streets, the epicenter of the Summer of Love. When Beth's mom attended, Beth says, "it was very much hippie, smoke weed with your teachers, very nontraditional classes, maybe have sex with your teachers on school trips. . . . There was a lot of weird shit going on." But the years that intervened had changed the school much as they had changed the city. By the time Beth got there, the school had been through some rebranding. It was still committed to progressive education, but it now gave each student a laptop. When the head of school described whom the school was intended for, he gave barely a nod to its untraditional past: "If you are an academic achiever, a creative thinker, a math or science stand-out, a skilled artist or athlete, a brilliant writer or a civic-minded individual who chooses to measure your success against your own potential, Urban is the place for you."[32] Tuition for the 2015–2016 academic year was $40,050, plus a $650 laptop fee.[33] That is about twice the median household income for a family of four in the neighborhoods where Anthony grew up.

DREAMS DEFERRED

While he was in high school, Anthony began working at a local corner store—a job that paid him "four bucks an hour," about half of the legal minimum wage in Chicago at the time. He didn't mind the pay, though, since initially he just worked for the extra spending cash: "There were a lot of things at school that I just didn't have that I wanted . . . as far as clothing and things of that nature." When his dad lost his job, his work became more central to the family's survival. What he had been spending on the accoutrements of high school distinction now went to pay the bills: "It kind of turned into me trying to barely put some food on the table." The meaning of a job can change without the work itself changing at all, as when one's dependence on it increases. Anthony's changing financial responsibilities to his dad and brothers made his job suddenly feel much more significant.

But by the time he graduated from high school, Anthony had begun to run into problems with the drug dealers who hung out on the corner near the store—it seemed to Anthony that they resented him for being "that nice guy" who had the legitimate job. He began feeling scared to go to work. And so when he applied for a job at the

Forest Park Walmart [#2204], and got a call offering him nighttime hours, he jumped at it, even though his commute was nearly two hours by bus and train, each way. Working at the Forest Park Walmart got him out of the corner stores, out of the neighborhood, and far away from the eyes of the dealers who were making him uncomfortable. It seemed like a perfect solution.

Aside from the commute, Anthony's early experiences at Walmart were pretty good, all things considered. He started working in the gardening department and got along well with his managers. When the department manager had a heart attack and had to take a few months off, Anthony reports that he became the de facto department manager himself: "I was kind of the one in charge of the department. You know, every day an assistant manager or a comanager would come and they would give every department at Walmart notes, so I was that guy that they gave all the notes to, you know, get with everybody else in the department to get them done." The next September, "when the kids were starting going back to school"—and Anthony wasn't—he began to work in the back room on inventory as well. A new store manager noticed his hard work and gave him full-time hours in the back of the store on the day shift. After Anthony became certified on the power-lifting equipment, he increasingly assumed a leadership role there too. He felt like he was on his way up, like he could slowly climb to corporate.

Walmart gave Anthony what he was looking for: a sense of distinction and a sense of community. In those early months he would stick around the store after his shift was over just because he didn't have anything better to do:

> [Tahira] was a zone manager at Walmart. She used to always tell me at the end of the day, "Go home, Tony." And I'm like, "I'm going! I'm going!" I'd end up sticking around for, like, an hour or two, because like I said I didn't really have a social life, so Walmart was my life. So she would just say, "Go home, Tony." I'd say, "I'm going," and I'd walk around a little bit more. Then I finally, like, she'll finally shoo me out the door and say, "Go home. Go do something."

He was soon approached about being in the commercial. As Anthony remembers, "It was supposed to be a true associate testimony, you know, saying, 'I'm a real associate working from a real Walmart store. They treat me good. This is a good place to work.'" For the shoot they flew him to San Francisco and to Walmart headquarters in Bentonville. Anthony *did* feel like it was a good place to work. He believed wholeheartedly in the imagined future that the commercial laid out for him. After the filming, the producer asked Anthony where he could see himself in the company: "I answered that I wanted to go to corporate."

But back at Forest Park, Anthony's pay did not keep up with his responsibilities. He was doing a lot of the hardest work in the back room, but his pay had remained the same: $8.65 an hour. He asked the store manager whether he could have a supervisor position, and was told that he could not be promoted because of problems with his work attendance (Anthony had called out for about a week because of a leg problem that had made it difficult for him to walk). Instead, Anthony wound up training a new associate on the equipment, who was then given the supervisor job in his place: "I taught him pretty much everything I knew, and in about two months he got the position that I wanted."

Things came to a head during the Christmas season when Anthony was unloading "a bunch of trailers" by himself. He had accidentally locked himself outside the building, and knocked on the door to get a manager's attention to let him back in. "She was sitting in her office, and she couldn't get up for two seconds to unlock a door for me. . . . I was frustrated, and I kind of yelled at her."

The things that came to make Anthony the most frustrated about his work at Walmart—what he remembers most clearly—were not the things that we often hear about the company: the low pay and poor benefits, or the unpredictable schedules. It was the disrespect he felt from his supervisors: the way he was overlooked for a position he felt he deserved, how a manager refused to lift a hand to help him.

The day after he yelled at his manager, Anthony was fired. But he didn't take the news sitting down. Instead, he used the connections he had established at the company to get around the formal termination. While he had been filming the commercial, Anthony had met Walmart's director of corporate affairs. And so he emailed the director, along with higher-ups in the Chicago region. Within 24 hours he had been placed at the Pullman store, much closer to his home, where he had been working ever since, now in bakery. Shifting stores meant giving up the "power and authority" he had at Forest Park—he had been the only associate at his level with keys to the building and all the equipment—but he had gotten "tired of working my butt off for nothing."

THE COMMODIFICATION OF EXPERIENCE

Ever since Beth can remember, her mom had been encouraging her to become politically engaged: "My mom has this sort of deep passion for [and] anger about issues of social justice." Beth's mom related to her work as a vocation and seemed eager to pass on this orientation. Trained as a nurse, she was involved in local organizations providing health education and services to low-income women. At first, Beth says, she just wasn't interested. But something seemed to click for her partway through high school, when she joined a group called Students for Women's Equality and Rights (SWEAR). The school had prohibited SWEAR from staging *The Vagina Monologues* at the school—the administration was not enthusiastic about "vagina" being posted around the halls during campus tours. SWEAR, outraged by the administration's seeming hypocrisy, had found a loophole in campus regulations, which was that *original* student work could contain sexually explicit content. So the students wrote their own show. "And so we just had all of these workshops, where we wrote a lot of pieces, and we worked on the pieces, and then we performed them all together, and it was very, very powerful." She had taken the lessons of Terra Mia and converted them from pottery to politics. The group was "huge in shaping me as a human," she says. She doesn't think she would have called herself a feminist during freshman or sophomore years in high school, but by junior year "it felt so obvious." Not that the thought had occurred to her explicitly, but it is also true that SWEAR was more likely to get her into a good college than Terra Mia.

When she arrived at Barnard, then, Beth already had the idea that she wanted to commit herself to social activism—that this could provide her with a purpose, a feeling of distinction, as well as a sense of community. Given her experiences in high school she assumed that this would have something to do with women's rights. In her introduction on the opening night of the program, she explained that, instead, she had "fallen into" a group on campus called Student Worker Solidarity. But it wasn't exactly a coincidence. This was the group that some of her closest friends were a part of, and it also seemed to be where the activist action was on campus. The group had been cofounded a couple of years before by Jackie— a participant on the Los Angeles team and friend of Beth's—and had an impressive track record of generating student and community support for workers on and off campus. Beth says, "It wasn't the kind of social justice work I thought I was looking for, but it turned out to be a really important community and helpful for me to see action and not just discussion around issues like this."

The gap between the worlds of the students engaged in the Summer for Respect and the Walmart workers they would meet was more than economic. People who end up at elite colleges like Barnard and Columbia often learn, somewhere along the line, that experience is fungible, that it can be useful for purposes that are distant from purposes around which it is putatively oriented. High school guidance counselors at elite private schools, for example, are skilled at convincing students and their parents that sending kids to build a house in Ghana (or a similar experience of community service) gives them a leg up in the elite college sweepstakes. They are right about the leg up. With those kinds of experiences behind them, kids can write personal statements that resonate with college admissions officers. It doesn't really matter what kids do—whether they build a house or work in a soup kitchen. What kids do has little to do with their subsequent opportunity. But what the kids *learn* does, and what they learn is how to make experience fungible. This is one thing that Beth, Max, Wendy, Michelle, Alexis, Kevin, and the other students shared despite their heterogeneous paths to the project. They had learned how to commodify experience. This could be the experience of Terra Mia, the experience of becoming an activist, the experience of counseling at summer camp, or even the experience of growing up poor.

This alchemy, once learned, does not disappear after admission to an elite college. And it lurked in the background of the Summer for Respect project too: such a project could be a valuable line in a developing resume. This should not be read as cynicism about students' motives. Kids who build houses really do want to make the world better. Beth and the others were genuinely committed to altruistic, egalitarian ideals. They wanted to make the world a better place, to figure out how to continue to live out their commitments after college. It's just that they also knew—they would have learned—that such altruistic commitment could continue to distinguish them from others in an economy that was far more uncertain than it had been for the young activists of the 1960s. Back then, stable careers for graduates of elite colleges were so easy to come by that it was easier to be disdainful of them.[34] Our students' altruistic commitments were, structurally, necessarily more shaky. And the fungibility of experience provides a potential escape hatch from collectivist commitment.

BRIDGEABLE DISTANCES?

A couple of months before Anthony's interview with Beth, he had been approached by an organizer with OUR Walmart whom everyone called "the Rev." OUR Walmart, a voluntary association made up of current and former Walmart employees, was founded in 2010, and had been slowly growing in size and reputation at the point that we initiated conversations with them. At the time we met them, the organization was best known for its annual Black Friday strikes at

Walmart stores, which threatened to turn the busiest shopping day of the year into a day of reckoning for the world's largest retailer. But it was also working to build its membership within stores, to help Walmart workers come together to advocate for one another against the everyday indignities of their jobs.

A coworker from the produce department was talking to the Rev and called Anthony over. As we will see, most people joined the organization through someone that they already knew. Anthony recalls that the Rev put it to him bluntly:

> He said, "If you're not satisfied with your check at the end of the week and you don't think you're going to be able to make it, you need to be part of OUR Walmart." He explained to me the things that they were doing and how, you know, how they are here for us. That's when I'm like, well, [I've been] just sitting here and hoping that things will change because of me being with Walmart for a couple of years [and instead] I'm seeing that it just gets worse. I've learned the pattern of deceit and the terrible things that comes with it, and something like this is a group that I really need to be a part of.

Anthony had heard of OUR Walmart while he was still at the Forest Park store. There, managers had warned him to stay away from the group. During that time he was "always pro-Walmart, you know, everything was for Walmart." So he did not want to have anything to do with the organization. It was only after he started asking for something from the company—a few extra days for his leg to feel better—that he "saw the second side, I guess the Dr. Jekyll and Mr. Hyde effect of it. So that's when I saw the bad face of Walmart, and that's when OUR Walmart didn't sound so bad." At the time of the interview he had recently participated in a one-day strike with OUR Walmart at the Pullman store and felt pride at "standing up for myself."

Anthony turned his interview with Beth in the hotel in Chicago into an account of newfound empowerment with OUR Walmart: "I feel like my voice has actually been heard, especially now that you're doing an interview with me. It's like I feel like my voice and

my opinions are actually being heard." Oral history is often empowering to those whose testimonies provide the raw material for a
project. For narrators, it can be a vehicle for achieving a sociological
imagination, for seeing how one's life unfolds against a backdrop of
larger social and institutional processes.

As it happened, Anthony's involvement in the organization would
be short-lived. He saw the need for change at Walmart but never
grew close enough to others in OUR Walmart to see his fate as bound
together with theirs, to become a part of a collective movement that
could take on the company. Instead, the same frustrations that
made OUR Walmart appealing to Anthony also spurred him to look
elsewhere for work. Anthony's commitment to collective action was
contingent. Soon after the interview he left Walmart, and left OUR
Walmart as well.

Anthony had stuck around Walmart longer than most. Annual
turnover rates at the company and in other low-wage jobs like it
hover around 50 percent. This means that when you enter a Walmart
on any given day you are likely to confront a distribution of employees who are much more content at the company than the sum total
of people who have ever worked at the company—people who have
not yet seen Dr. Jekyll, or whose basis of comparison makes Walmart
seem okay, or who *have* managed to find a sense of purpose or community there. High turnover is a form of unnatural selection; assuming that the company does not spend too much searching for new
hires or investing too much in them, the easy exit protects the company from people who might, in other circumstances, feel invested
enough in problems at the company to try to fix them.[35]

At the time of Beth's interview with him, Anthony was still optimistic about his future. But the aspirations he expressed in the
Walmart commercial—school, IT, engineering—had been overshad-
owed by more modest, proximate ones. He wanted to move out of
his aunt's house, where he was still living: "As a 20-year-old man
I shouldn't have to worry . . . if I'm not able to stay with my aunt
anymore, whether or not I'm going to be out on the street." He also
wanted to raise a family, but he was worried about being able to

provide for them: "I can't raise a child not knowing whether or not I'm going to be able to support not only myself, but that child." The woman he was most interested in had a daughter of her own, and she wondered whether Anthony would be in a position to support her, if she needed it. And Anthony knew that he could not give her that assurance: "Right now where I'm at as far as working, I don't see myself being able to support a family."

Anthony seemed to know on some level that Walmart was not going to give him the stability he craved, but he also didn't seem quite ready to give up on the fantasy that he just might be one of those who were "working [their] way up" to corporate. At the end of the interview, when Beth asked Anthony if he had any questions for her, it was as if he thought Walmart might be redeemed—and that *he* might be the redeemer:

> Do you—would you happen to think that taking an associate that possibly started at the bottom—like, you know, they say that the new CEO, he started off pushing carts. Let's say if we had possibly an associate who came from an impoverished area, who's been with the company for a while, who steadily moved up and steadily saw the actual discrimination and the harsh working conditions, do you think then possibly becoming the CEO in the future could make a difference?

It is hard to let go of fantasy. The interview ended and Beth and Anthony got back into the rental car. It turned out that the car—the Ford Fusion—was Anthony's dream car. He and his brothers were car fanatics. Here is Beth's account of the interaction:

> *I then asked him why the one we were in was his dream car. He gave me what I would later realize was a classic Tony answer: he explained how it was a practical car, with good safety features and a long life, but also sleek and cool. He was more in tune with his responsibilities and the potential for having a family than most boys his age but he wasn't immune to the seductive and ever-elusive coolness of popular masculinity. He asked me what my dream car was and I didn't have an answer.*

In the short term, Anthony's interview with Beth affirmed his commitment to OUR Walmart by making him feel like his voice was heard; longer term, though, it made him acutely aware of the experiences that Beth had had that he had not. Later, Anthony would tell us that the interview with Beth—just meeting her and realizing that she was not so different from him—made him wonder if he could go to college too, or at least find a job like Beth's in which he got to drive around in a rental car like Beth was doing. That dream was realizable. By January of 2015 Anthony had found a job at Enterprise Rental Cars near Chicago O'Hare.

The distance between a 19-year-old Barnard freshman and a 19-year-old Walmart associate might seem unbridgeable. One of the things we consider in this book is when such distances work, and when they fail, for both sides of the interaction—for the student activists who have committed their summers to the project of helping Walmart workers achieve respect, and for the workers, whose summers are not things they control sufficiently to imagine giving them over to someone other than the company they work for.

WHERE WE ARE GOING AND HOW

The 20 participants in the summer project, scattered across five different regions of the country, were charged with two quite different roles over the course of the nine-week project: one as researcher; the other as labor organizer. The students were asked to conduct interviews with Walmart workers; they were also charged with helping to build OUR Walmart in whatever ways their local sites required.

These two roles sat somewhat uneasily alongside one another. Most obviously, every time a student took half a day to conduct an interview was a half-day in which he or she wasn't knocking on doors, visiting stores, staffing tables, shuttling workers, making follow-up phone calls, or doing any of the other daily practices urgent to OUR Walmart. Organizing and in-depth interviewing operate on different timescales; the former thriving on urgency, metrics, results, the latter eschewing them. Some staff in OUR Walmart didn't understand why the students were doing the interviews in the first place and, more often than not, were not going to go out of their way to make room for them.

There was a deeper tension too. After all, most qualitative researchers aspire to elicit from people the meaning to which they give the experiences they have had—not to impose such meanings on them. Storytelling is important to organizers too, but the organizer is often listening with a moral already in mind, working to mold individual stories into a common collective story in which we are stronger together than we are apart. In-depth interviewing is to organizing what psychoanalysis is to Alcoholics Anonymous.[36] Among organizers, then, there is often a legitimate concern about an individual going "off script," threatening the collective interpretation on which the organization is based. But going off script—or rather, being reflexive enough about one's own script so as to recognize when one's subjects' understandings diverge from one's own—is of foundational importance in qualitative research.

This is reflective of a broader tension between academic work and projects for social change, between the pursuit of academic knowledge and the pursuit of the public good. It was this tension on display during the first week of training, when Kevin—a student who would go on to work in Cincinnati—began asking questions about the ratio of workers to community supporters at OUR Walmart's rallies, which led to a quiet suspicion among OUR Walmart staff that he was a company spy. It was this tension on display when Nicole, a student from the Los Angeles team, interjected during a call regarding a survey of customers to ask questions about methodology, only to have her priorities questioned by the organization's leadership. For those in academia, whether students or faculty, knowledge is often considered an end in itself, the academy a (blessedly) autonomous field. For those in the thick of battle, information is artillery.

Of course, these two ways of engaging with the world can also be complementary. In-depth interviewing can help deepen the relationships between interviewee and interviewer; it can give the interviewee an opportunity to reflect on the choices they have made and the contexts in which these choices are situated. More simply, an in-depth interview can make someone feel "heard," as Anthony had put it, when the daily life of work at the company could feel silencing. Respect is something won not only through collective power and institutional change—the raison d'être of organizing—but also interactively, through processes of individual recognition. Not to mention that such interviewing might help an organization better understand the life situations and common sense of the communities they hoped to engage. Beyond the interview, as we will see shortly, there are many ways in which academic knowledge might contribute to social justice work.

Conversely, an organizing ethic may enrich interviewing as well. An in-depth interview risks reifying and reproducing the world at the same time it helps us understand it. While a certain reflexive understanding *may* emerge from the interview, it certainly does not have to—in which case it can make the world seem more stable and static than it is. An organizing ethic can help the interviewer challenge people's self-understandings, push them to interpret the past in alternative ways and imagine new futures. It can also help to connect stories to one another, concatenating these individual stories into a larger whole. More broadly, academics tend to eschew engagement with questions of values in their work, preferring to stay on the safer ground of description and explanation. An organizing ethic can force academic work to be more explicit and reflexive about the values underlying it, help it see the ways in which it tends to reproduce the world and how it might unsettle it.

This tension sits in the background of what is to follow. But it is what students learned about Walmart workers and labor organizing, and what we learned, that takes center stage.

In chapter 1 we consider how people's ties outside work (or the absence of such ties) frame how people make sense of their work. It is here that we meet some of the 1.4 million associates working at Walmart. It is just a descriptive taste. But it is a taste that we have confidence provides a fuller picture of the whole. It is these people whom our students meet. It is these people whom organizers try to mobilize. And it is these people whose work building community is what we need to understand. We focus on how people got to Walmart, the social worlds from which they came and that serve as reference points for how they make sense of working there. That is not by accident. How one's life course has unfolded—how we got to where we are—is the key thing that one has to know in order to answer the question: What am I doing here?

For many, we find, work at Walmart looks pretty good when compared to the situations they were in before; a shredded social safety net and expansive criminal justice system has made life outside the low-wage labor market worse and Walmart, by comparison, better.

We then turn, in chapter 2, to what that "here" is, that is, we turn to what work is like at Walmart. We cannot explain Walmart workers' relative quiescence only in relationship to bad outside options. Somewhat surprisingly, workers at Walmart find pockets of autonomy in which they are able to exercise a sense of creativity and feel a sense of investment in the work they do. And they form relationships with one another, and sometimes with customers, that provide community and recognition. Moreover, the possibility of exit—of leaving Walmart—makes it feel like a choice to stay. So what does make workers feel a sense of indignity and injustice? The arbitrary authority of managers. This is a story of creativity in a desert, of building community and a sense of personal distinction in a context in which every decision, put into place by operation engineers, buried in algorithmic bunkers in Bentonville, Arkansas, seems designed to destroy the capacity for community. It is a story of intense observation and supervision, but also of pockets of freedom and autonomy. People find meaning on the shop floor through their ties with coworkers and customers. This often serves to bind workers to the company in ways that make it easier for their bosses to take advantage of them.

In chapter 3 we try to solve the puzzles presented in chapter 2. We argue that workers' capacity to find pockets of autonomy, the depth and breadth of their social relationships at work, and their frustrations with the arbitrary authority of managers can all be explained in part by structural features of retail work and the low-wage labor market. Here we explore server systems and their relationship to unjust authority, monopsony power in the labor market, and the just-in-time production of service with a smile. We also delve into workers' ambivalent relationship with customers, who are socially close to workers (many workers are also customers) but structurally distant: it is often in the name of customers that workers are treated poorly by their managers, and customers wield a form of supervisory authority themselves.

Chapter 4 turns to the role of the labor organizer. We distinguish what an organizer does from the "framing processes" predominant in many contemporary analyses of social movements. We explore the recognition among contemporary labor leaders of the importance of social ties in the organizing process—as conduits for influence and information and as bases for collective identity—and the significance of interpersonal respect as an issue around which to organize. And we analyze how the history of the American labor movement—its early domestication and bureaucratization in response to vehement state and employer opposition—has left it profoundly ill-equipped to capture the imaginations of workers today.

We consider the nature of workers' structural power in service-sector jobs like those at Walmart compared to workers in those industries on which the modern American labor movement was built in the 1930s; we consider the gap between the material benefits that unions traditionally have offered their members and the considerations of respect, control, and community that seem to animate workers at Walmart today—and, we shall see, has often animated workers in the past; we consider at the microlevel the kinds of relationships on which labor organizations have been and might again be built, the processes by which dyadic relationships between individuals become solidaristic groups, the quasi-religious feelings of effervescence that emerge out of such groups, and the necessity but insufficiency of these feelings for winning power.

This chapter is also where we first encounter at the microlevel the idea that friendship ties may be orthogonal to organizing. Where friendship and community identity are overlapping, movement organizing may need to find another basis.

Chapter 5 returns to the students who participated in the Summer for Respect to see what we can learn about organizing, solidarity, and collective action from their experiences. Where existing literature tends to regard "social movement unionism" as a relatively uniform set of practices, we observe wide variation in conceptions of organizing and social change across the five sites— variation which, in turn, helps to explain the very different ways that our students made sense of their experiences in the field. And yet we also see ways in which the summer shaped the students regardless of the specific sites where they worked. Drawing on interviews, social network data, and brain scans, we show that the nature of collective identification among students changed over the course of the summer and that this evolution may have implications for new labor organizing. Drawing on brain scan data, we show that friendship and trust are distinct phenomena arising in different brain regions, and we show how this distinction may be important for both scholars of collective action and for organizers.

Finally, chapter 6 explores the future of the labor movement as it experiments with new ideas and new technologies to build community and power among those who work in low-wage jobs at Walmart and beyond. The problem for OUR Walmart is and remains one of scale. The leaders of OUR Walmart saw this from the organization's inception. Recognizing that people today are as likely to strive to build community online as they are at work—especially when their schedules are unpredictable and turnover is intense—they understood that they should connect to people in these online spaces, and build *new* kinds of online spaces in which online communities might facilitate building collective power. As importantly, they would find out, such online infrastructure was also resilient to organizational shocks, meaning that OUR Walmart was able to survive even when its funding was pulled by the UFCW soon after our students returned from the field.

This chapter observes the tremendous potential of such online spaces, and also their perils. In the absence of concerted moderation and facilitation, an online community of Walmart workers can become a place of virtual friendship at the exclusion of help, advice, and trust; people can come to the group to share funny and moving and banal things about their lives—watercooler talk—but not to cooperate. We see here the tension between collective action and "good feeling," between solidarity and friendship. And we see how moderation makes the difference, how principles of relationship building and organizing can be brought into such online spaces, and how linking online and offline organization can yield an enduring, impactful, and resilient framework for the future.

A FEW WORDS ON METHODS

In these endeavors we make use of many different kinds of methods at many different levels of analysis. They are complementary, and what we learn from one approach is almost always refracted through the prism of another. First we make use of interviews students conducted with workers and organizers in the field. We also conducted interviews with the students themselves, and complement those interviews with material drawn from their field observations. Second, we make use of our own observations from the field; conversations with Walmart workers, union organizers, and the leaders of OUR Walmart; and some of OUR Walmart's internal records, deidentified to protect confidentiality.

Third, we draw on over 600,000 posts made by more than 20,000 workers over a few years to a discussion board of current and former Walmart employees. The board gives a rich sense of everyday life at Walmart, which we try to capture qualitatively. But we also analyze these data more systematically, using co-occurrence methods for distant reading of texts to uncover the nature of conversations among workers and how those conversations change over time, as the composition of the community and the norms for appropriate discussion topics change.

We also use reviews of Walmart written by over 9,500 hourly associates on the website Glassdoor.com, a website founded in 2007 that allows employees to anonymously review their employers. Reviewers are able to rank an employer on a number of different dimensions, as well as to describe the "Pros" and "Cons" of their jobs. We use these data specifically to understand the most salient positive and negative parts of working at Walmart among the selective sample of workers who review the company. Alongside the Glassdoor data we analyze more than 35,000 Yelp.com reviews written by customers about their experiences at Walmart. This allows us to investigate in more detail how the experience of shopping at Walmart varies across different geographic regions and demographically distinct neighborhoods. We find, for example, that Walmarts in poorer communities and communities of color are more likely to receive negative reviews from customers; perhaps unsurprisingly, these are also many of the Walmarts in which workers express the most dissatisfaction with the way they are treated. Together these "big data"—discussion board, Glassdoor, Yelp—confirm some of the impressions we have about low-wage work based on our more qualitative data; and they also help us to appreciate the extent to which the experience of Walmart—for both workers and for customers—varies across its more than 4,000 U.S. stores.

Fourth, we draw from a survey we conducted with over 6,000 Walmart workers, the overwhelming majority of whom we recruited using online advertisements to anyone who indicated that Walmart was (or had been) their employer. The survey was designed to take approximately 15 minutes, and consisted of questions about a number of different domains: one's background; one's history of work at Walmart and elsewhere; one's social relationships inside and outside the store and the extent to which these overlap; one's experience of hardship before (and during) one's time working at the company; one's feelings about a variety of causes and organizations; one's voting history; one's general outlook toward the world. These surveys allowed us to focus particularly on how Walmart facilitates and breaks down social relations; and how individuals feel in their stores and their communities.[37]

Fifth, turning the focus back toward the students, we use standard network survey data at multiple points in time to capture the evolving relationships of the students over the course of the project. Finally, we make use of data not previously seen in sociology—data from fMRI scans of our student volunteers. We conducted these scans twice, once at the start of the program and once at the end. We had the idea (described much more fully later) that we could learn something about how students' ties with other students—both the ties that they expressed having and implicit ties measured by neural response to others in their group—shaped their individual and collective experiences. We were right that we could learn about that. Along the way, we may have learned why friendship is a poor predictor of organizing success, and that, years ago, the organizer Saul Alinsky seems to have predicted the basic principle by which the human brain organizes multiple social relations—namely, that the brain distinguishes between friendship and trust.

Combining the social network surveys, our in-depth interviews of students, data on OUR Walmart organizing in different sites, and the fMRI scans, we are also able to ask and start to provide new answers to such fundamental questions as: How does solidarity emerge? What do people seek in their relationships with others? When do communities cohere and when do they come undone? What group-level or environmental processes make for *success*, whether success is defined in terms of productive Walmart workers (by managers), motivated members of OUR Walmart (by organizers), or a cohesive community of participant-observers (by us with regard to our students). In short, we learn from this work something about organizing, about when it works and when it fails.

Throughout, we try to learn what people get out of their work, how they make community work for them, how they struggle to understand and change the things that are holding them back.

SOCIAL STRUCTURE IS A SET OF PROCESSES WITHIN A MULTITIERED FOUNTAIN

A set of binary oppositions are often used to describe the field in which social science operates—macro and micro, agency and structure—even if most people basically recognize that these distinctions are neither sustainable nor meaningful. To this list we could add "qualitative" and "quantitative" data, the stuff that is described as getting "mixed" in "mixed-methods research."[38] The implicit assumption of the large literature on mixed methods is that there are actually data in the world that come to us as "qualitative" or "quantitative." If this were true, then this book could be seen to "mix methods." That said, the idea that there are two types of data in the world makes little sense. Are the neural signatures of future liking qualitative or quantitative data? Are the 600,000 posts on a discussion board qualitative or quantitative? More useful for us than thinking about types of data is thinking about how to capture multiple views of many different levels of structure. These issues—multiple views and multiple levels—are intimately related.

Proust remarks somewhere that it is better to travel across a single land with a thousand pairs of eyes than a thousand lands with a single pair of eyes.[39] This idea is echoed by Burawoy in his description of reflexive sociology, the goal of which is to "collect multiple readings of a single case and aggregate them into social processes."[40] These multiple readings are readings from different standpoints, where standpoints can be people, or levels of observation, or neurons firing, or patterns of interaction in historical context. Any real world is best described as a complex set of interwoven tiers. Because information doesn't just walk up to us and announce itself, and because it doesn't exist in the world as "qualitative" or "quantitative," waiting to be discovered, the work of the social scientist is to nurse an observation into a crystalline form that for a moment can be apprehended from multiple points of view.

These views are designed to put together a whole object—a social structure, a field. But the act of putting multiple views together is not like the parable of the blind men, whose partial observations of the elephant yield a rope, a wall, a tree trunk, a fan, and so on. Social structure is no more an assemblage of different things than an elephant is an assemblage of ropes and fans and tree trunks. The complex social worlds we try to describe and gain access to in this book are, as we see it, sets of interwoven social processes, mechanisms, interweavings.

THE FIRST STEP IN UNDERSTANDING

We've talked to a lot of our colleagues about this book about Walmart and most of them tell us that they have never been to a Walmart, or just went once, in an emergency, on a road trip or something. It's a weird sort of anticipatory social desirability bias. Most of our colleagues have never been inside a factory either. But the first thing that they would say if we told them we were writing a book on a factory would not be, "I've never been in one." Perhaps urban intellectuals and artists and professors and their fellow travelers feel closer to factory workers they have never seen than to Walmart workers (and shoppers). Perhaps they want to tell us that Walmart is something else, that it is somewhere else, that it is not theirs.

It is our intuition that many people in our networks conflate their disdain for Walmart as an abusive employer with a class-tinged disgust at the company's *low class*. They don't shop at Walmart because it is cheap and dirty and tacky and sterile . . . and also because it treats its workers badly. A thin form of solidarity is an intellectually justifiable excuse for revulsion: revulsion at an imagined mass of the downtrodden who work there and shop there; the senior citizen forced to demean himself by greeting people at the door; the intellectually disabled; the pimply, skinny high school dropout. But these are imaginary figures cobbled together by the cultural elite from stereotypes of people different than they are. All types of people work at Walmart.

But it turns out that many people who work at Walmart do not experience working at Walmart as unjust. Many find that it makes a real community. And many people find working at Walmart creative and meaningful. Even its narrow economic impact is somewhat ambiguous for the poor. In some ways it *does* make it possible for people to buy that hamburger and cup of coffee by making everything so much cheaper. Walmart workers and Walmart customers are often the same people. Any time people complain about Walmart's low wages and poor working conditions, the company highlights how much it is helping poor families save.[41] This isn't all just spin. The company has risen to prominence as a result of its *everyday low prices*—its profit margins per item are tiny; it makes its money on its massive scale.

And so, if not revulsion and distance, then what? We end by considering how our readers might contribute in new ways to renewing low-wage workers' organizations in the United States. The first step is understanding. We think that if we can understand Walmart workers, labor organizers, organizing, the nature of work, and the ways in which people build community out of the most meager resources, then we can understand how places like Walmart work; and we can better understand why efforts to organize Walmart workers to win better wage and working conditions have not yet succeeded, and we can understand how such efforts might succeed in the future. We think that if we can understand our students' experiences—their successes and failures, their inspirations and frustrations—we can learn new lessons about the challenges of and possibilities for wider community involvement in workers' rights. In any case, those are the goals.

1

PATHWAYS

Almost every day of the summer, Kevin and Max—two members of the Ohio team—would drive together from their makeshift apartment in a college dorm in northern Cincinnati up I-75 to the Walmart stores in the suburbs of Dayton. They were something of an odd couple. Kevin was a white guy from Walnut Creek, California, an extroverted and slightly nerdy dude with a loop earring at the top of his right ear, who had been so inspired by the *Odyssey* during his first year at Columbia that he had a quote tattooed on his left arm in Greek: *polytropōs* or "many turns," the first adjective that Homer applies to Odysseus. A rising senior, he had no prior activist experience. While Kevin was a newcomer to social justice activism, Max—a transgender student from New Haven—had activist roots: Max's grandma had worked alongside Angela Davis as a Black Panther in Oakland, California. *The Communist Manifesto* was around the apartment when Max was growing up. This asymmetry in experience was coupled with another, more practical asymmetry: Max did not have a driver's license, so Kevin was the one driving, and it did not go unnoticed by either of them that the white man was always behind the wheel during the three to four hours they'd be in the car every day.

The highway would take them past lush farmland and industrial buildup: *The land here is so rich that a deep green tone exists every place where there is not an asphalt parking lot or a building*, Kevin wrote. Max remembered driving by the *factory that manufactures chemical flavorings and scents*—with the car windows down it was *always possible to tell which are blueberry days*. A few miles outside Cincinnati they'd pass an enormous 52-foot statue of Jesus, arms outstretched, which sat astride the Solid Rock Church, one of several megachurches dotting southwestern Ohio. And as they got closer to Dayton, they'd pass another massive structure, this one crumbling and just visible from the freeway—Kevin described it as *a giant vacant body . . . like the heart was just ripped out of the place*. This structure, with *its steel shell peeling white paint, its parking lot sprouting weeds*, had been the General Motors Moraine Assembly plant.

On December 23, 2008, the GM plant—4.1 million square feet, larger than 70 football fields—had shut its doors for the last time. Almost 3,000 local residents had been hourly workers there. Once one factors in the jobs lost among those businesses in the vicinity of the plant, as well as those up and down the supply chain, about 33,000 people lost their jobs as a result of the plant's closure. The closure had a devastating impact on the local economy, with a cost estimated at over $700 million per year. Local charitable organizations were stretched to their limits helping people find food and shelter.[1]

In the scheme of things, though, the closing of the Moraine plant was merely one more indignity for a Rust Belt long in economic decline. Back in 1900, Dayton had had more patents per capita than any other city in the United States—the Silicon Valley of the early industrial era.[2] In his Dayton saloon, James Ritty had invented the cash register in 1883—"the incorruptible cashier," he called it—as a way to prevent his employees from pilfering.[3] And in their Dayton bicycle shops, around the turn of the century, the Wright brothers dreamed up their flying machine.[4] Air conditioning, magnetic strip technology for credit cards, stealth technology for airplanes, barcode scanners, the electric wheelchair: they were all invented in Dayton. And industry followed invention. John Henry Patterson bought the patent to the cash register and built the National Cash Register (NCR) Corporation in Dayton, which would spread the machinery of commerce around the world. By the 1960s, GM, AK Steel, Delphi, Mead Paper Company, and many other manufacturers were institutions in the area, as were the large labor unions that represented the workers within them.

The decline of U.S. manufacturing, beginning in the 1970s, hit cities like Dayton particularly hard. Companies began to outsource their manufacturing, either outside the United States or to places in the country where labor was cheaper; companies also invested in technologies that made skilled manual workers redundant. NCR, for example, employed approximately 15,700 factory workers in Dayton in 1969; just seven years later, in 1976, only 2,000 workers remained.[5] In 2009, the company moved its headquarters from Dayton to Duluth, Georgia, taking with it the remaining 1,200 jobs.[6] As one last slap in the face, NCR—the cash register company that had been so integral to Dayton's industrial past—has recently been producing the self-checkout devices being installed in Walmarts across the country, threatening to displace a new generation of workers.[7] At different times, each of the other industrial giants in the area has followed a similar path, closing factories and laying off unionized workers.

In mid-June of 2014, at the Walmart Supercenter in Franklin, Ohio [#3784], a 20-minute drive from Moraine, Kevin met Jenny Molten, who worked in the photo department there. Jenny remembered the days after the Moraine plant closed: "A lot of people . . . came into our [Walmart] store because they were locked out of their jobs or shut out or the plant closed." They came to Walmart looking for work, hoping to rebuild their lives: "People have lost their homes, people have lost their . . . their property, their assets, everything that they worked hard for in their life, it's gone." If they got jobs at Walmart at all, these jobs paid "basically pennies, compared to what they [used to make]." Jenny's grandfather had worked at GM for 40 years before his retirement in 1999. Before she had her kids, Jenny had also worked in factories associated with the automobile industry, like Pioneer and Faurecia. But those jobs had disappeared. Most of the workers who reported to the Moraine Walmart Supercenter, a mile and half from the shuttered GM plant, or any of the other supercenters in the area, made less than $10 an hour.

Over the course of the summer Kevin and Max would meet others at the Franklin store with similar accounts of downward mobility. Joan Wharton had spent over 12 years working for the AK Steel Corporation. The work had been backbreaking, but she was paid more than $20 an hour and had union representation. Now, at the Franklin Supercenter, she was making $9 an hour, less than half of what she had been making before, trying to support herself and her husband, who was serving time in prison for drug possession: "I've got all the responsibility of a family without all my family being here," she says. Gerald, an "old head" in Kevin's words, who worked in the photo section alongside Jenny and would later become a central figure in the effort to organize the Franklin store, had previously been a shop steward at AK Steel as well.

These workers' accounts of downward mobility—of the hollowing out of U.S. manufacturing and consequent dispossession among the white working class—is a story in which Walmart plays a triple role: first, as the antagonist, the dispossessor, the company that takes advantage of and speeds up the flood of cheap goods from far-flung parts of the globe; second, as the employer of last resort, the place that will pay you half as much to hawk cheaper versions of the goods you once produced yourself; and third, as a last-ditch provider, the place that will sell things cheaply enough for you to squeak by on your paltry paycheck. It is Fordism in reverse, with the same result of stoking consumer demand: rather than pay you enough to buy the car you are producing, Walmart will pay you so little that you are compelled to shop there.

As we shall see, over the course of several weeks, Kevin and Max spent time getting to know workers like Gerald and Jenny and Joan and were able to build the beginnings of an OUR Walmart chapter in the Franklin store. Many of these workers knew firsthand the benefits of labor organization—they or their parents or coworkers had been unionized before. Many of these workers were trying to support families on less than they had been paid in the past and had a clear sense of being worse off than they had been before. Against this background, OUR Walmart may have felt risky, somewhat uncertain, but it often seemed worth the fight and within the boundaries of what seemed possible. They had had secure jobs before; it did not seem preposterous to think they might have secure jobs again.

Less than 15 miles away from the Franklin Walmart is another Walmart Supercenter [#1503], this one on the outskirts of Dayton in a shopping center just across the boundary that separates the suburb of Centerville from Dayton proper. Kevin and Max tried just as hard to recruit OUR Walmart members in this store too. But they had no luck. They could barely get anyone to speak to them, much less spark interest in the OUR Walmart organization. The tension that Kevin and Max felt in the Franklin store—their sense that people were aware of things not being right—was missing here.

Their intuition was that it had something to do with the different demographics of the places. Centerville seemed fancy to them. Compared with the Walmart in Franklin, the associates at the Centerville store seemed either much younger or much older. Kevin and Max were onto something. The average household income around the Franklin store was about $46,000 in 2012, whereas it was close to $80,000 around the Centerville store. Granted, both of these figures are far above the pay of the average Walmart worker, but the difference between them is also striking. What it meant was that the people who worked at the Centerville store tended to be more socially distant from the "average" worker, locally, than those who worked at Franklin. In Centerville, Walmart workers were disproportionately high schoolers, retirees, moms working a few extra hours for pin money: people who likely thought of their jobs quite differently than those trying to provide for their families, as it seemed like many were doing in Franklin. The Centerville workers were building different kinds of careers at Walmart because they were coming from different places. And because they were doing something different, they built a different local culture there—one less oppositional to Walmart—and hence were disinterested in efforts to stand up to the company. It turned out that Max and Kevin's intuition is substantiated in aggregate data on the OUR Walmart campaign across the country: stores located in poorer neighborhoods were, all things equal, more likely to have more people sign up for the organization.

We also see support for Kevin and Max's intuition in the results of the Facebook survey that we conducted with Walmart workers. Those associates least happy at Walmart, as a whole, were between the ages of 22 and 50—years in which people are often looking for regular work, trying to build careers. Those under the age of 22 were happier; those over the age of 70 were the happiest of all.

This chapter makes the simple but important point that in order to understand what work means to the people who work at Walmart, one has to appreciate the diversity of people who wind up there, the range of social situations that drive them to the store, and the ways that these different reference points result in different understandings of relatively similar experiences after they arrive. We have to understand the ways that these workers understand their alternatives; the social situations they were in before they began work at Walmart; the kinds of jobs that their friends and family members have or aspire to. In short, what they actually feel is possible.

To put Walmart in perspective, if the company were its own city, it would be the seventh biggest city in the country, just behind Phoenix, Arizona. And the city of Walmart workers would be filled with people of all ages, ethnicities, and motivations—older people on the brink of retirement who are working there because they have always worked somewhere, or because their old jobs disappeared, or because they just want to have a place to be, or because they want to be close to their children and this was the only game in town. Young people who are paying the bills while they go to community college, or who are thinking they *might* go to college if they just save up a little more money, or who have already climbed to customer service manager (CSM) after only six months and are sure they can climb higher, or who got stoned too much in high school and may *still* be stoned even now as they wander somewhat aimlessly around the toy department. There are 40-something women who are trying to support their families on Walmart wages, who are comparing notes with other 40-something women in the grocery department about what kinds of dairy products they can buy with their WIC benefits;[8] 50-something women who are bored to death at home while their husbands work and are so happy to be around other people; men who prefer pushing carts in the parking lots to anything indoors, since you don't have to talk to customers outside, and the managers leave you alone too, and you can even (occasionally) get drunk on the clock; people who have just found a home after months of homelessness, who have recently been released from prison, who have returned from military service, who have escaped abusive relationships, who have struggled with mental illness.

In this chapter, we introduce you to some of these people. This is not only to highlight the diversity of experiences of people who work at Walmart, but also to illustrate the ways in which people's social ties outside the store frame the way they make sense of the world inside. Just as the trace of a stable, unionized job—the memory of it, but also the familial obligations and social status that went along with it and persist after the job itself disappears—can make one acutely aware of the inadequacy of Walmart wages and arbitrariness of Walmart supervisors, so can acute loneliness make Walmart feel like home.

GOING DOWN

The story of the Moraine GM plant and the workers left behind in its wake is a story familiar to sociologists and social critics—the background for movies like Michael Moore's *Roger & Me* and books like Amy Goldstein's recent *Janesville: An American Story*. For those alarmed by growing economic inequality, one of the comforting aspects of this sort of story is that it appears as though critique is its natural outcome, a result of the mismatch between the life to which people are accustomed, and so imagine for themselves in the future, and the life into which they have been plunged.[9] People have been screwed over; people should be pissed.

We did hear these sorts of stories in the field. Within the first few minutes of Kevin's conversation with Gerald in the Franklin store, Kevin remembers, Gerald *went off, calling Walmart a bunch of "labor stealing motherfuckers," calling this or that manager an "asshat," and expressing his frustrations with the "lunatic" half of the store* that opposed advocating for themselves. The notion of Walmart stealing one's labor does not arise out of the ether; even to conceive of one's work as "labor" seems a throwback to a time when Marxist language was less absent from workers' common sense than it is today. It seems likely that Gerald had learned to "labor" during his time as a steward at AK Steel, that he was applying the factory's language, its way of seeing, to his new, more modest digs.

Ann Regnerus was another Walmart worker our students met in Chicago. Ann had never worked in a factory, but in a craft similarly vulnerable to displacement. She and her husband, Bill, had until recently been comfortably middle class and still lived in a modest home in the suburbs of Chicago. For 30 years, Bill had owned a gravestone-cutting business that he had inherited from his stepfather. Even accounting for the uptick in cremations, this is a business sector that is pretty secure to economic fluctuations, simply because every year since the founding of our country there have been more people born than in the previous year, and for that simple reason more people die and need a gravestone. Ann and Bill ran their business together in Orland, Illinois. As inequality became more marked in the United States, they had begun to specialize in "high-end work" like those fancy black stones with hand-etched photos in them, because Bill was tired of doing "dumb stones," he said. He "just wanted people that wanted something beautiful." That was not a good business decision. The Great Recession hit their clients hard, which in turn hit Bill and Ann hard: "When they give you 30 [thousand dollars] on a stone that's 50 [thousand dollars] . . . and then don't have the other 20 thousand, and the stone cost you 35, what do you do?" They went under.

The transition from small-business owner to low-wage worker was painful for both of them. For two months, Ann says, they barely ate. She remembers a friend of theirs giving them a coupon for a turkey, which they froze so they could economize and eat in pieces. They finally got on food stamps, but not before standing in line, at dawn, outside the welfare office.

It turned out that outside the office was better than inside, where, Ann remembers, they were subjected to the kinds of interrogation meant to distinguish the worthy from unworthy poor: "Because even though they're chastising you for being poor, they don't believe that you're poor enough to deserve anything, so you need to carry your paperwork with you and prove it. And, you know, you're in this situation where it's, like—every stranger on the planet is looking through your personal financial stuff, you know? And then they're judging you and questioning you." On another occasion in the office she remembers being told that she wasn't allowed to speak—Bill, as head of household, was the only one permitted. "I'm, like, are we in America?"

They found jobs through a temp agency driving cars for CarMax, a massive used-car retailer. Ann was depressed. "I wasn't smiling and the boss said, you know, 'Well, why don't you start smiling, you know? Look happy!' And I'm just, like, well, you know, it's still America, you know? I may have to work here, but I don't have to be happy about it. I thought. And then, next time we heard from Labor Ready, they said, 'Oh, but they requested that you not be asked back.' Because I didn't smile." In today's low-wage service work you are not allowed to convey anything but cheerfulness.[10] She and Bill had been working overnight shifts at the Walmart in Crestwood, Illinois [#3601], since 2010. It was no better—"unbelievably abusive," "Orwellian."

Are we in America? This was Ann's refrain. Before, she had had a sense of control over her days, and now that sense of control was gone. She had to supplicate herself to the bureaucrats at the welfare office who told her to be quiet, to bosses who wanted control not only of her time but of her feelings.

The strangest thing for Ann was when she looked around at the other clients in the welfare office or her coworkers at Walmart and saw their seeming acceptance of their situations. In the welfare line, it seemed to her, everybody was "beaten down and broken down and just obedient." Of her coworkers at Walmart, she felt, "It's almost like they have Stockholm syndrome. They identify with their oppressors." But the resignation was confusing for her. "I just don't understand what's going on—is it all the antidepressants that got in the water supply?"

People like Ann Regnerus look back at the halcyon days when "America was America," when they were better off than their parents, who were better off than their grandparents; when there were enough sort of wealthy people to memorialize their deaths with a better class of gravestones than their "dumb counterparts." That America did exist, but not in 2007. Partial memories of a lost America tend to be associated with partial penetrations of the actual situation.[11] Many of the people Ann Regnerus imagines having gotten Stockholm syndrome had been quietly working away in hard, low-paying jobs for years, jobs in which they had likely felt obliged to smile at people just like her.

GETTING OUT OF THE HOUSE

But accounts of industrial displacement as the pathway to Walmart, while present, are not the only or even the predominant stories among the Walmart workers with whom we came into contact. In fact, we found, most workers' everyday counterfactuals—the lives to which they compare the lives they actually lead—are not middle-class jobs characterized by security, high wages, and respect.

One striking feature of retail work as a whole, and the Walmart workforce in particular, is its gender composition. As of 2014, over

70 percent of Walmart sales associates were women.[12] Throughout its history, Walmart has counted on a supply of female workers for whom work at the company was not the family's primary source of income. The Ozarks of northwest Arkansas, where the company began, was no manufacturing hub, but its agricultural industry was undergoing its own technological transformation in the 1960s that preceded the changes in manufacturing that were to come to the country as a whole. As Nelson Lichtenstein writes, "Farm women, who had once had their hands full with the chickens, the cows, and the canning, now found that electrification and better roads made wage work attractive, available, indeed necessary."[13] For these wives and daughters, retail work provided second and third incomes that could supplement a family's earnings.

As importantly, work could provide an escape from the banality (as well as brutality) of home life. For women relegated to the domestic sphere, work at Walmart was sometimes experienced as liberating. Take Sue Rogers, 54, from the suburbs of Dayton, Ohio. She had met the man she would marry, another kid from town, when she was just 16, and had her first child at 18. Looking back, she says, "I lost a lot of fun time there. I should have [been more careful], you know, but things happen." Her husband was a "good husband, a good provider," she says, but was also a "workaholic" and "was rarely ever home." So Sue stayed home and raised her two daughters, trying to give them the same stable childhoods that her parents had given her—now updated to include the requisite after-school activities of suburban living: soccer, choir, cheerleading, karate, volleyball, baseball, and even the Miss America contest. Sue, embodying a certain suburban cliché herself, joined a bowling league with her mother-in-law.

When her kids left home, though, she seemed to give herself permission to feel the resentment that had been there on some level for years. She was frustrated with her husband's emotional unavailability and chafed at her dependence on him. While the kids had been at home, Sue had worked sporadically delivering pizzas for a local pizza joint: "I just enjoyed it. I drove and delivered pizzas because

I knew New Lebanon. I've been there all my life. I knew where every place was at." It gave her something to do. After her kids had left home she looked for more steady employment and found it at a Walmart in Dayton [#1504]. The proximate reason for her employment was that she wanted a car, and her husband said she would have to pay for it herself:

> I got a job so I could get me a car and I paid for it myself. See, because when the kids left, he was trying to teach me responsibility about myself because I never had—with the kids and everything, I never worked. So I never had no opportunity to make my own money, pay my own bills. He paid for everything. He did everything. . . . That's what his idea was. So the next year I got a brand-new car, a 1998. I purchased a new Malibu and I paid for it out of my money.

Sue was craving independence from her husband (it is hard not to hear the condescension in his voice as he "teaches her" financial responsibility), and when her kids left home she seized it. Her work at Walmart wasn't as much about having Stockholm syndrome as it was about having something to do and call her own.

Likewise, Mayra Rodriguez, from Montebello, California, didn't wind up at Walmart because of any sort of economic desperation. She needed to get out of the goddamn house. Mayra had been a stay-at-home mother for years, while her husband worked construction. He got injured at work, which gave her an opening to convince him to allow her to look for work: "I was just tired of staying home. . . . I was tired of *Blue's Clues* and *Sesame Street* and *Bob the Builder* and all that stuff. No more. I just needed to get out. So, I got a part-time job. And it kept me occupied. It got me out of the house for a couple of hours." It was an ongoing negotiation, though. If she was at work, then he had to take care of the kids, and he didn't like it. He made her quit her first job, at a debt-collection agency, because he "didn't like taking care of the kids during the day. He missed having his wife home, taking care of that." But she couldn't stay at home any longer: "I stayed home until it wasn't going to work for me to be home anymore. I had to get out of the house. I had to." And so she applied for work at the Paramount Walmart Supercenter in California [#2110] and got a job working in the lingerie department. Her husband conceded. By then the kids were older.

Sandra Lopez wasn't at Walmart entirely for the money either. She found a job at the Walmart in Pico Rivera, California [#2886], because "I was bored at home." She continued, "By then my son was in school full-time and I just needed to keep busy, because I think you go crazy at home. I do." She was excited to get the additional money with which she could "do nothing," and did not feel like she needed the job to support herself or her family. Walmart wages were pin money, spending cash. Working there was a way to feel useful. For money she could continue to lean on her husband, a man to whom she affectionately refers as her "complication."

"Labor" is a way we describe a particular use of time. By selling time to an employer, a worker turns time into labor time, an hour of work in exchange for an hourly wage. The wage, at least in theory, compensates the worker for the "costs" of using time in this way, costs that include the opportunity costs of all the things that the worker could have been doing but was not able to do because she was at work.

But what if there are no real opportunity costs? Or, phrased differently, what if one's time is not experienced so much as a commodity to spend as an affliction to pass? Those with small children who experience the interminable wait for bedtime can appreciate the distinction. Years ago, Arlie Hochschild captured this idea in *The Time Bind*, when she described the ways in which work was becoming more like home and home was becoming more like work.[14] Hochschild focused on workplaces that were becoming more family-friendly—offering things like flextime, maternity leave, lactation rooms—a trend, for upper-class professional workers, that has gone into overdrive in the era of work sites conceptualized as campuses, with cafeterias, exercise rooms, nature trails and benches for quiet contemplation.

But of course, depending on how bad it is at home, a workplace need not offer very much to feel better than home. According to these women's accounts, working at Walmart was more desirable than the sequestration of family life. Work provided a legitimate reason to get out of the house. Now, we should also consider that being a wage earner likely had symbolic importance for these women as well, that they would not have been content to volunteer at Walmart, or it would not have felt quite the same—a subject to which we return subsequently. Nevertheless, our economic models of the labor market risk collapsing when time at work is more desirable than non-work time.

Such an idea also offers a different perspective on the rising economic insecurity of the last half-century. Married women's workforce participation took off in the 1970s, alongside declines in manufacturing, as wives were forced to make up the lost wages of husbands.[15] As of 2012, approximately 60 percent of married couples with children were dual-income households, up from just 25 percent in 1960,[16] and yet median family income remained practically unchanged. The easiest way to interpret this is that couples today are working twice as hard for the same amount of money. The decline in manufacturing had upended the gendered division of labor on which the working-class family had established itself, putting new stress and strain on lower-income Americans as women were forced to leave the home to make ends meet. This is all true.

But there were benefits to this forced labor-market entry as well. As Lillian Rubin writes in *Families on the Fault Line*, an interview study of working-class families published in 1994, "Universally, the women I interviewed work because they must. Almost as often they find a level of self-fulfillment and satisfaction on the job that they're loath to give up."[17] What may have begun as a response to economic necessity became a valued part of women's self-conceptions.

Moreover, married women's increasing workforce participation likely helped to facilitate a realignment of power dynamics within the family. The traditional family division of labor had always been an unequal one, premised on women's subordination to and dependence on their husbands. The decline of manufacturing may have created the material opportunities for a women's movement that could further challenge women's subordination to men. Changing norms about and opportunities for women at the workplace could, one imagines, give them new leverage within their relationships with men.

Thus, more women could experience the freedom that Sue and Mayra and Sandra were able to experience; more women could go get jobs at Walmart. Seen in this light, the declining fortunes of men in the labor market offered the economic opportunities—and potential justifications—for women to do what they may have wanted to do all along: get out of the house. As women lost economic ground as their families lost ground, within their families they may actually have gained it. It is probably not a coincidence that economic models developed during this period began to peer inside the family to consider its functioning as a result of utility-maximizing decision making between spouses rather than treating the family as a unitary whole in its relationship to the market.[18]

That said, it's not entirely clear whether these opportunities have been realized, and there are many good reasons to think that men have pushed back against these arrangements, using familiar conservative rhetorics that aim to preserve their status. Thus it is no accident that movements to reassert control over women's bodies have become stronger and more violent over the same period. What is more surprising is how some women have reproduced their own subordination—whether by taking on, and downplaying the significance of, the second shift at home,[19] or doubling down on gender roles at home when their husbands are forced to do "women's work" in the labor market,[20] or voting for a widely reported serial sexual harasser in the last presidential election rather than elect a woman.

BECAUSE YOU CAN ONLY PUTTER SO MUCH

We have focused on married women's boredom at home pushing them into the Walmart workplace, but women are not the only ones who pass time at the store. We see it in Anthony's decision to stick around after his shift because he had nothing better to do. We see it in the discussion board post of an associate from Kentucky who writes on Thanksgiving that after *an extremely lonely afternoon, seeing as I have no one around for Thanksgiving, I cannot wait to go into work and be around people*; and in the agreement she gets from other Walmart workers in Louisiana, West Virginia, California, upstate New York, Texas, Indiana, and Florida. Work provides community for people, and work at Walmart is not an exception.

Boredom and loneliness and needing to be busy and needing money to supplement meager SSI checks all lead elderly people to think about working at Walmart. As of 2005, approximately 220,000 workers there—just shy of 20 percent of the company's total workforce—were over the age of 50. The company has been known to send recruiters to senior centers.[21] Certainly, increasing economic insecurity is partially responsible for keeping these older associates in the workforce. But many seem to rely on Walmart as much for giving them a place to be as for giving them a regular paycheck. In the automotive section of a Walmart in Vestal, New York, an older man tells us that he has been with the company for 20 years, much of which time he was also working in the accounting department for the local Catholic Charities. He could have retired long ago, he said, but he kept postponing retirement. He was now finally close to retiring, but only because his wife had passed away and his new girlfriend insisted he spend more time with her. An older woman cashier at the same store had moved to the area to be closer to her sons while they went to college at SUNY Binghamton. They had left, and she didn't feel like moving again, and she wasn't quite ready to retire, not completely, and there weren't so many jobs around here; and anyway it wasn't as bad as people said to work at Walmart, and she mostly got weekends off (though we were speaking to her on a Sunday). Older workers have been found to be more likely than younger workers to find emotional rewards in their work, and many older workers—particularly women—who postpone retirement say that they do so because of the social connections they feel with their coworkers.[22]

The prototype of the elderly low-wage worker in the United States may be the Walmart greeter, that person who stands at the front entrance of every Walmart store and says hello to customers. Legend has it that the greeter position was invented in 1980 by Lois Richard, an associate at the Walmart in Crowley, Louisiana [#310], in the midst of an uptick in shoplifting at the store. Lois and her husband, a local police officer, were talking about the problem one evening and it dawned on her: a friendly face at the front of the store could both make customers feel welcome *and* make customers feel watched.[23] Senior citizens were considered the perfect candidates for these service-cum-surveillance positions. As *Time* magazine put it in a 2012 article, "Smiling seniors playing golf or mah-jongg under a bright warm sun served as Americans' dominant image of retirement 30 years ago. More recently, the vision has been of smiling retirees greeting customers in front of a Walmart."[24] For a few people, when the problem of elderly poverty collides with the problems of elderly isolation, Walmart can serve as a solution for both.

These workers—women supplementing their husbands' incomes, older people looking for a way to pass the time or pad their retirements or both—are those for whom jobs at Walmart were made. People at the periphery of the labor market, who may not have noticed or cared so much that Walmart was violating the basic principle of the wage relationship that Adam Smith had first articulated: that workers would exchange labor power for the means of their subsistence, so that they could come back to work the next day. For some of these workers, Walmart wages seem to appear not as wages at all but as something more akin to pin money: spending cash; money to play with; income earmarked for something other than one's necessities, which are covered by one's spouse or one's SSI check. It's a shell game, of course. But we all have these kinds of monetary shell games.[25]

But when a husband dies, what was originally a welcome diversion, a way of getting out of the house, can come to feel central to one's survival. This is what happened to Elizabeth Masters from the Walmart in Paramount. When she began working at the store she didn't give much attention to the pay; combined with her husband's income, it made her feel downright flush. It was only after her husband's death, in 2009, that she realized "[I] couldn't make it on my own . . . I have been late every month on my rent for the last four years, since his death." It happened to Sue Rogers too. Since her husband had died, the job that she had welcomed as an escape from the monotony of monogamy became central to her financial well-being: "I don't make enough to cover my bills sometimes," she says. And the job was now differently related to her family life too. Before, the job had been there to fill a void in her family life; now she understood it as an impediment to her closest relationships. Since her husband died she would like to see her children more but just doesn't, mainly because her work schedule, combined with her daughter's, made contact next to impossible: "I can't seem to get with her because she's a nurse, so she's got wicked hours too, and so do I." Here the issue for Sue is not the number of hours—Walmart polices overtime quite carefully—but the irregularity of her schedule. All one needs to do is contrast the deeply structured temporality of the factory—its routines organized to maximize efficiency—with the randomness of customer shopping habits to realize how disruptive the Walmart schedules can be for people trying to build lives outside the store.

WALMART PROVIDES AN ESCAPE FROM SERIOUSLY BAD SITUATIONS

Walmart's early success arose in part from women of the Ozarks who—like Sue, Mayra, and Sandra—were on the periphery of the labor market. This early success was decades before Walmart had grown to become the largest employer in the world. Today, the irony is that the Walmart employment model has become central to the U.S. economy, while its employment model continues implicitly to rely on workers peripheral to it. Put another way, the Walmart employment model relies on and reinforces workers' peripheral attachment to the labor market. Its employment model continues to work because it has become so central—jobs like the jobs at Walmart are, in many places, the only game in town.

This fact shapes the pathways of other workers who see that Walmart jobs are good jobs, relative to the other choices that confront them. For these workers, Walmart provides a chance to escape seriously bad situations as well as to build a community more rewarding than the others available to them. Associates are not choosing between unionized jobs at GM and Walmart. Assuming that there are jobs to choose from, Walmart workers are choosing between Walmart and McDonald's, Target, or Costco (if they are lucky). When people consider "choosing" not to work, in turn, they confront unpaid labor at home, a welfare state in retreat, and a criminal justice system in ascendance. They are comparing work to loneliness, isolation, sitting on a porch watching absolutely nothing ever happen, or playing video games.[26] Or they are comparing their jobs to the hardships they have escaped: prison, unemployment, eviction, homelessness, intimate partner violence, selling drugs outside a corner store.

Based on rates of acceptance, it is often harder to get a job at Walmart than to get into Harvard. When two Walmarts opened in Washington, D.C., in 2013, more than 23,000 people applied for 600 jobs.[27] This kind of competition has implications for organizers and for those who want to change their situations at work. When good jobs are scarce, people actually end up accepting wage deals that are worse than the minimum wage. Consider, just as an example, that Anthony was willing to commute four hours every day to his first Walmart job in Forest Park; if we add that time to an eight-hour shift (even without including the bus fare), it suggests that he was willing to work for a wage 33 percent less than the wage Walmart was paying him.

Many of the workers we talked to, especially the women, are at Walmart because Walmart was an escape valve. Anna Jones, 59, from the Englewood neighborhood of Chicago, had struggled with drug addiction in her youth, but had been clean for the past 12 years. It had been a steep climb up. Anna was living in a homeless shelter in 2007 when another woman at the shelter recommended she apply to work at Walmart. She got a job working maintenance on the evening shift at a Chicago store [#5965]. The job was a lifeline, and finally, six years later, she had saved enough to rent a room of her own with a housemate in a shared apartment:

> I don't have my furniture yet. I have an air mattress, but I am so glad to have my own place to live. I mean, you just couldn't even imagine! If you've never been without a home, you don't know what it's like. I kid you not. I'm, like, in a palace! Being in my own place, man, it's like heaven! I'm telling you, heaven on earth! I'm so proud to have my own place, I'm too happy!

One might point out that if there were any semblance of a social safety net, then Anna would not have been homeless in the first place. Likewise, if there were such a safety net, then Linda Tanner, 60, another Chicagoan, might not have felt so stuck in her abusive marriage. Though her husband had a decent-paying job, "He never even tried to put a roof over our heads." Instead, he would spend his money on alcohol and then come home and beat her: "The last time he jumped on me, it was pretty bad. He took a plastic flashlight and cut my head open right here. And he went to jail." That was when she decided that she had had enough. Like Anna, she and her children had been forced to spend time in the shelter system before she found a job as a cashier at a Walmart on the South Side of Chicago [#5781]. She remembers that feeling when she walked into her own apartment for the first time: "I walk in and said, 'Yes, that's right, I made it, I got us out!' And I felt so proud of myself."

Tracy Ryan also used a job at Walmart as a pathway out of dependence on an abusive husband. For two decades she'd been stuck at home with her three children, suffering under the brutality of the man she married at the age of 20. Over the course of 22 years he tried to kill her at least twice. Her mouth is now "messed up"—she is missing her front teeth—lasting evidence of his abuse. And the dates of his aggression are seared in her memory. He first went to jail on December 23, 2011, and was released August 10, 2012. While he was away, she says, "I forgave him," but the abuse soon "started all over again" once he returned. He went back to jail on April 8, 2013; she finalized her divorce on December 10 of that year. Newly single with three kids, Tracy needed to find work and found a job working the overnight shift at the Walmart in Bedford, Texas [#1178]. She recalls how her early nervousness about working at Walmart gave way to a sense of pride:

> In a way, it felt good. And yet, it felt strange. I felt out of place. Like, "OK, I can't do this." . . . But the more I went to work every day I'm, like, "OK." I met more people. "OK." I'm, like, "OK, I'm paying the bills. I'm working instead of worrying about how it's going to get paid. I'm doing it." It felt good. . . . Now I like working.

Tracy came to feel a sense of control of her life that she hadn't had when she was so dependent on her husband. She felt like she was "living instead of sitting at home worrying." It would be a mistake to suggest that Anna or Linda or Tracy have any false consciousness about their economic situations. They have an accurate diagnosis of their relative standing: jobs at Walmart have truly saved them from situations that were far worse.

At the same time Walmart offers these associates an escape from bad situations, these bad situations bind associates to the company, making them more dependent on it and likely making it easier for the company to ask more of them. In our survey of current and former associates, the more hardships that people had faced before getting a job at Walmart (going hungry, getting evicted, having one's electricity turned off, etc.), the more likely they were to still be employed at Walmart at the time they took our survey. Likewise, of those who no longer worked at Walmart, those who had experienced more hardships were less likely to have quit voluntarily and more likely to have been fired.[28] Those who came to Walmart out of desperation found it harder to leave.

Not inconsequently—as developed more fully below—when changes to national social policy make large segments of the population more desperate, Walmart is well situated to take advantage of it.

WALMART MAKES MONEY WHEN THE WELFARE SYSTEM RETRACTS

Among those critical of Walmart's low-wage employment model, one of the most widely cited arguments against the company has to do with how it takes advantage of state public assistance. It pays its workers so little, gives them so few benefits, that they remain dependent on welfare—on WIC, SNAP, Medicaid, public housing. As of 2013, one estimate suggested that for each Walmart Supercenter, the government paid an average of somewhere between $900,000 and $1,744,590 per year to keep its workers afloat.[29] Scale this up to the company's operations across the country, and taxpayers are paying approximately $6.6 billion a year to keep Walmart workers housed, fed, and healthy.[30]

This argument relies on an underlying set of normative assumptions about what an employer should do, namely that a job *should* pay enough for a one to support oneself. Absent this assumption, one could (and conservatives do) make the argument that Walmart actually *reduces* the amount that the government has to pay, if the alternative is that people would be without work altogether and on the public payroll. Not to mention the low prices, which we will get to later.

Walmart's relationship with the welfare system is actually razor-edged. Too much (e.g., adequate) welfare provision for the poor, particularly if disconnected from work requirements, hurts Walmart's capacity to hire, because it makes it possible for women (and others) otherwise forced onto the labor market to spend more time at home caring for their children, or doing anything else. More precisely, it drives up the reservation wage, the lowest wage people would willingly accept for working. On the other hand, too little welfare, and people working at Walmart simply cannot survive on the meager wages and benefits that the company provides.

Walmart's rise to national prominence corresponded with a particular transformation in national social welfare policy, "welfare-to-work," that more or less resolved this conundrum in favor of low-wage employers. Such a model made *not* working more punishing because it tied eligibility for benefits—like income assistance—to having a job, through programs like the earned income tax credit. This meant that companies like Walmart could get the advantages of welfare (i.e., could substitute wages for public benefits), without its costs (i.e., the raising of the reservation wage). If it seems like such a policy was designed to benefit low-wage employers, this may be because it was. Low-wage employers actively lobbied for such changes.[31]

Over Walmart's entire history as a publicly traded company, its market capitalization rose most dramatically in the years directly following the passage of welfare reform in the 1990s (see figure 1.1). This was also the most sustained period of abnormal returns for the company in its history. Between 1997 and 1999, the years when welfare-to-work first went into effect, Walmart stock

FIGURE 1.1 Market capitalization of Walmart.

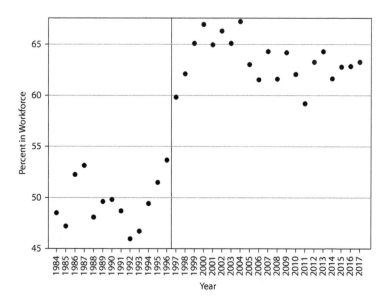

FIGURE 1.2 Percentage of low-education, unmarried women with young children in U.S. labor force.

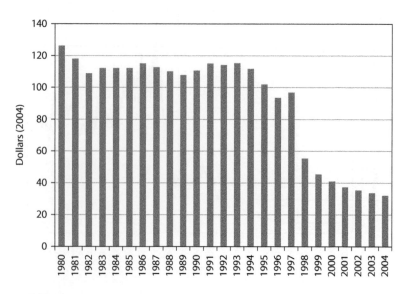

FIGURE 1.3 Annual cash assistance per capita (AFDC/TANF).

outperformed the market as a whole in a way that it has not done before or since.

As a result of welfare reform, Walmart likely profited both from an increase in the supply of low-wage labor and an increase in the demand for the cheap goods that Walmart sold.[32] On the one hand, welfare reform drove poor women with young children into the low-wage labor market in unprecedented fashion (see figure 1.2), meaning that companies like Walmart could push their workers harder (if not also postpone wage increases). On the other hand, as more families faced more desperate economic situations, they may have turned increasingly to Walmart to meet their basic needs. The year of greatest abnormal returns for Walmart during this period, 1998, was the year in which federal cash assistance dropped the most dramatically (figure 1.3).[33]

Welfare reform is the backdrop against which we can understand the stories of many women with young children who wind up working at Walmart. Giana King, from the Watts neighborhood of south Los Angeles, had eight children in a row, beginning in 1991 at the age of 24. For almost 15 years she stayed at home with them while her husband worked a minimum-wage job. She felt stuck at home, and they felt stuck as a family, barely making it on a combination of his wages and their food stamps: "With you not being able to afford childcare, you have no choice but to be a stay-at-home parent if you don't have family members that are willing to babysit for little or nothing. And then they're probably in the same situation that you're in and maybe have two or three jobs, so nobody can really help each other, because we too poor to help each other." The tension in the household became too much. Her husband was emotionally abusive, had a lot of anger "because of the pressure on him to be the bread-winner"—an ideal to which he could not live up. It eventually drove them apart.

Faced with raising eight children alone and even less financial stability than she had before, Giana "had to get a job that would allow me to stay on welfare." Since President Clinton had signed welfare reform in 1996, welfare was less a safety net than a prod—to receive benefits a recipient would have to get a job or at least get "job ready." Through CalWORKs, California's program, Giana found a job at the Walmart in Crenshaw, Los Angeles [#2960]. Oftentimes she left the kids with her mom ("I was lucky, because I had a mom that watched my children for me"), but sometimes she would have to leave her 15-year-old in charge of the seven younger ones, "which could [have gotten] us in trouble with Child Protective Services."

Walmart's job application, Giana remembers, asked explicitly about whether the applicant needed help obtaining government assistance. The company made the assumption that Walmart workers would need more than the company was going to give them. And workers did. When Giana began working at the company she realized that, like her, almost all of the other female associates were on welfare too. She would occasionally work as a cashier, and so would check out the employees shopping for themselves. The women would always have their EBT cards on hand along with their Walmart IDs and company discount cards. New workers had been forced onto the job market by welfare reform, but Walmart and other low-wage employers did not give them enough to get off of welfare.

But like Tracy, like Sue, like Mayra, Giana loved her job. She was eager to make a mark at the company, and took every chance at job training she got—Giana thinks she must have learned how to staff 11 or 12 departments in her first six months at the company: she could work the registers, mix paint, cut keys, mix the chemicals for the photo lab. She was popular with the higher ups since "they really loved the fact that I was easily teachable." And she was soon promoted to be a department manager for health and beauty, one of the largest departments in the store. Now she would order merchandise, stock merchandise, supervise other associates, even help create a schedule that would keep her department humming. "I was convinced that, yes, I'm going to probably be CEO of Walmart if it's this easy."

At a macrolevel, Walmart seems likely to have profited from new welfare requirements that tied benefits to labor market participation—a social enclosure analogous to the physical enclosure of the commons in eighteenth-century England.[34] The absurdity of the fact that the largest, and one of the most profitable, companies in the United States requires that its workers collect welfare simply to make ends meet is worth repeating. And yet, for many individual women struggling within this new welfare regime, Walmart was not the problem; it was the solution. There was community and opportunity there.[35]

DREAMS

I have exciting news. My 19 yr old daughter just got hired [at Walmart] *yesterday.* [S]*he has applied for almost 2 yrs. She will be an overnight stocker. She is leaving McDonalds where she is an overnight cashier/dishwasher.*
—DISCUSSION BOARD POST FROM WALMART ASSOCIATE

The group for whom the meaning of work at Walmart seems the most unsettled consists of younger workers who have most of their lives ahead of them and yet have little sense of what these lives will hold. Unlike the others we have discussed, whose reference points are relatively clear (Walmart is worse than a unionized factory job; Walmart is better than domestic tedium, domestic abuse, or homelessness), these are young people who are at Walmart now but often don't have any clear sense of how their present will connect to their future.

At the store in Vestal, we ask an older woman in the apparel section for help finding the essential oils. She has no idea what we are talking about. To be fair, this is a somewhat esoteric request, and that is the point of the question. But a younger woman with a lip ring and pixie cut is standing beside her and doesn't miss a beat. Though she has been working at the store for only six months—compared with the older woman, who, she tells us, has been there for years—she has gotten the merchandise figured out and leads us to the oils without a problem. On the walk over to the oils (we settle on eucalyptus), she tells us how she is about to be made an assistant department manager, and she has lots of ideas about how to reorganize things. She does not have much patience for women like the older woman in apparel—it's as though they deliberately don't know where things are so they don't have to help, she says. That's not her style. She wants to move up.

One of the most important economic changes of the past 50 years is the declining likelihood of a child's income exceeding that of his or her parents. A child born in 1940 had a 90 percent chance of earning more than his or her parents, whereas a child born in the 1980s has only a 50 percent chance. A man born in 1940 had a 94 percent chance of earning more than his father, compared with a 41 percent chance for a man born in 1984.[36] Upward income mobility is still possible in America, but it's no longer the norm. This does not mean that people stop trying. They just don't succeed as often.

Can people climb at Walmart? Some people do. The company asserts that 75 percent of its store "management teams" started as regular associates.[37] And the idea of a job ladder at Walmart is certainly attractive to new hires, particularly young people. Juan Meza, a young Latino from Los Angeles, had previously been working at a hot dog restaurant that had been "all ghetto and stuff. Like, dirty and shit." He had quit that job to work at a dollar store instead, but that too felt like a dead end. When he got the call letting him know he would be hired as a stocker at the Duarte Walmart [#2401], he was thrilled. He recalls, "I went into [Walmart's] orientation expecting, this is the real top-dog game. Like, this is going to be professional; this is a big company. I'm going to make . . . a life out of this." The orientation affirmed this idea: "They sold Walmart. . . . 'We're a Walmart family, there are plenty of opportunities to move up.'"

In our survey of Walmart workers, a majority (59 percent) said that when they started they expected they could rise "high in the company." This expectation was significantly stronger among African Americans at the company (68 percent), and even stronger among African American men (80 percent). Take Jamal Green, a young black man from Cincinnati, Ohio. He was the bookworm in

his family. His siblings were all "bigger and stronger," so his grandfather—with whom he lived—had told him he had to "learn how to
use your words." He started reading the family's set of encyclope-
dias. By the time he was a teenager, he was helping other kids with
their homework and took pride in how others regarded him: "I think
I would shock people [with] how intelligent I was, even as a teenager." He started college at the University of Cincinnati but soon
dropped out: "I wasn't—my mind, well, my heart wasn't in it." He
found a job at the Walmart in downtown Cincinnati [#1521], and was
determined to stand out:

> I was the best cashier, you know what I mean? Not to brag or any-
> thing, but we had a—what they call SPH, and that's Scans Per Hour, so
> they time how fast you're moving. And I just kind of took it as a sport.
> LeBron James would score 44 points in a game, have 10 assists, and 15
> rebounds. So, I'm, like, I can get my SPH up to 1,000, up to 1,500. And I
> had it so high it was at 2,400 scans per hour. . . . My store manager was
> telling me that that's the highest in the whole district.

Twenty-four hundred scans per hour is 40 scans per minute, which
means entering a bar code an average of every second and a half,
while also bagging and dealing with payments. He remembers an
event in 2012 when store managers selected the best cashiers from
a variety of stores to compete in the "cashier rodeo." Jamal took the
whole thing very seriously, gave "110 percent," and won the competition for his store. He was going places: "Everybody wants progress,"
he says. "You want to move up. I definitely want to, from whatever
situation I'm in." He was excited when his manager approached
him about becoming a CSM—a promotion that would come with a
90-cent wage increase and new responsibilities (CSMs are responsible for preparing and auditing registers, training cashiers, and
handling any customers' questions about the prices of merchandise
during the checkout process).

Like the woman with the lip ring in Vestal, people like Juan and
Jamal were determined to stand out from the pack and make their

mark at the company—to move up to management. In almost every store, moreover, there are role models for people like Jamal and the woman with the lip ring, youngish people who have made it up. In our visits to Walmart stores people told us again and again that with enough grit and determination you could move up, that it was even *easy* to do so. A comanager on the discussion board posted in response to someone complaining about the lack of opportunity: *Not true. I went from hourly to assistant to co in 2 years. Just depends how much you want it.*

WHO KNOWS WHAT YOUR PROMOTION CHANCES REALLY ARE?

But the idea that 75 percent of managers began as regular associates is somewhat misleading, since it says nothing about the percentage of associates who are able to work their way up to management. It's sort of like saying that 100 percent of lottery winners are human beings. What are the actual odds of rising?

First we need to know the composition of store management. What positions are available? Each Walmart has a store manager, who makes an average of $102,351.[38] This is a high salary for a store manager, almost double the national average salary for store managers of all sorts, and far higher than store manager salaries at places like Starbucks ($49,239), Dollar Tree ($45,067), and RadioShack ($33,919). But it helps to remember that the average Walmart Supercenter employs more than 350 associates (225 for regular Walmart stores), compared with 20–25 employees at the average Starbucks. The store manager salary at Target is comparable to that at Walmart ($105,966).

Large Walmarts also hire comanagers, who make an average of $65,472. Below these positions are the assistant store managers, who make an average of $43,500 a year. Together these three positions—about 12 people in all, give or take a few depending on the store's size—make up a store's "management team." These 12 are the only people on salary out of the 200–400 employees in the building. If 9 of those 12 were once regular associates, this means that at any given moment there are—on average—about 30 hourly associates for each "regular associate" who has made it to management. Figuring out the odds of one's promotion to management is very difficult and would involve knowing all sorts of things that the average associate would not easily know; for example: the average tenure of managers once promoted, the number of associates interested in mobility at the store whose tenure at the time is longer than one's own, the bias in promotion rates by age and gender, the number of new Walmart stores opening up each year, and so on. The first figure is important because one cannot calculate vacancy rates without knowing mean tenure. The second figure is important because it tells you where in the queue you are, all else being equal. The third figure is important because the promotion rates for women at Walmart are much lower than they are for men, even though Walmart associates are disproportionately women. The fourth figure is important because much mobility at Walmart is driven by expansion. If a new store comes on line, the 12 managers have to come from somewhere.

But more important than one's not knowing all the relevant figures that determine one's likelihood of promotion is the fact that the vast majority of those factors—and all of the things that create vacancies and therefore opportunity—are entirely out of one's control. The best one can do is put oneself into a position where there is a chance to be promoted if a vacancy arises. For promotion to assistant manager that means working at Walmart for 2.86 years (for men) and 4.38 years (for women), on average. For promotion to store manager, that means working at Walmart for 8.64 years (for men) and 10.12 years (for women). This does not mean that any associate working 10 years becomes a store manager. It just means that the pool of people one is competing with have tended to work for roughly that long. Since the average associate stays at Walmart 3 or 4 years (shorter for men, longer for women) this means that even after a decade of service the chances are high that one will not get promoted to management.

Some young people at Walmart have dreams of upward mobility but no plans to stay at Walmart. They see themselves as passing through the job on their way to better things. At the Wilkes-Barre Walmart, a young white man in a bright yellow jersey with an earpiece and walkie-talkie was standing just behind the cashiers. He had begun as a cashier himself only two months before, he said, but had already been promoted to CSM. There are only four positions higher in the store, he told us, but he wasn't interested in pursuing them. This was just a stopgap for him. He was going to apply to medical school next year.

RUNNING IN PLACE

But plans change. The median age of workers in the retail sector has crept up over the last 20 years, from 29 in 1984 to 33 today.[39] Many people assume they are going to leave Walmart but don't leave as soon as they thought they would, or leave only to return. On the anniversary of an associate's first day of work at Walmart, the screen congratulates the associate as he or she clocks in for work. This was a rude reminder for Rebecca Sanaith, who was finishing up her second year at the Walmart in Lakewood, California [#2609]. She had applied for work there to get some distance from the "ghetto life" of her mom and siblings—her mom's dependence on welfare, her sister's life as a single mother: "Growing up in the ghetto, they say statistically you have kids when you're young. We didn't have a dad, so it was just like—I just knew I didn't like that life." She needed space, and the job did serve that purpose, in that it had allowed her to move into her own apartment. She was doing overnight shifts on the remodeling team, working full-time while she was also taking classes at Cal State Long Beach. "That's when my grades started dropping," she recalled. But it seemed worth it. Living on her own "was awesome." The year 2014 was the first since 1880—more than 100 years before—when living with one's parents was the most common arrangement among young adults ages

18–34.[40] So, again, a room of one's own is an accomplishment. It's just that Rebecca didn't want to end up at Walmart. At the time of our interview it was approaching August 25, 2014, her second anniversary at the company. "I remember that date, because every year when it says, 'Happy Anniversary,' I just cringe, and I'm, like, 'Oh, my God!' [laughter]. I tell myself at the end of this year, I'm going to leave, hopefully."

The average tenure of any Walmart associate that one meets in the store is likely to be much longer than the average employee's tenure at the company. This is partially because the people who don't stay as associates very long are not there to be met; it is also because there are thousands and thousands of people who have worked as associates at Walmart for two decades or more. Today, a host of young people are at Walmart simply because there is nowhere else to go, and Walmart offers at least a first step toward the independence they associate with adulthood. They stay because there are not that many other places to go. And they get older.

Another role that Walmart played in some young people's lives was as a place to try to get one's life back on track. Walmart was one of the earliest large retailers to adopt "fair chance" hiring policies, making it easier for those with criminal records to find employment.[41] Katrina Jackson, a 27-year-old black woman from Fort Worth, Texas, had celebrated her twenty-first birthday in prison. She hadn't been in trouble in the last six years, though. "I told a lot of people, once I got out of jail I was going to change my act, and I did. I have not been in trouble ever since. And I—I really commend myself on that, because I was a little hardheaded." After prison she was hired almost immediately at a Walmart in Arlington, Texas [#5416], working inventory control on the overnight shift. As a younger woman she had been enmeshed in a pack of siblings and extended cousins and it had been overwhelming: "That's one of the hardest things for people to do is to depend on other people," she says, "because people do let you down." Now she was independent: "It's wonderful for me now. . . . You know, you don't have to worry about somebody—feeding nobody, looking after anybody, nobody else paying your rent, nobody walking in and out of your place." Being responsible for herself alone was a luxury, an accomplishment:

> [It's] a great feeling. You really can't explain it because it's just like, I'm going to my house. I'm going to open up my door, open up my refrigerator. If there isn't any food in my refrigerator, it's because I ate it. If there's no toilet tissue in the bathroom, it's because I used it up. . . . If my bills are late, it's because I paid them late. I might have messed around and blew a little more money than I should have, but it's because I did it. It's not because I was providing, or you know, somebody was taking from me or I was being used.

Katrina's close friend in the inventory department, Marquan Reed, also had a felony on his record. But he looked at the job a little differently than Katrina. Rather than a lifeline, he felt tethered to it:

> The reason why I've been at Walmart so long is I have a charge on my record. There was two decent jobs that my background denied me from getting. . . . I'm stuck. That's why I kind of gave Walmart a better attitude, I tried not to worry about so much what was going on, try to just block that out and work. When I go home I leave everything there.

Walmart was one of the few places around that would hire him in spite of his criminal record, so he was trying to change his attitude about the place. At the time of our interview with him, Marquan had been at the store for about two years, and had recently been rejected for a job working for Dr Pepper. He had half a mind to leave Walmart even without a backup plan, but his superego kept getting the better of him: "I realized, okay, you're an adult, you need an income, do your job." Being stuck with no other options "was about the most frustrating part."

An emergent argument among criminal justice advocates and scholars is that the formerly incarcerated make good employees who will go the extra mile for their employers and are unlikely to leave.[42] But what goes largely unexamined in such accounts is the coercion underlying this performance: the threat of re-incarceration, whether explicit (for instance, in a parole requirement that one remain employed) or implicit; the fact that since most employers are prejudiced against hiring those with criminal records, the employer who *will* hire them is able to push them harder given their lack of other options.[43] Marquan's account highlights the extent to which one's involvement in the criminal justice system can compel one to stay at a job one hates.

The criminal justice system can also scare people into silence at work. Based on an analysis of OUR Walmart's administrative data, combined with zip code–level prison admission data, we found that associates who lived in high-incarceration neighborhoods were far less likely to sign up for the organization than others, after controlling for a host of other local factors. Katrina, who had spent her twenty-first birthday in prison, remembers just how fearful she was when she began getting involved with OUR Walmart: "I was like, 'Oh my God, I don't even know if I'm supposed to be working at Walmart,' [so] I wanted to basically be like a silent partner" in the organization. Katrina got involved despite her fears; in those neighborhoods in which prison loomed large in people's experiences, most people did not.

THERE IS NO SINGLE PROTOTYPE
OF THE WALMART WORKER

Employees' very different understandings of work at the company can be explained in part by the very different trajectories they took to get there. For some older workers, who took advantage of the well-paying industrial jobs available in the mid-twentieth century, Walmart feels emblematic of the erosion of the white American middle class of which they were once a part. For others, Walmart can feel like a path toward freedom from abject poverty or domestic abuse, or a solution to the loneliness and boredom of domesticity.

For some younger workers it can feel like an initial step toward a brighter future, or a step back from the brink of becoming a statistic. For other younger workers it can feel like the best of bad options. These perceptions are not all mutually exclusive, meaning that working at the company can also feel confusing, conflicted, a version of freedom but maybe not the version to which people had originally aspired.

For many employees, relative to other jobs that they can realistically get, working at Walmart is not so bad. It is, for most, preferable to McDonald's or other large fast-food restaurants. It's better than working at small retail outlets that are likely to close down, fail to pay properly or regularly, or not grant vacation time at all. For elderly people seeking to pass the time and capture some pin money, the absence of regular full-time hours is a benefit. For people with a criminal record, Walmart is what there is, basically. And for many women, Walmart is not just an escape from a bad situation at home, it is a positive escape into a community of other women, an opportunity to make new friends, to see oneself in a different light.

These different pathways into Walmart mean that at any given moment in any given store the workers there have widely disparate attitudes and expectations. Those trying to get ahead will discover they can because many of their colleagues have no interest in that and simply want to pass the time. Those who want to pass time are content to have others strive for promotion. Those trying to build community will discover others in the same shoes. They can look forward to going to work. Even social isolates can be happy if they land a job pushing carts in the parking lot, far from most coworkers and managers and customers. One parking lot attendant told us, "I like it outside because you get to drink." These different pathways also mean that Walmart's low wages have different significance for different workers, making it unlikely that wages alone can serve as the basis for collective struggle.

But these different pathways don't mean that the job is easy. It is not. What happens once workers enter the door is the subject of the next chapter.

2

THE SHOP FLOOR

SHELFIES

Years before she began work at the Walmart Supercenter in Paramount, California in order to escape from *Blue's Clues* and *Bob the Builder* and her children, Mayra Rodriguez would tag along with her grandmother on regular trips to "expensive department stores." Her grandfather, who had served in the military, used low-rate mortgages available through the GI Bill to invest in real estate, so by the time Mayra came along her grandmother had discretionary income to lavish on her: "She would dress me up like a doll when she could. I mean, nice stuff. Oxford shoes. Expensive dresses, which I hated." Mayra may have hated the emphasized femininity of the dresses but she appreciated the luxury—these were "very expensive stores," she says. Quiet, clean, classy. Between stores they would go to nice restaurants and, once home, they would spend hours picking out the perfect outfits for Sunday services. It's not hard to pick up the admiration in Mayra's voice as she describes her grandma: "She had to convey an image that her husband was successful. And she carried herself in a certain way, and she expected to be treated in a certain way, you know? A lady wherever she went. . . . I hope some of it rubbed off."

Her grandmother "wouldn't [have been] caught dead in a Walmart" during those years, Mayra says, though later she softened on Walmart, at least in part because of the "little motorized carts" that could help her get around the store. Mayra worked in the women's apparel department at the Paramount store, where she was responsible—among other things—for keeping the women's lingerie section stocked and orderly. This was the part of the department that "took care of ladies' jammies, purses, and scarves and belts and stuff, all the accessories and stuff that my grandma always had to have matchy-matchy." Mayra made it her personal mission to bring the section up to her grandmother's exacting standards: "I try to keep it nice for my grandma. That was my motivation the whole time."

It was about more than grandma too. It was about creating an environment—an aesthetic experience—in which people could feel that the "impossible [was] possible." She continues, "When you shop, you're supposed to take your mind off of reality and just go into where you could be, what you could look like, what you could make your home into." It was as though Mayra wanted to recreate her childhood experience of luxury in her one little aisle of the Paramount Walmart. In *her* aisle, she wanted people to be able to escape into fantasy; and she took pride in being the kind of worker, the kind of designer, who might make this escape possible.

Wandering into a typical Walmart on a typical Saturday afternoon, when lines at the registers seem to snake for miles and the shelves are half-empty and the associates are on their knees stocking and seemingly avoiding eye contact, it is difficult to appreciate the amount of pride that some associates take in their work. It becomes easier to appreciate when one returns to the store early the next morning to find the shelves full and organized and—given an aesthetic defined by sheer quantity—inviting, the floors glistening. And if one logs onto the discussion board one will find hundreds of pictures that associates have taken to document their labor.

These are the Walmart "shelfies." A worker from the apparel department shows off her meticulously folded and color-coordinated sweaters: *Y'ALL THIS TOOK ME SO LONG BUT LOOK HOW PERFECT IT IS. I'm gonna cry when I come back tomorrow and it's destroyed.* Another associate posts a picture of hundreds of perfectly placed acrylic paints, bemoaning that she didn't get a *before picture* to show just how much work she put into it. Another expresses pride at building her *first feature today*, a special display of Toll House chocolate chips in various flavors and colors. And it's not only shelves. A deli associate posts a picture of perfectly rolled meats. She was *sad and proud at the same time.* Proud because she was able to roll the cold cuts into such tidy meat popsicles *because it shows that we go above and beyond* for customers. Sad because her commitment was unmatched by her coworkers—she had to do the order last night, since she was off today and her coworkers *refused to roll the meats as requested.*

An associate in apparel may be the shelfie queen. Between November 10 and December 17, 2016, she posted a full 72 shelfies of the apparel department—jeans, t-shirts, flannels, sweatshirts, khakis.

Together, the photos are a torrent, a merchandise kaleidoscope—repeated shapes and colors of fabric, cereal boxes, chicken stock, hair products, essential oils, flowers, fruit, toys, cardboard. But as remarkable as the pictures themselves are the responses to them. For every banal *Good job!* or *Very nice* there is another comment that is thoughtful, specific, and constructive. For instance, there is an emergent consensus that there is too much space between the shelves of the Toll House chocolate chips feature, that there might have been room for another shelf. Writes one associate, *my boss is a stickler about airspace he would've yelled at me for that but I think it looks great.* Another agrees, adding, *you can't sell air*, before assuring, *you did a really good job though.* A third writes *Good job!!!* before echoing the airspace concern and suggesting that an entire endcap of chocolate chips might be overkill and that half of the shelf *should be a different item that sells well with chocolate chips, like a cake mix or something.* Twelve more associates comment on the airspace; a few compliment the "striping" of the colors of the different kinds of chocolate chips, although even here there is some dissent: one associate thinks that all of the milk chocolate chips should have been placed next to each other in order to be striped properly.

People find meaning in their work and discover ways to express themselves through it. An associate working produce writes, *There's a pride in it. When I stock the wet wall* [vegetables with mist]*, I make sure to display each item well. Few things shine like a beautifully stocked wet wall.* Another agrees: *Coming on to nothing but empty spaces and then filling everything you can, and taking a step back and looking at it like . . . WOW I did that? It honestly does feel pretty good.* The associate responds, *I take pictures of that type of work.*

The shelfies are visual documentation of work well done—they stop time, stabilize a moment of order in what is a constant battle against entropy. Posted to the discussion board they are also appeals for recognition from one's peers. It is not just that the associates are thinking about a specific aesthetic, alternating green and yellow dish detergent or building a structure out of boxed products that looks like a Jenga game. They are actively thinking about and commenting about and working on their products in order to better sell them. One associate comments that since she became department manager of the deli her sales were 23 percent up over the previous month (though there is probably seasonality to deli sales and so month over month comparisons may not be a particularly useful metric). Another strongly believes that product moves faster when the shelves are completely full. She is probably right. Who buys the last carton of milk unless it is right before a snowstorm? The last sweater looks like it was rejected for a reason as well. There's a science to selling, and many of the associates are invested in perfecting it.[1]

One of the things that distinguishes the service sector from other kinds of work, about which we will say more later, is that the unpredictability of customer demand tends to make it more difficult to routinize than other sorts of industries. This can create pockets of autonomy in which workers are able to exercise creativity and feel a sense of investment in the work they do; pockets in which a department manager, who makes somewhere between 40 cents and a dollar more per hour than an entry-level associate, feels so committed to the job that, she writes, [I run] *my department like it's my own business.*

SERVICE WITH A SMILE

A long history of scholarship on the labor process documents how the mid-twentieth-century workplace was one in which raw coercion had given way to "manufactured consent." Human resources departments and strong labor unions had created structures like internal labor markets and incentive payment systems to align workers' interests with the interests of their employers.[2] Walmart works to produce the same effect on a more meager budget. Here, quarterly "MyShare" bonuses, based on storewide sales and metrics like customer satisfaction scores, play a role in aligning workers' interests with store profits. These bonuses can range from nothing—if a store had poor sales, poor service, or too many worker injuries—to a maximum of around $500 for a full-time worker, every three months. But this still can't explain individual workers' investments in store sales, since any one worker would still have an incentive to shirk.

Rather, it is recognition that seems to drive workers more than any additional pay they may receive from bonuses or promotions. It's Jamal Green feeling like the LeBron James of the cashier crew. Even those cashiers who aren't regional champions can get their daily stats and compete against themselves and their coworkers. At the end of a shift, each is able to see his or her own "productivity totals"—scans per hour, seconds per item, percentage of items scanned (rather than entered by hand). An associate posts a picture of her daily report because she was in the "high 1400s," higher than usual for her and she *wanted to share 'cause I am super proud of myself!!!* Another day, another group of cashiers are comparing notes about the tricks of the trade that can help them get their numbers up—stopping the clock while between customers or while looking up an item. Others discuss whether the number of scans or errors per hour is the most relevant statistic. There are lots of ways to achieve distinction, and slow and steady has its adherents.

Years ago, Walmart figured out how to use information technology to maximize the efficiency of its sprawling distribution system. Today it uses similar technologies to reflect employees' performances back to them—mini-measurements that both reinforce the idea that employees are being watched and give them a series of small accomplishments to which they might aspire. These are complex strategies designed to appear and be experienced as nudges[3] while masking their surveillance functions. They are the analog to wearable technologies like the Fitbit or the Apple Watch, except that the outcome is labor productivity rather than personal fitness and Walmart is aggregating the data for its own uses rather than some distant technology company, which is aggregating the information about your steps and heart rate in order to sell it to a company—like Walmart—that can pitch you the perfect pair of running sneakers.[4] Nudges work on both the production and consumption side of the service economy.

A cashier gets her second recognition in three months from the company, this time a framed Award of Excellence for "going above and beyond and providing superior service to our customers" (she received it for convincing lots of customers to apply for Walmart credit cards). Beginning in March of 2015, Walmart instated a volume-processing item (VPI) program in which associates could "adopt" an underperforming item and try to increase its sales—winning awards at the store, market, and regional level for the associate who increased sales the most. An associate would get one point for every "sales dollar increase" this year versus last during the same time period; one point for every "unit sold increase"; and two points for "every profit dollar increase." The highest performer at each store would get $50 and a certificate at the end of the quarter; the market winner would get $75 and a certificate; and the regional winner would get $150 and a certificate. Associates compare notes on the best products to upsell: four-pack chocolate milks, 88-cent store-brand hair ties, popcorn tins, Bounty single-roll paper towels, tilapia fish.

All of these little achievements are indicative both of associates' drive for personal distinction and of the real sense of community they find among their peers, a community without which being a fast scanner or fastidious stocker or a genius at the VPI would likely feel less important. Just as wearables' self-observation and self-motivation work best when people share their results with friends, the surveillance-cum-measurement data work best when others can see them. Ironically, the discussion board, developed in part to help workers see through to the control functions of seemingly neutral incentive systems, provides a new and deeper community to share ones' achievements with, masking the surveillance implicitly built into the incentive structure.

A SENSE OF PLACE

This community was the other thing that struck Mayra about her work at Walmart. Mayra thought her work at Walmart was "just going to be a job," but instead she "fell in love." For the first time in her life, it seemed, she had found a community of peers with whom she felt she could be herself. "I just fell in love with the people that worked there. And the customers [who] were there." Before Walmart, "I was a mom. I was home with my kids. I had my kids. I had my husband. But I didn't really have friends, you know? Just— that's what I found." [5]

This was Sue Rogers's experience too—Walmart gave her a community and a sense of emotional intimacy that she had been missing in her marriage. For Sue, like Mayra, the job offered a quasi-family:

> I knew everybody there in that store. . . . Everybody—it was like a big family. Everybody I knew, and we had good times. We had functions all the time for Children's Miracle Network [a nonprofit that supports

children's hospitals]. We had functions all the time set up. We had Halloween parties where we would be dressed up and go around giving the kids candy that come in the store. . . . They even have pictures of us doing the chicken dance going up and down the aisle.

Sue found a group of friends at work with whom she spent more and more time. Friday nights they'd all go to the local Applebee's where they would "sit around and cut out and laugh, you know, have a good time." She would invite her husband to join them, but, she says, "He didn't want to go out and do things. He would come home, sit in his recliner, drink his beer, read his paper, and go to bed." She continues, "It made me feel like he didn't want to be with me." They got separated. And it was okay.

Associates see one of their coworkers has a broken car window and within two days collect more than the $300 needed to fix it, treating their coworker to a *$25 Applebee's card, $25 Subway card, $50 gas card, $56 in cash and we paid the $300 to get her car fixed.* When Walmart associates die the whole store often grieves. Some stores set up memorials in the aisles; others collect money for funeral expenses; the staff of one store walks together into the parking lot holding pink balloons and casts them, collectively, up into the air.

Coworkers are often literally one's family. In our survey, 42 percent of respondents said that they had a family member who also worked at Walmart (or had worked there at some point). A third of respondents (33.4 percent) had a family member who worked at the very same Walmart where they worked. And if associates don't have family at the store now, there is a good chance they might in the future, as romance often flourishes in the aisles. The discussion board is full of stories of people hooking up at Walmart. Workers with workers (*I was in electronics* [he] *was in dairy*), workers with customers (*thought he was cute he was a customer in my line on reg 7*), and customers with customers. In early 2013, the most frequent place that people reported having had "missed connections" on Craigslist—catching someone's eye, flirting without exchanging numbers, not quite getting up the nerve to ask someone out—was Walmart.[6]

This was particularly true across the South—Texas, Louisiana, Arkansas, Alabama, Mississippi, Florida, Tennessee, North Carolina. In New York, by comparison, it was the subway; in California, 24 Hour Fitness. For large swaths of the country, Walmart is the place where people are most likely to meet new people. It's our new public commons, only it's private.

Before she started at Walmart, Ximena Fields had been unhappily married for over 23 years. She was working as a service writer in the automotive shop at the Walmart in Grand Prairie, Texas [#896], when she met Alfred, who worked inside the regular store: "It got to where he would come . . . everyday or something like that just so he could come in. I know it was just to come in and talk to me. But, eventually, we would give each other a hug and kiss on the cheek, and then it escalated from there." She left her husband and she and Alfred began a life together. By the time the students showed up in Dallas, Ximena and Alfred were inseparable. Once they told Louisa about a time they had been in such desperate economic straits that they *had sat in the car and squirted ketchup onto saltines for lunch.* Louisa remembers thinking *it could have been a morose story, but instead they were laughing, tears streaming down their faces.*

The overnight shift is particularly fertile for friendship, and more, among associates. The customers are scarce and most of the managers have gone home. Throughout the summer, Harmony, from the Cincinnati team, would spend many late nights in the parking lot of the Cunningham Road Store [#3749] with Frank Brown and Doris Goodman, another couple who had met at work. During one 2 a.m. lunch break they *sat in the back of their white pickup, far away from the fluorescent lights of the break room, smoking and playing music out of Doris's phone. Doris dangled her feet off the bed of the truck while Frank rummaged behind the seat for an old photo from the '80s. We squinted at it under the parking lot light and laughed at the state of his hair.* Southern Man *came on and I blurted out, "I love this song!" Doris nodded. "Neil," she said, "that's what's up."*

At its best, people feel both a sense of individual recognition and community from their peers at Walmart. We can see evidence of this in the ways that associates review their jobs at Walmart on a job site like Glassdoor.com. Glassdoor is a website founded in 2007 where employees are able to anonymously review their employers. It's like Yelp, but from the perspective of workers. Between 2007 and 2015, more than 9,500 hourly Walmart associates used the site to review the company. Reviews include "Pros" and "Cons," as well as an overall rating of the job (on a scale from 1 to 5). We used simple text analysis strategies to explore the most common words that workers use on Glassdoor to describe their jobs. The most frequent noun used to describe the "Pros" of the job, by far, is "people." Among workers as a whole, it's the "people" that make the difference.

We can take this one step further by looking at the "Pros" nouns that are most strongly associated with higher overall job ratings. The word most highly associated with how much one likes one's job is "culture," with words like "environment," "team," and "family" close behind. These are the associates who see the store as theirs, not someone else's. These are the ones who not only can perform the "Walmart cheer" on command—"Give me a 'W,' give me an 'A,' . . ."—but also know the specific cheers associated with *their own stores*: "#3261, keep the others on the run!"; "#1823, Hanover is the place to be!"; "#2136, the store that really kicks!"; "#2860, where it's cooler in Pooler!"

GHOST STORIES

There are associates so connected to the specific histories of their stores that they report on the ghosts haunting the aisles: ghosts who will occasionally push things off the shelves in the backroom when no one is there or pull on a worker's cart when she walks by the garden center; who will throw tires off their racks in the tire and lube express (TLE) department; who will turn the registers off and on; there's the girl in white walking past the general merchandise docking bay; the ghost of a construction worker who fell through the skylight during a store's construction. A woman named Abigail, killed by her husband in a house on the lot where the store now sits, who *loves to pick on overnight managers. Especially if they are mean.* To believe in ghosts at one's Walmart one has to believe that the place has a history, depth, significance.

It's not surprising, then, that some of the ghost stories concern Sam Walton, the larger-than-life founder of Walmart. An associate writes that a voice came over the walkie-talkies one night telling him and his coworkers, "Sam is not happy," though all the walkie-talkies were present and accounted for. Another associate said strange things started happening at her store only after *Mr. Sam had passed, so we like to say that he is haunting us.* A few others remark that all the stores are haunted by Mr. Walton, as he is *rolling in his grave at what the corporation has become.*

Among many associates there is a sense of belonging that comes from sharing this weird, idealized past—a past when Sam Walton was running the show, when Walmart was smaller than it is now. It's not hard to wrap one's mind around the myth of Sam Walton, but it is somewhat harder to wrap one's mind around the fact that the story *works.* It's a Horatio Alger story: young, striving entrepreneur with novel ideas and real concern for and understanding of real people lifts himself up from humble origins, never forgetting who he was or who helped him along the way.[7] The cult of personality that developed around Walton is supported by his famous sayings, a small sampling of which are:

Appreciate everything your associates do for the business. Nothing else can quite substitute for a few well-chosen, well-timed, sincere words of praise. They're absolutely free and worth a fortune.

If you want a successful business, your people must feel that you are working for them—not that they are working for you.

Commit to your business. Believe in it more than anybody else.

If you love your work, you'll be out there every day trying to do it the best you possibly can, and pretty soon everybody around will catch the passion from you—like a fever.

If people believe in themselves, it's amazing what they can accomplish.

These and a host of other equally vacuous aphorisms are routinely referenced by both disgruntled and satisfied associates in support of their view that Walmart has either betrayed its initial mission or stayed true to it. Either way, many Walmart associates share the same founding myth, and sharing that story solidifies the sense of community that they have, a sense that Walmart is theirs. The weird thing is that this loyalty to Walmart actually extends beyond their store, beyond their colleagues and friends who shop there, to other Walmart stores that they happen to visit. Associates often discuss how *Sam would roll over in his grave* (Sam is often rolling in his grave) if he saw how rude the cashiers were at some other store, or how messy the aisles were, or how anything was not working as well as it does at their own store. The sense of belonging to something bigger is palpable.

Bethany Moreton links Walmart's cultural power to its historical roots, which she argues has made the company particularly adept at mixing market dominance with populist morality. Sam Walton built the company out of the Ozarks of northwest Arkansas, a region that, in the late nineteenth century, had "hosted some of the nation's most vigorous popular protests against huge economic 'combinations'"; and in the 1920s and 1930s had been swept into a vigorous "antichain" movement against the spread of retail chains from Northern cities. Sensitive to the region's heritage of agrarian populism, Walton looked for financing locally—entering into "partnerships" with local "investor-managers," and seeking loans from a large Arkansas bank rather than from New York.[8] Even as the corporation transformed itself into the largest employer in the world, it sought to maintain a "populist corporate image"[9] of thrift, anti-elitism, and quasi-egalitarianism. Its "Home Office," which remains in Bentonville, Arkansas, is an assemblage of nondescript buildings about as far from the glitzy "campuses" of Silicon Valley as one can imagine. There, Walmart buyers negotiate with suppliers in unremarkable conference rooms. Its executives are known for flying coach, for renting cheap cars, for sharing hotel rooms, for working out of minimally furnished offices. Staffers at headquarters report bringing pens from home rather than asking the company to buy them; when charging meals to the company they are allowed to tip at only 10 percent. For years Sam Walton would visit stores in his 1975 Chevy pickup truck.[10] The message for customers is of the company doing everything in its power to keep costs (and prices) down. The implicit message for associates seems to be one of shared sacrifice—of everyone, from the top on down, stretching every dollar in the name of low prices. That Walmart's CEO Doug McMillon made $22.4 million in 2017, well over a thousand times the earnings of a full-time Walmart worker earning $10 an hour, is obfuscated by a common, spartan aesthetic. Sam Walton may have been a specter all along. But in many ways this ghost continues to do its work, and Walmart's aisles—which made us feel small—make others feel at home.

FRIENDS MATTER

Some of workers' sense of community comes from the simple fact that many Walmart associates, especially those outside the larger urban areas, live in neighborhoods near the stores where they work. And that means that they know their coworkers from settings outside Walmart—because they went to high school together, go to church together, belong to the same clubs, root for the same local teams. Part of this sense of community comes from the fact that the customers they see at their stores are their neighbors and friends. And part comes from making new friends.

This sense of community is strongly associated with how one feels about the job. Seeing customers that one knows from other parts of one's life; having friends at work; being able to ask one's coworkers for help—in our survey data, each of these is positively, significantly, and independently associated with one's job satisfaction, even after controlling for things like race, sex, age, whether one currently works at Walmart, and how long one has (ever) worked there.

Working with one's friends matters. When Joan Wharton, from the store in Franklin, Ohio, described her daily work, it sounded a lot like a social club: "You looked forward to going in there, because you knew you had fun." Her coworkers were some of her closest friends—Bonnie would offer the latest pictures of her granddaughter ("She's so proud of her. She's so cute"); Linda would be talking about her garden, or she'd be drinking her coffee from Thornton's and singing; Kitty—"I love Kitty—if it wasn't for Kitty, I would walk away"; and some of the guys too: "We've got Joe there, young Joe. And Noam—oh, Lord. He's something else!" The days passed easily:

> All of us are really close-knit, and we're all friends. All of us coworkers. We've been there for a long time, we all get along. We all have a sense of humor, and we would see what we had to do for the day, and we would all be laughing. We would all talk or holler at each other if we needed this, or we needed that. We would holler, like, an aisle or two over, and cut up, and laugh. And we would all be singing while we worked, or whatever. And everybody helped each other; we would all work together.

Stories about one's "regular" customers also abound. These stories are often told with a mix of annoyance and pride, the way people complain about receiving too many emails or faculty members complain about having too many students who want to take their courses. An older male associate in the Walmart in Vestal, New York, describes how he can't be in his store in plainclothes without being identified by his regulars who then ask him for help. He's considering retirement, but he has two older customers who have made him promise to give them his phone number if he does so that they can call him with questions. A cashier at the store in Oneonta, New York [#2262], tells us she buys her own groceries at Stop & Shop because "if you are a Walmart associate then you are always a Walmart associate and everyone knows I work here." Her regulars won't leave her alone and company policy is that if someone asks you for help, even while you are off the clock, you have to "be nice and represent the store." It was just easier not to go there at all on her day off. An associate writes online that he's feeling aggravated: *I'm here shopping with my wife in regular clothes not work clothes & keep getting asked where stuff is! Hello I'm not on the clock. Let us be!* Another, former associate writes that she had stopped working at Walmart more than a year ago and *was shopping in my old store yesterday and got asked for help*. Others write that customers ask them to help them even when they are shopping at *other* nearby stores. The consensus seems to be that one is better off staying away from one's store on one's day off. But it's hard to stay away from all retail stores altogether, and one associate's theory is that *when u work retail for awhile they sense it*.

Workers may go to such lengths drawing boundaries between their roles as workers and their roles as customers because the boundaries are so blurry. Walmart workers are Walmart buyers, and not only because of the discount card that entitles people who have worked there more than three months to 10 percent off most merchandise, though this certainly helps. Among our survey respondents who currently work at Walmart, 84 percent report doing their own shopping at Walmart once a week or more, and 96 percent report shopping there more than once a month. Among respondents who no longer work at Walmart (and so do not get the discount unless they have a spouse working there), 53 percent still report doing their shopping at Walmart once a week or more, and 80 percent report shopping there more than once a month.

GUNS AND ROSES

It is not unusual to see workers in uniform discussing their schedules or their weekends or their moods with people in street clothes who seem just a little too familiar with the store to be shoppers. At the store in Catskill, New York [#2351], a man in street clothes comes up to an associate and gives her a big hug. A second worker turns to the man and says, "That's what she needs today." And then her voice deepens: "I'll tell you what she really needs." There's a fleeting moment of tension—was she talking about sex? So she continues: "I mean weapons. She needs weapons. So do I." Apparently, the day has not started out so well. The man smiles: "I've got weapons!" The associate replies, "Can I borrow them? I'll bring them back without fingerprints." The man must be an associate himself— the three know each other, he understands why they might joke about arming up to take on the day. This is not a customer service interaction. Yet these types of interactions—ones that don't fit the archetype of customer service, but aren't obviously interactions among workers on the clock—are commonplace. An associate stands in the aisle of the Taylor, Pennsylvania [#4276], store with a mop in her hand, talking about scheduling with three people in street clothes who seem a lot like her family. Another associate at the same store turns into an aisle with a man who must be her boyfriend or husband. They walk down the aisle together, briefly take one another's hands, and then release them before they reenter the central corridor of the store.

Some customers are friends, some customers are coworkers, some customers become more than customers across repeated interactions over months and even years. And for some people who work at Walmart there is a real sense of pride and satisfaction in the social interactions that make up the workday. James Drake, from a store in Lancaster, Texas [#471], described his own muscular arms as his "customer gun boats" and reminisced about the people from his neighborhood who would come and shop in the store. Chelsea Mays, a cashier from a store in Cincinnati, Ohio, said the customers were the best part of her job: "My customers make me laugh. I have customers, they come in the door to look for me when I come to work, so they can get in my line, because I make them laugh." Jeffrey Rivers, who worked as an assembler at a store in Texas, also conveyed the closeness he felt with some of his customers: "They say, 'We'll come back and we'll try and find you so you can help us out.' I help my customers out all the time." His customers returned the favor—he wasn't supposed to accept tips for helping people assemble equipment they bought, but his customers would insist:

> Every time there'll be customers I will see, after I get off work, and [I'm like], "I can't take money for helping out." But [they say], "You off the clock?" "Yeah." "Here you go." They all hand me a little bit of money. I'm like, "Naw," I'm trying to force like, "Nope, nope, nope, nope." They, like, drop it, and I pick it up. Hey, me personally, I'm not going to leave money just lay there.

An associate writes that being a cake decorator is her *dream job* since every time *someone leaves with their cake and a smile on their face, it makes the rest of the crap all worth it.* Another writes that she had a customer follow her from one store to another when she transferred two years before. A third says that she knows most of her regulars by name—then adds, *Its pretty cool actually to have that personal connection with your customers.* A Spanish-speaking associate intervenes in a conversation about how there is no one paid to translate at the store: *I don't mind doing it, it feels good being able to translate and speak both. I know my parents struggled a while back and I would have to translate for them and being able to help others is great!* An associate in electronics says that he has *hundreds of customers that come directly to Electronics just to see me.* He recounts a story about the advice he gave a customer about 4K televisions, who *told a few friends of his to come see me about TV's instead of going to Best Buy because I'm clear and concise. . . . That's why I'm called Mr. Television.*

This feeling of community is distributed unevenly across Walmart workers and Walmart stores. White workers, on average, report having many more friends at work than workers of color, even after controlling for a host of other factors.[11] Those who have worked for more years at the store also report having more friends (though one wonders whether this is a cause or an effect of job tenure). Workers of color and workers from poorer families tend to talk to their managers and their coworkers about their personal problems less frequently, ask for help from them less frequently, and work in stores in which they run into customers they know less frequently. The social benefits of work at Walmart are unequally shared.

There are likely two different reasons for this. First, it may be a result of the particular kind of power that Walmart has in certain low-income communities and communities of color, where the company is one of the only employers around.[12] In whiter, wealthier communities, the people who work at Walmart are less dependent on the wage (e.g., retirees, high schoolers), have more options, and choose to work at Walmart in part because of the social amenities— friends, customers they know. In poorer communities of color, the people who work at Walmart are more dependent on the wage, have fewer options, and so have to work at the store regardless of whether it is a pleasant social experience or not. Second, it may simply reflect the fact that communities of color tend to be concentrated in more urban areas and as a consequence associates are less likely to know one another, travel further to work, and share fewer overlapping associational foci.

FAIR ENOUGH WAGES?

For years, Walmart has been the poster child for the low-wage employer. Really it's been more than the poster child—it's the model that has helped set the bar so low for workers across retail and adjacent industries. And it has done so at a time when retail workers have been increasingly productive. Between 1987 and 2014, labor productivity across the retail sector doubled. But average real wages across the retail sector were flat, meaning that workers were not able to claim for themselves any of the increased productivity they were making possible for their employers (see figure 2.1).

Given this fact, it might come as something of a surprise that low pay is not the most common complaint among Walmart employees who post reviews on Glassdoor, among those who participate on the Walmart associates' discussion board, among the many interviews we conducted with workers at Walmart, or during any of our visits

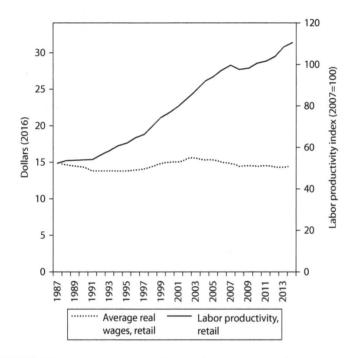

FIGURE 2.1 Average real wages and labor productivity in the retail sector.

to Walmart stores. This is not to say that people weren't struggling financially. People were often just scraping by. When Carmen Bond worked the register in Huber Heights, Ohio [#1495], she would often be hungry. "I knew that if I was to buy some food, then I probably wouldn't have enough for gas. Or I'd probably be a couple of dollars short for rent." She'd scramble for change in the cushions of her car, then go to the deli in the store and ask them to weigh "62 cents or 79 cents" of something. The vending machine at the store would sell soda for 50 cents. "Water was a dollar. And I couldn't even afford to buy water. I had to buy pop." One time her hours got cut so drastically for a couple of weeks that the precarious balancing act was simply impossible: "I had to burden my parents and ask my mom for help. And I felt so small. Like, I felt like I couldn't do it myself. I felt like less of a person." It was humiliating to have to turn to others, or even share her hardship with others, so she avoided doing so when possible.

But Carmen and others didn't seem to place too much blame on Walmart. The outside options were just as bad or worse. When there are no other jobs, then Walmart is a better alternative than not working. As the economist Joan Robinson once quipped, "the misery of being exploited by capitalists is nothing compared to the misery of not being exploited at all."[13] Joan Wharton, from the Franklin store, says, "You just have to suck it up, and just take whatever they dish out to you. Because if that's the only way you've got to support your family, like I said, I was raised: 'Don't be no quitter. You just have to suck it up. Just forget about it, suck it up, bitch. Go on.'" Richard Walker, who worked in the grocery at the store in Lancaster, Texas, remembers, "I didn't go in there saying $7.75 is great. I went in there and said I needed a job, and I took what I could get." Naomi Adams, who worked inventory at a store in Arlington, Texas, said that there were days she just wanted to walk out, but "I have to keep a roof over my head. So I suck it up and do it." If there are other jobs they don't pay much better, and may even be less secure. At least Walmart mostly pays the wages it promises when it says it is going to. In the peripheral job market this is not always the case.

Walmart's massive profits depend in part on the low prices it pays for workers' labor. This is something that most workers at Walmart know intuitively but rarely articulate explicitly. Karen Ford might be the exception that proves the rule. A cake decorator in Cincinnati, Ohio [#4609], she was more vocal than most about getting too small a piece of the pie (or cake):

> The cheapest [cake] is $7.98. . . . A quarter sheet now, without a kit, is $14.98. A quarter sheet with a kit is $19.98. Now, for every hour that I work, if they sell one cake, they have paid my wage for that hour. But in the hour that I work, if they sold four or five cakes in that hour for $14.98, they done almost paid my salary [for] a day! You understand what I'm saying?

Karen had overlooked the fixed capital investment that Walmart had priced into the cake and the cost of the ingredients. Some tiny fraction of the electricity, debt payment, rent, the congealed labor and materials embedded in the making and maintaining of the physical store, the labor of greeters (security guards), and so on, all of it ends up in the cost of the cake. So does the cost of the flour and eggs and sugar. Still, all of those elements don't come up to $14.98. Karen was right that she was making money for Walmart.

Meanwhile, Karen was barely making enough to scrape by. She would put $5 worth of gas at a time in her car. She would sometimes go without meals so that her kids would have enough to eat. And she believed strongly in the ideal of "an honest day's work for an honest day's pay. . . . If I'm working, then I feel like I have the right to work and live. You know what I'm saying?"

But even Karen, who had partially reconstructed the labor theory of value as it pertained to baked goods, in the next breath was quick to qualify her criticism of Walmart pay.[14] She added, "They don't owe us anything, you see what I'm saying? You can't be ungrateful, because do you know how many people it is that don't have jobs? It is a job. And you know what? I'm going to tell you something. No one is indispensable. At Walmart, they'll get rid of you, because there's four or five people ready to take your place." It was clear to Karen that she was not making enough. But it also seemed clear to her that she had to be grateful for what she got. It was difficult to blame *Walmart*, anyway, for the fact that other jobs paid next to nothing, and Walmart was the best she could do. As Paul Lee from a Chicago store [#5645] put it, "people are so desperate to have a job that they'll work for almost anything just to have food on their table." Not only that. They'll work for almost anything and keep relatively quiet about it.

This is a sleight of the invisible hand of the labor market: people are free to leave Walmart anytime. The pernicious psychological flipside to this exit option is that it implies—even for workers themselves— that those who stay are choosing to stay. They are accepting the terms of the deal: therefore, Walmart doesn't owe them anything.

For the typical American worker, the labor market is an abstraction, a weather pattern. Getting mad at Walmart for its low wages when low wages are everywhere is like getting mad at the rain.

PETTY DESPOTS

So where do Walmart workers direct their frustration? Toward the real people who make the abstraction of the labor market tangible: store managers and comanagers and assistant managers. They are all identifiable. They have faces, names, walkie-talkies strapped to their belts and collared shirts that distinguish them from everyday associates. While the wages and benefits one is offered may feel like the result of distant and uncontrollable forces, the manager is standing right in front of you. And while Walmart's low wages may have different significance for workers coming from different situations, the experience of a manager's arbitrary authority—the experience of the Walmart regime—is common.

Returning to the Glassdoor text, while workers identify the "people" at work as the best part of the job, the most common noun workers use when describing the "Cons" of work at Walmart is "management." The "Cons" nouns most strongly associated with liking one's job less are "respect" and "treat." In other words, among those who like their jobs the least, their unhappiness is due to the lack of respect they feel at work; the way they feel they are treated.

Take Joan Wharton, who—you'll remember—had previously worked at AK Steel for $20 an hour and now worked at the Franklin, Ohio, store for $9. Joan discussed the nearly 60 percent drop in pay almost in passing. The difference she most noticed between working at AK Steel and Walmart? The management. With the union at AK Steel, "there's union contracts, union rules, union representatives. Things that you had to go by, that the workers and the employers all had to go by." If you were treated poorly by a manager, you could "go talk to a rep." At Walmart, though, managers "feel like they can step on anybody they want. They feel like they can talk to anybody any way they want. They can make you do anything they want." There were no boundaries to what managers could ask of workers at Walmart. "They can make you do 20 jobs and give you your nine dollars."

Managers at the Franklin store didn't like the camaraderie that Joan and her friends had established. So they ended it. "We're not allowed to sing anymore," Joan says. "We're not allowed to holler. You know, 'Hi, how are you doing?'" Instead, she says, "We're to go where we're supposed to go, keep our mouths shut, do our work, and get it done now." Now, Joan reports,

> All the close-knit family that we've had in there, and all the helping each other out, and the enjoyable days of going in there and being with, like, our little family together, doing our thing? It's over. It's like being in a jail or something. The management has literally sucked the life out of everybody in there.

Workers weren't even permitted to banter with customers: "You're talking to customers, laughing with customers. They don't even like that." They weren't allowed to call customers "hon" or "sweetie" either. "You have to watch everything you say, every move you make, everything you do in Walmart." The story at Franklin is echoed elsewhere, not everywhere, but the experience of having management suck the life out of a store is common enough. Willie Bell, from the store in Lancaster, Texas, said, "Walmart now is ran on intimidation . . . If you open your mouth, you won't get fed. You keep your mouth closed, and you go with the flow."

Like Joan Wharton, Mayra Rodriguez from the store in Paramount, California, had loved the community she found at the store. But she also soured on the job, because she felt as though managers were intent on breaking up the second family she had established:

> When you work there, you're not just an associate. The person that works next to you, they're more like your aunt, your cousin, your brother, your sister. So, when you get somebody gone, you're breaking up a family. And then when their income is affected, you're breaking up another family.

Managers seem to think that when workers have fun at work—when they talk, holler, visit each other's aisles—that time otherwise spent on productive activities is being wasted. They also seem to think that informal friendly relations among workers create the possibility of a countervailing moral community that might threaten their control over the flow of work. This may be particularly true in retail where, other than the flow of customers and products into and out of the store, there is no structure that organizes labor. The significance of this absence—the absence of an assembly line, of a fixed structure of activities—for the exercise of arbitrary managerial authority is not trivial. Coupled with a scheduling system that is designed to make every minute in the store exactly the same with respect to the staff/customer-material ratio, one can see why management sometimes uses the rhetoric of customer service to break up friendship groups that emerge spontaneously.

And such was the case at Paramount, where soon enough a new management team came after Mayra. She started getting "coachings" from her supervisors that she felt were entirely without merit. Mayra never understood why she was disciplined. Her theory is that they were trying to get rid of her "because I was making more than some people." She says, "I was fenced in. And I didn't see it coming. But by the second coaching, it was already—something's up. Third one, 'Oh my God, what did I get myself into?' And then, the last one, which was like, 'Really?'" So she lost her job.

Mayra might have been unlucky. The new management team went after her quickly and hard and she was unable to outlast them. One thing that Walmart employees know is that managers are regularly moved from store to store. This means that if they can get a quick assessment of the despotic qualities of new teams rapidly enough they can "keep their heads down" for a year or two (which, granted, is an incredibly long time to have to experience the unbridled control of anyone) and outlast them. When this happens, new management teams enter stores where the average worker has worked significantly longer than they will anticipate being there. Like political appointees to cabinet positions, who have to figure out whether they can move potentially entrenched civil servants (the answer to which is "yes" if they are smart, and "no" if they are hacks), these management groups often have to deal with equally entrenched worker communities. And this fact tempers, for many, what changes they seek to put into place.

REPETITION IS MORE COMMON THAN REDEMPTION

Because most managers are male and most associates are female, the destruction of a shop-floor community can replicate the isolation that women have historically experienced in the transition from family of origin to family of destination. For some women, the community that had originally felt like such a nice escape from the banality or brutality of home life started to feel all too familiar—a home away from home, but not in a nice way. This was, at least in part, by design. At the company's founding, Sam Walton had fostered a culture that reinforced the ideals of the patriarchal family from which the women of the Ozarks came, so that Walmart would be understandable to the communities into which he sought to expand. Male managers, often much younger than their female counterparts, would look after and take care of the women at the registers and in the aisles.[15] Sex discrimination was in the company's DNA. In *Dukes v. Wal-Mart Stores, Inc.*, the largest civil rights class action case ever filed against a private corporation, women recounted how they began to confront their managers about being passed over for promotions in favor of less-experienced men. They would sometimes be told explicitly that the men had families to support; that the men were out to make careers at Walmart while the women were not. Giana was offered a $0.40 raise to become a department manager; she remembers many of the men getting $1.00. The plaintiff in the *Dukes* case argued, "Wal-Mart has been living in the America of thirty years ago."[16] The gendered hierarchy within the store also meant that management's domination often took the form of men treating women badly. Rose Robinson, from the Walmart on the South Side of Chicago [#5781] put it simply in an interview: "It's things that I seen in that store that hurts. And you know, coming up, I was hurt enough. So, then a woman of sixty-five now, I'm not looking to get hurt again by nobody."

The awful boss is a cliché, the stuff of sitcoms and movies—think *The Office* or *The Devil Wears Prada*. The usual setup in such movies is that some people are just nasty and/or incompetent and that suddenly one morning they are "the boss"; and life is hell until they find redemption. Real life is different from the movies (it is more similar to sitcoms). First, repetition—which is the premise of the sitcom—is more common than redemption. In the sitcom the nasty boss is nasty until the show is canceled; in real life, bosses don't often find redemption, they are just transferred (or even promoted). Labor contracts and the laws that undergird them set some boundaries on the kinds of requests that bosses can make of workers and the avenues through which workers can seek remedy. But those boundaries are clearer for demands that involve the allocation of one's effort to satisfy the personal needs of bosses—doing their laundry, running their errands, and so on. For demands that are cast in the language of the job, of furthering organizational goals, the boundary between fair use of labor and exploitation is much blurrier.

THE INCOMPLETE CONTRACT

Absent a collectively negotiated labor contract, with respect to actual work in the organization (as distinct from personal services), there are almost no limits to what employers can and do ask of those low-wage employees for whom there is no serious exit option. As we will discuss in more detail in chapter 3, this may be especially true in the retail sector, where little structures the flow of activities other than the movement of people and goods, which—given the ways in which schedules are structured—is effectively randomized. The experience of working in a setting where there are few rules governing what one can be asked to do is translated back as "being in a jail," as Joan Wharton (whose husband is in prison) put it.[17] Comparisons to prison and slavery are deployed with particular regularity by black men at Walmart—Trevon Wilson, from the store in Forest Park, Illinois, said the company "wants you to be in jail" or "on the sale block." Randall Stewart, from a Chicago store, said a manager spoke to him as though "if you walk away from him, he'll hit you with a whip." Owen Taylor, from a different Chicago store, said Walmart treated him "like a slave without the shackles." Just as, for some women, Walmart comes to feel like the abusive spouses they sought to escape, for these men Walmart feels analogous to the institutions that historically have defined black American life.

Such a sense of powerlessness vis-à-vis one's employer is a reality for many at the bottom of the U.S. labor market—a phenomenon Elizabeth Anderson describes as "private government" in her book by the same name: "Private governments impose controls on workers that are unconstitutional for democratic states to impose on citizens who are not convicts or in the military."[18] The political scientist Alex Gourevitch notes that, since most labor contracts are written in vague language, they give the employer "residual authority to specify those undetermined terms and conditions of employment."[19] This indeterminacy is true across a wide range of employers but is presumably the most extreme at places in which workers have neither collective representation nor bargaining power at the individual level: places, in other words, like Walmart. Gourevitch continues,

> Disputes about "the job" can be very wide-ranging. Are the political views, Facebook postings, off-hours recreational activities, and health conditions of employees a reasonable basis for being fired? Is it part of the job to be required to pee in a cup for drug-testing but also be denied bathroom breaks? Can a worker be denied the right to read a newspaper during lunch? Should employees have to listen to the political opinions and participate in political activities of their employers, or is this irrelevant to the employment relationship?

Anyone who believes that constitutionally protected rights like free speech are protected at work need not work too hard to be disabused of this idea. In the aisles of the Walmart in Catskill, New York, on the weekend before the 2016 election, two young white men were pushing a cart of baked goods, laughing with each other about how one of their coworkers had called out sick—"I bet she's out there getting another vote for Hillary," one said derisively. We walked up to try to join in the banter, but they clammed up. "We're not allowed to talk about the election with customers," they said sheepishly. This may not be all that surprising, but it *was* a striking contrast with the experience we had the next day at a small store selling "authentic Polish pottery" in a small development near the Walmart in Wilkes-Barre, Pennsylvania. Here, when we mentioned we were from New York, the owner was quick to respond, "Oh, no! That's a bunch of liberals over there. We're Trump supporters here." Polish Trump supporters who had been immigrant coal miners—now that the coal industry had declined—were selling their immigrant pottery. When we told him we were not going to buy any of his authentic pottery because he would then give the money to Trump, he sort-of-jokingly threatened that his two friends Smith and Wesson would help us get out of the store and that the last New Yorker who came through was lying behind the counter. The owner of the strange authentic Polish pottery store was able to own his strange political beliefs. Associates at Walmart have to be clandestine about them.

Workers' health, formally protected by law, is often not protected in practice within private governments like Walmart. For instance, by law, employers are required to provide medical care for those injured at work. In practice, though, large employers like Walmart are permitted to self-fund their workers' compensation programs rather than pay insurance premiums to an outside insurer. In these cases, the company has a particular incentive to keep claims down—to contract its medical work out to those who will look out for the company's bottom line. Among those Walmart workers who took our survey, 38 percent reported having been injured on the job. Of those, only 12 percent report being covered by workers' compensation. It is hard to know what this means precisely, since many injuries wouldn't be serious enough to warrant workers' compensation. But in Colorado, Walmart settled a class action suit filed by approximately 7,000 employees alleging that the company had conspired with a subsidiary to limit medical care to save on costs.[20]

Work at Walmart can be hard on the body, yet getting sick and missing work while working at Walmart is often grounds for punishment—again, at the discretion of management. The formal attendance policy has been changing so rapidly in recent years that many associates are unclear about what it is at any moment. It does not help that Walmart historically has regulated access to this information—according to one report, many associates were only able to access company policy while on the clock and were told that their viewing of company policy was itself being logged and tracked. [21] This keeps people unsettled, on their toes, unsure of whether or not they can safely get sick so they err on the side of attendance at all costs; it also lets managers make decisions by fiat. When workers are in the dark about formal rules, managers are able to enforce them (or not) at their whim.

Anthony Thompson remembers that in order to avoid "points"—given for unexcused absences—he would do his two-hour commute to Forest Park, Illinois, even when he was "sick as a dog." On these occasions his manager would often make him work his normal shift in the bakery for at least four hours before allowing him to go home. Trevon Wilson had worked at the same Walmart in Forest Park for five years when he began to feel unwell: "It got to the point where I was throwing up every day, and I was on the register throwing up, and they kept telling me I couldn't go to the bathroom." Ultimately his supervisor began sending him home, since "they said I couldn't spend my shift in the bathroom." He went to the doctor, where they diagnosed him with severe anemia: "They were, like, 'You were going to work like this? We're surprised that you even had the strength to lift your head off a pillow.'" By this point he was too weak to go back to work and kept calling off his shifts for about a month. "Then they just stopped putting me on the schedule. They didn't call me to see, 'Are you okay? Are you still alive?' or anything.

They just fired me." He received a letter informing him that he was no longer employed. "And then I called their corporate office, and they said they didn't have to notify me."

There are countless stories of workers and former workers that echo Hunter's experience. Just to pick one: Giana King was proud of becoming the department manager of the health and beauty department in the Walmart in Crenshaw, Los Angeles, after only six months. Giana would now come in overnight to rearrange shelves for new items, do maintenance jobs as they came up, and help to schedule the eight associates below her. For her troubles she got a 40-cent raise. At the time, though, she felt "just having that manager status on my résumé kind of made up for them not giving me" more. She pressed on even as they cut the number of associates who worked under her, first to six and then to four. "So I found myself doing double shifts, coming in overnight, trying to make up the work that my opener left so the closer wouldn't have too much on her. And I end up pulling my shoulder, have a rotator tear." When she went to her supervisors about the pain in her arm, she got little sympathy. "Every manager that I went to basically told me [there was] 100 people waiting in line for my position. And if I couldn't do it, step down and somebody else would." So she kept going. One day she went to reach for a bucket of "go-backs"—the products that people had taken off the shelves but decided not to buy—and "as I was bringing it down to the floor, my whole left side just pulled. And all I could do was yell."

Her pain having spread to her neck and back, Giana went to one of Walmart's contracted workers' compensation doctors in Los Angeles. The doctor's office told her that they weren't authorized to talk about anything other than her arm. So she hired her own workers' compensation attorney. And then, she says, the company really "started treating me like crap. Like you're broken. You're a throwaway paper plate or something." She needed major surgery.

Adding to the complication of having to lose wages if one is hurt is that injuries don't just impact one's own pocketbook—they can impact the pocketbooks of all the workers in the store through the store's bonus policy. Walmart gives out quarterly bonuses to associates at each store; and stores that have no compensation claims, no injuries, are allocated more money. So when a worker contemplates reporting an injury, in the back of his or her mind is the fact that a claim might hurt his or her coworkers.

Thus the soft moral authority of peer sanctioning works to keep Walmart employees "healthier." The system has some other "benefits" as well, one of which is to heighten Walmart associates' intolerance for customer behaviors that appear to put the store at risk of not preventing a "controllable" incident from occurring. An associate from Indiana sees a kid riding a bike around the store. She intervenes. *The mom gave me a hard time but that's my MyShare if she hits someone with it.* While the bonus system may incentivize workers to strive for higher store-level profits, it does so without distinguishing between different kinds of costs. From the perspective of an associate wondering about why her MyShare bonus is so low this quarter, customer theft is equivalent to coworker injury.

While Walmart escapes some of the costs of worker health through such inside health-care provision schemes and peer sanctioning, the real savings come from workers who come to work sick or hurt because they can't afford not to. One writes that she had to *leave work on Sunday because I was coughing up blood.* She went to the ER and learned that she had pneumonia and had bruised her ribs from the coughing. But she went back to work—in the produce section of the grocery department—with an *ace bandage around my ribs* because *I can't afford the points.*

Jasmine Fourzan, from the Walmart in Lakewood, California, holds Walmart managers responsible for a miscarriage she had in 2012. "I'm sure, without a doubt, it was because of Walmart, because they made me work in the freezer and then the dairy, where the temperature is really cold, and I was lifting heavy boxes and pulling pallets." Jasmine's miscarriage fits a troubling pattern of miscarriages among Walmart workers, many of whom say they have been denied requests for light duty or other accommodations during their pregnancies.[22] Mary Washington, from a Walmart in Chicago, was pregnant and working the overnight shift when she realized she was bleeding. She told her supervisor that she needed to go to the hospital, but relates that "[my supervisor] wouldn't let me go. I had to work the next nine hours." So, she says, "I worked the next nine hours, because I was afraid that if I walked out, that I would get fired." As her pregnancy progressed, she stopped being able to do the heavy lifting required of her as a stocker in grocery. But she felt like she couldn't tell her managers. Instead, "behind the manager's back," she would get help from her coworkers who "noticed that I was struggling." Her one other small act of resistance during this time was to wear a jacket when she was working in the freezers ("I'm anemic and I'm on medicine for it"), though her manager would chide her about breaking dress code nearly every day. Rose Robinson said that, in addition to Mary, three other coworkers from that same store had miscarriages on the job.

HAVING NO MONEY MAKES "RANDOM SHIT" HAPPEN MORE OFTEN

As of this writing, regardless of pregnancy or illness or family emergency, Walmart does not accept doctors' notes as excusing absences. Sick time, vacation time, and holiday pay are all considered interchangeable "paid time off" (PTO) that employees earn in proportion to the hours they work. Associates with different levels of seniority have different exchange rates—a new employee has to work 17.3 hours for an hour of PTO, while an employee who has been at the company for more than 20 years has only to work 6.8 hours. For a recent hire to take off one 8-hour shift for any reason without disciplinary repercussions, she would have to have worked 138.4 hours in advance. At first hire, then, full-time Walmart workers get about 15 days of PTO per year.

For workers without small children, for workers with another earner in the household, for retirees who may have paid off their mortgage, fifteen days off can work fine—maybe feel downright generous. One associate on the discussion board wrote, *It amazes me that people are fired for* [poor] *attendance* given how many days off are allowed. Another writes, *Be responsible. Show up to work.* A third says, [I]*f you miss 9 days in 6 months or 4 days in your first 6 months, MOST employers are going to let you go. It's not just Walmart.* And that is likely the case.

But the context created by minimum wage jobs is anything but stable and the capacity to absorb the kinds of shocks that routinely occur in all of our lives (a kid gets sick, the dog is picked up by animal control, the plumbing needs repair, the car needs service) without resources is extremely limited. And if the PTO balance is empty, an illness or family emergency can quickly lead to points (*demerits for adults,* as one associate puts it) that can in turn lead to coachings[23] and eventual termination. Every absence is a point; a no-call/no-show is four points; being more than 10 minutes late to work (or leaving more than 10 minutes early) is half a point; more than two hours late (or early) is a full point (same as an absence). Associates who have been around more than six months get nine points in a rolling six-month window before they are terminated; for new hires (those within the first six months of employment), four points leads to termination.[24]

It is more complex if, as is often the case, there is no other adult in the household able to help. And when you live at or near the minimum wage it's just a fact that more bad things happen. The car you rely on is older and less reliable; the housing stock you live in has an older furnace, older plumbing, and less insulation. If babysitters are too expensive or are unreliable because they live in the same situation you do, if taking the car to the shop means that you have to take a two-hour bus ride and that means your kids have to get themselves to the bus stop on their own, if the subway stops inexplicably for 20 minutes, if gunshots kept you and your kids up all night, if anything happens, the absence of resources means that the chances that you will be late or need to miss a day are high. Random shit happens; it just happens more to poor people than rich people. And when it happens, it is more devastating.

When the checking account has $17, or $5, or $3.82, or $0.76, or $0.32, or when there is no checking account to begin with—there is not a lot of give. Even one of the associates who chastised others for missing so much work returns to admit that she thought the company should accept doctors' notes: *I ended up getting the flu for the first time in my life within my first 3 months at Walmart. Not just once but TWICE! I was so afraid of getting fired I worked with the flu. I thought I was dying!—Actually I remember wishing someone would just kill me. In my case, and the case of others in a contagious condition, Walmart's management should make that exception.* Going to work with the flu is a surefire way to get one's coworkers sick, not to mention one's customers, whose interests are better served by a healthy workforce. A woman reports that her coworker in the deli had been *extremely sick* when a customer asked her why she did not go home instead of sneezing on all the food. She responded that she would *get in trouble*, and—when the customer reported the interaction to the store manager—the employee was disciplined for having told the customer about store policy.

The heterogeneity of experience is staggering. There are more than a million people working at Walmart. Every day thousands of kids get sick, thousands of cars break down, hundreds of people experience a death in their families, hundreds of pipes fail, and countless public transportation routes are unexpectedly delayed. In some Walmarts, managers seem to notch their belts with strict enforcement of the rules. But if all managers worked to rule, forced turnover would likely be higher than it is and the PTO system would collapse under its own weight. And the formal equivalencies—the exchange rates between hours worked and hours earned, infractions and points, points and consequences—belie the discretion that managers have to override the bureaucratic rules when they want to.

This disjuncture between the formal policies and the everyday practices of managers—the fact that managers can choose to look the other way—is what creates the experience of interpersonal domination among workers, the feeling that their managers are the rulers of little fiefdoms.

Not all managers are monsters. Alongside the stories of people being *fired for having pneumonia and* [being] *in the hospital for a week* are stories of managers looking out for their employees. A woman who had problems with blood pressure was told by her assistant manager that *if I really needed to go she would take care of it.* The manager also allowed her to take an unscheduled break: *I did that and was able to make up the day* without points. One associate from Missouri tells the story of a market manager who, upon hearing of an associate's uncharacteristic absence, feels worried enough about her to drive to her house, knock on her door, get in touch with the police when she doesn't respond, and discover—after breaking down her door—that she had fallen and broken her hip. He then *sent our two assembly guys over to fix her front door out of his own pocket.*

But this is not the point; managers' capacity to make life miserable or tolerable for associates—not their actual use of this capacity—is what defines domination. Even stories of managers letting workers off the hook, or of higher-ups going the extra mile, reveal as much about managers' power over workers as they do about their generosity. A manager does not have to ask an associate for permission to take care of a health problem (though she may have to ask someone above her); an associate would likely never think to break down the door of a manager's home.

THE CAN DRIVE SUMMARIZES EVERYTHING

The Internet exploded just before Thanksgiving in 2013 when it was revealed that the Walmart in Canton, Ohio [#5285] was holding a canned food drive for its own employees. Signs attached to the tablecloths on which the bins were placed read: "Please Donate Food Items Here, so Associates in Need Can Enjoy Thanksgiving Dinner."[25] The obvious, and troubling, implication was that Walmart workers were paid so little that they needed food assistance in order to celebrate the holiday.

The can drive has an ongoing, if less well known, equivalent in the form of the Walmart Associates in Critical Need Trust, a fund that—according to its tax filing—"provides monetary support to associates or their dependents when they experience extreme economic hardship due to situations outside of their control." During the fiscal year ending January 31, 2013, according to tax records, the fund provided over 14,000 Walmart workers with cash assistance averaging just under $1,000 each. That is $14 million, or 87 percent of the salary of Walmart's CEO that year. The largest contributor to this fund: Walmart associates and managers, who contributed approximately $5.3 million to help their fellow associates.[26]

Like the canned food drive, Walmart's fund for its neediest workers likely wouldn't be necessary if Walmart didn't put people in such desperate straits to begin with. And the process for accessing the funds was *a little humiliating*, wrote one employee. An associate writes that her husband just passed away and she is *trying to get help with cremation expense.* She went to the store manager, who told her that the fund was for people behind on their bills, but that *funerals weren't considered critical need.* Another responded that she was able to use it once for an electric bill but *had to go through a lot to even get it, I don't think it's worth it.* It finally went through only after she *sat in the dark too long.* Another says that she [d]*idn't get it when I needed it* after hip-replacement surgery, and another says that she was denied and that *I don't think they approve it at my store.* As with schedules, shifts, promotions, the system is formally rationalized but no one really knows how it works, so those who do not benefit feel as if the beneficiaries had it rigged from the start. It is very unlikely that they did. The outcome is an expression of the fact that when Walmart does look after its associates, it is often through a framework of altruism rather than one of reciprocal and universal rights and obligations.

One associate writes how happy she is that her assistant manager gave her a Christmas card with a lottery ticket. Another writes that her *store manager sent out Christmas Cards to each employee and personally wrote Merry Christmas and signed his name.* This makes her *love* [my] *store.* Another responds, *These kinds of posts make me happy and sad . . . I'm happy for you, but sad that our store doesn't do stuff like that.* Expectations are low: people are genuinely grateful for the manager who gives a little spare change out of the Critical Need Trust when one's wages aren't enough to keep one's lights on, who gives a card and a pat on the back at the end of the year, and who provides a good meal in the break room when one is working on Thanksgiving.

3

THE STRUCTURE OF DOMINATION AND CONTROL

Walmart is known throughout the corporate world for revolutionizing the logistics of retail—the processes by which goods move from the point of production to the trunk of a customer's car. More than any retailer before, it has broken down this process into its component parts and maximized the efficiency of each. It was one of the first retailers to make use of the barcode to keep track of its inventory; one of the first to integrate its operations vertically, cutting out wholesalers; one of the first to use its own fleet of trucks and develop its own network of distribution centers close to its stores so as to minimize the inventory it kept on-site and reduce both overstocking and outstocking.[1] Not only does it collect detailed information about every product it sells across its stores over time, but through its Retail Link system, Walmart shares many of these data with its suppliers—a process that helps suppliers modify their production and marketing techniques, while also making them acutely aware of whether they are living up to Walmart's sales expectations.[2] In sum, Walmart has used its market power, combined with information technology, to squeeze its suppliers—sometimes to the edge of insolvency—and pass those savings on to its consumers, profiting itself on the sheer volume of stuff that comes and goes.

Given such systematization, how does one make sense of what we find at the Walmart in East Windsor, New Jersey [#3266]? It is almost 2 p.m. on a Saturday afternoon in March. The fitting-room associate, who runs the intercom, has announced that all associates starting their shifts are to meet by the jewelry counter for a 2 p.m. meeting. A few people begin wandering over to the counter around 2:05, but the meeting does not begin in earnest until at least 2:10. An assistant manager—a 30-something West Indian woman—tells the assembled associates that they will be "zoning" (i.e., straightening out) the grocery section for the first hour of their shift. But before she can finish her instructions, she gets told, via her headset, that she is needed at the registers in the front. A slightly older white man takes over. But before he has time to say much of anything, he is cut off, this time by a customer who approaches with a shopping cart, asking the assembled group to point her in the direction of the cutting fabric. As the man running the meeting turns his attention to the customer, the meeting melts away before it has really begun.

Watching men roll large pallets of goods across a Walmart shop floor, it can feel as though Walmart is its own sort of assembly line: a steady churn of stuff from truck, to bin, to cart, to shelf, to register, and out. This is right on one level, but it misses two dimensions of the retail sector that make it different from the assembly line, both of which we saw in one mundane moment of disorganization in East Windsor. First, retailers like Walmart (and many other service-sector companies) are server systems, meaning there is unavoidable uncertainty in the flow of customers and items.[3] Second, at retailers like Walmart and across the service sector, the traditional two-way relationship between workers and managers is replaced by a three-way relationship among workers, customers, and managers.[4] These new relational dynamics change dynamics of control in subtle but important ways as well.

In this chapter we suggest that the experiences of Walmart we observed in chapter 2—the sense of creativity, autonomy, and community that some workers find there some of the time; the frustration with the arbitrary authority of managers that many workers come to resent—are structured by these features of work in the service sector.[5]

SERVER SYSTEMS AND UNJUST AUTHORITY

The central structural fact about retail work is that it is a server system. Customers flow in at unpredictable times and purchase unpredictable things. They make unpredictable demands on the workers who serve them. Or so it seems. But there is a typical flow. People are more likely to buy doughnuts in the morning than TVs. Ammunition is more likely to be sold during hunting season than it is the week before Christmas. Each of the million products sold at Walmart has its own schedule, each day, down to the hour. And product schedules are correlated with one another. The schedules for peanuts and soda are more similar than the schedules for hosiery and avocados, because customers—whose bundles of goods make up their shopping baskets—generate each product's schedule.

Down in Arkansas, some cluster of corporate operations research engineers have designed algorithms that pore over the hourly sales data for each store and predict optimum, store-specific minimum staffing levels for each hour the stores are open. Those minimum staffing levels are then transformed into schedules for assistant managers and department managers and associates. The minimum staffing level is that specific level that maximizes profit, moving the most product out the door with the least labor. Somewhere along the line, these corporate engineers have figured out just what the optimal wait time at checkout is for each store. A little wait may be better than none at all, because people make impulse purchases of items displayed at the registers while they are waiting in line. But if the lines are too long, people may just leave. The retail industry, led by Walmart, figured out a long time ago what the airlines recognized more recently: customers are willing to absorb a lot of the costs of business to save a minimal amount of money. These engineers also know that people buy products when those products are fully loaded on the shelves, and so they need to make sure that associates can keep their areas stocked. The goal is to reduce idle time for staff to zero by shifting it onto customers without that shift becoming so obvious or burdensome that people stop going to Walmart to buy things.

How much Walmart can shift this burden onto customers varies by location. People tend to wait in longer lines in poor communities and communities of color. What Walmart (or any retailer) can get away with is strongly correlated with the mean household income or percent of African Americans in their catchment areas, presumably at least in part because there are fewer alternative places to buy things. In these places Walmart has market power over both its workers, who do not have many other places to work, and its customers, who do not have many other places to shop. Figure 3.1 shows the association between the average Yelp review for a Walmart and the characteristics of the neighborhood in which it is located. The reviews are significantly worse in poor communities (figure 3.1A) and communities of color (figure 3.1B).

Using the same analytic techniques as we did in our Glassdoor analysis earlier, we also investigated which words are most associated with reviews in African American communities versus those most associated with reviews of stores in white communities. In stores in predominantly African American zip codes, reviewers are more likely to use words like "worst," "unorganized," and "nasty" to describe their experiences. In contrast, in stores located in white zip codes, reviewers are more likely to use words like "typical," "friendly," and "smaller." The single word most highly correlated with reviews of Walmarts in communities of color is "ghetto." Shoppers at different Walmarts have starkly different experiences.

No algorithm works perfectly. And so the everyday problem that Walmart faces even with the most precise algorithms available is the simple fact that shit happens. The minimal server-allocation system can take into account a whole host of disruptions and slowdowns

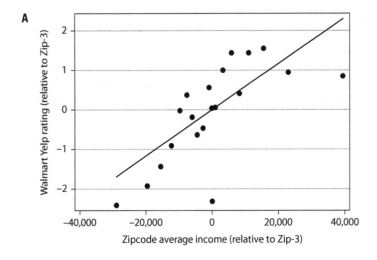

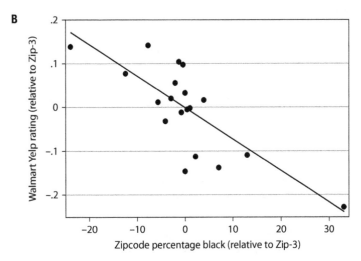

FIGURE 3.1 (A and B) Average Yelp reviews reflect neighborhood quality.

caused by patterned customer behavior, but it cannot account for all of the strange things that the 100 million customers who come to the store each week might (and do) actually do. When one of those things happens, giant queues can form at the register. And when that happens, people with full baskets can just decide to walk out, abandoning everything in their carts, thus leaving even more chaos behind them and elongating the queue.

And so while Walmart has rationalized much of the logistics to maximize the efficiency of the flow of goods through its system in light of varying demand, there is a huge element of uncertainty in the production process to which Walmart responds by allocating to their managers a high degree of discretion over staff allocation. If lines appear at the registers, managers shift associates off the floor to work them; if cashiers are suddenly idle, managers have associates move stock. Outside of Wilkes-Barre, Pennsylvania, on the Monday morning before the 2016 presidential election, for example, there was such a run on guns and ammunition that additional staff had to be allocated to what was usually (at that time of day) a relatively sleepy department. This helps to explain the puzzle that while Walmart is hyperrationalized, many associates do not have the kind of stable job descriptions we expect in a bureaucracy.

DIRECT CONTROL AT THE POINT OF PRODUCTION

Contrast the situation at Walmart on any given day—shifting personnel, chaotic arrivals and departures of goods and persons—with the typical factory characterized by the systematic movement of goods down an assembly line at fixed speed. Customers introduce an improvisational element to the service sector. It is uncertain exactly when they will come, what they will want, what they will do.

If associates feel under the watchful eye of managers who track their productivity with obsessive attention to detail, managers are—in turn—under the watchful eye of performance algorithms that drive them to sell more products. They also get to do fun things like decide strategies for increasing sales or set the parameters within which employees can experiment with what condiment goes best with fried chicken in Omaha or give advice on the displays the associates set up and later post "shelfies" of. Managers are the ones who frame how employees ought to respond to the requests and behaviors of customers—the customer who returns a box of condoms saying they did not work because she got pregnant; the customers who are trying to wire money to children they seem not to know or "lovers" they have never met; the diabetic who complains that Walmart is discriminating against diabetics because the sugar-free pecan pie is 50 percent more expensive than the normal one; the customers who come in with snakes or ride horses that poop in the aisles.[6] They are the ones who are responsible for scheduling employees so as to accomplish several different objectives at once—matching the somewhat predictable but varying flow of customers with the supply of labor; allowing employees some degree of say over when they work, how many hours they work, and what department they should work in; staying under budget. At the end of the day they are left to try to figure what combination of carrots and sticks they ought to use to incentivize labor productivity.

On the assembly line, the structuring routines built into the machinery limit the extent to which the manager can wield arbitrary authority over work. A manager cannot simply take people off one task and put them on another willy-nilly, as the line would likely stop; managers cannot change much about the structure of production, just its tempo. In this setting the inflexibility, predictability, and interdependence of the production process provide the foundations for worker voice: management demands that impede the functioning of the line will likely be seen as illegitimate; there are defined work rules around which workers might negotiate; and there is the credible threat that disobedience by a small fraction of the workforce will disrupt production for everyone by stopping the line entirely.

Control over labor encoded into the technical means of production—that is, the assembly line—does more than mute the discretion of supervisors. It directly enhances workers' structural power. Richard Edwards, in *Contested Terrain*, argues that employers' reliance on technical control in the early twentieth century, itself a response to workers' resistance to managers' arbitrary authority, created the conditions of possibility for the sit-down strikes of the 1930s and the growth of industrial labor unions: "Technical control linked together the plant's workforce, and when the line stopped, every worker necessarily joined the strike. Moreover, in a large, integrated manufacturing operation, such as auto production, a relatively small group of disciplined unionists could cripple an entire system by shutting down a part of the line."[7]

All of this is missing in the low-wage retail sector. In settings where the routine is dictated not by the fixed capital of machinery but rather by the ceaselessly changing flow of customer demand, workers can be moved from one task to another under the seemingly legitimate claim that such shifting is aimed at improving customer service.[8] In such contexts it is not difficult for managers to make life difficult for workers they have come to dislike or would like to see fail. Even those managers with the best of intentions toward all of their employees end up favoring some over others, if only because the some they favor are those that they trust to get the job done. From the perspective of the worker, though, the exercise of managerial discretion over their time and activities on the shop floor appears tainted by favoritism. That this perception makes it harder for workers to align with a single voice may be an unexpected benefit of the Walmart management strategy for labor control, as it surely acts as a powerful impediment for collective action.

UNFAIR MANAGERS AND THE RHETORIC OF CUSTOMER SATISFACTION

Against this background, it is not surprising that the perception of managers' arbitrary and unjust authority frustrates associates most. Under some theory of sales, every tiny little thing matters, and if one holds that theory, then pretty much everything employees do is up for grabs. Vickie Allard, from the store in Rosemead, California [#5154], remembers the moment when she was told by a younger male supervisor that she had to change her name tag from "Vickie," the nickname she had used since her father used it in her childhood, to "Victoria." She complied because "he's the boss, you know, what am I supposed to do?" But it stung. She wasn't allowed to decide the name on her own name tag? "That was the first time I had ever encountered such disrespect in a store or any, or any establishment I worked for." It is hard to imagine how one's name tag could influence sales one way or another. But under the prevailing understanding that managers have discretion over employees limited only by what is not related to customer service, a demand as absurdly illegitimate as the name-change demand might be justified.

It's the frustration of giving birth to a child and then having to pee more regularly than usual, only to be chided by one's superior, or being disciplined for *stealing time* for having diarrhea while on the clock. It's the casual banter with a manager that suddenly becomes serious: *I had to go get a* [scanner] *from a co manager. He jokingly said do you have a dollar. I jokingly said back I work at Walmart I'm broke. He then gave me a 10 min lecture on how I shouldn't say bad things about the company that he works for.* A long thread on the discussion board concerns whether or not it complies with dress code for an associate to wear a rainbow pin. On the one hand, the fact that Walmart sponsors an "associate resource group" in support of LGBTQ associates—Walmart PRIDE—is discussed as evidence that the pin would be acceptable. On the other hand, an associate responds that *if a customer comes up to you saying it's offensive to them then you have to take it off*; another says that its acceptability depends on the store and that her store—in Ohio—*had a guy who had to remove his rainbow pin.*

One of the recurrent problems facing associates is that they confront multiple levels of authority, many of which are not in sync. Vickie, for example, didn't know what she was supposed to do if an item's stock keeping unit (SKU code) was missing. Type it in herself? One assistant manager said yes; several weeks later she was written up for doing so; a few weeks after that she was chastised for doing the opposite. An associate like Vickie has several different managers to whom she might have to respond: her customer service manager (an hourly associate in charge of the front of the store), a support manager (an hourly associate one step up from CSM); or any of the salaried managers on the shift (assistant store managers, store comanagers, and store managers). People in these different positions likely have different problems they are trying to solve at different times, and so they respond to the same everyday uncertainties differently. April Williams, from a store in Dayton, Ohio, described the absurdity that would sometimes result:

> You have your immediate manager, who tells you something and you go off and do it. And then another manager sees you doing something, and you just finish up doing what your immediate manager told you to do, and another manager will see you, thinking that you're not busy, and give you something else to do. And your immediate manager will be, like, "Where are you at? Where have you been?" It's, like, "Well, manager level B told me to do this." "Well, I need you over here . . . I need you to do this." So it's kind of a struggle between your immediate manager level A versus your higher-level manager, level B, and then sometimes level C comes in and wants you to do something, and it can be—it feels like you're getting jerked in 18 different directions, and it's like you can't complain, because you do what the top-level manager, the highest-level manager that tells you to do something, that's the manager that you listen to.

Many times workers' frustrations also revolve around unpredictability and favoritism regarding work schedules. Walmart's scheduling policies, like its policies regarding sick time and paid time off, have been in flux. Consistent has been the company's aspirations to match work hours with customer traffic as predicted by the company's algorithms—what it calls in its most recent iteration "customer-first scheduling." The fact that customer demand varies based on all sorts of factors means that Walmart, ideally, would have all of its workers on call 24 hours a day, 7 days a week, and could match immediate changes in traffic (say, the announcement of an upcoming snowstorm) with immediate changes to people's schedules. But the flow of labor is not as flexible as the flow of merchandise. In light of widespread opposition to such just-in-time scheduling practices, the company has put in place a system in which workers can indicate the hours they are available and are given their schedules two weeks in advance, though these schedules may vary within (and sometimes even without) the hours that associates indicate they are available.

How do managers decide on which hours to give which associates? Should associates who are available more of the time be rewarded with more of their preferred hours, since they are willing to shoulder more of the uncertainty for the company? Should more senior associates get more predictable schedules or more total hours, or should the regularity and number of hours be distributed based on worker productivity or some other metric? Naturally some people appear to receive better schedules. And the scheduling matters, because that is how people get their hours. If they don't get hours, they have less money. And if they have less money, they are even more subject to the contingencies of the things that might happen to them, putting them at risk of being even less available.

In some perfect, algorithmically efficient world, the answers to these questions and more would all have been encoded in software, and managers could not be blamed for any favoritism. Even better for the company, perhaps, would be if Walmart could treat its employees like Uber treats its "contractors"—associates could log into work whenever they felt the inclination and would be paid more or less for each product scanned or shelf stocked or pallet emptied depending on the labor supply and demand at that hour. For now, though, hours are passed down from the home office in Bentonville to the regional manager to the district manager to the store manager, who then—along with those further down the chain of command—have to decide on matching particular hours to particular people.

It is easy to blame managers, and there are certainly bad managers at Walmart. But the problems are deeper, if only because managerial authority here is not constrained by anything inherent to the work. At the end of the day, managers are responsible for increasing sales at the lowest possible cost. The fact that workers do not have fixed schedules makes it easier for Walmart to make more money. It also makes it more difficult for Walmart workers to create and maintain community. It puts them directly under the eye of managers whose opinions and thoughts about them matter not just during their time on the floor, but also for how many hours they get and when, when they are trying to balance competing obligations.

CUSTOMERS

Under some circumstances, as discussed earlier, customers can feel like family for Walmart workers. This is particularly true at stores where regulars make up a relatively high proportion of shoppers and work schedules are relatively fixed, allowing for repeated interactions among the same customers and employees over time. It's also likely to be true where customers are literally workers' family and friends. These tend to be Walmart stores in more rural areas. But it is also the case that Walmart workers experience customers as their adversaries.

How does it come about that customers are seen as the enemy? How might we understand this opposition? After all, all of the energy devoted to aesthetic stocking, the shelfies, the desire to make even the worst Walmart a place that one's grandmother could feel okay about shopping in, seems oriented toward making things work for customers. That is all true. In the imaginaries of thousands of Walmart workers, aesthetics, distinction, control all seem possible, and those Walmart associates "go for it."

The problem is that these desires fundamentally contradict the real Walmart, which at the end of the day is about low prices. Walmart's primary concern is to offer the lowest prices within whatever turns out to be the competitive catchment area for the buyers who come into their stores. Buyers tend to come to Walmart not because it makes them feel good, not because they mistakenly believe that Walmart supports their community through charitable contributions, not for any other reason than they know that, on average, their shopping basket is going to be cheaper than the same basket purchased anywhere else and they can get all sorts of cheap things in one place.

A 2016 survey by Market Force Information found that Walmart was ranked the lowest across all grocery stores in virtually every dimension of customer preference, from cleanliness to checkout speed.[9] The American Customer Satisfaction Index recently gave Walmart 68/100, the lowest of all retailers. ConsumerAffairs gave it 1.2 stars out of 5. People don't come to shop. They come to buy. The millions of people who go to Walmart would be happier if it looked better, was cleaner, faster, whatever. But they are coming for the prices, not the atmosphere.[10]

From its inception, Walmart's business model has been premised on offering customers the lowest prices. The company's motto has reflected this priority, even as it has changed over time. First it was Always the Low Price. Always. After the Better Business Bureau challenged this claim, Walmart modified the slogan to Always Low Prices. Always. This one stuck until 2007, when the company changed its motto again—this time to Save Money. Live Better. At the time, the business press suggested that this represented a significant shift in the company's mission—it was no longer just about price at Walmart, but about what savings could make possible. But it was a shift in framing more than a shift in content, and the thrust was still the same—if you shop here, you will save money.

These are not the lowest prices possible. In today's market they are not always even the lowest prices around, as competitors, online and off, have cut prices in order to compete. But the prices are certainly low, and they are widely understood to be the lowest. And so the company's defenders, including people like Jason Furman—Barack Obama's chair of the Council of Economic Advisers—argue that Walmart should be understood as a hero for the poor,[11] a corporate Robin Hood. In 2005, a company-commissioned study from Global Insight reported that the company saved consumers $263 billion in 2004, more than $2,000 per household. This assumes all sorts of indirect effects on prices in other stores, but the effect at the individual household level is real enough. Some scholars have suggested that the Consumer Price Index—a basic economic indicator produced by the Bureau of Labor Statistics and used to measure inflation and set interest rates—ought to be adjusted in light of the savings that Walmart makes possible.[12]

Recall that the largest single period of abnormal returns for Walmart over the last 30 years occurred during the years surrounding welfare reform. The other peaks? All during recessions (see figure 3.2). Financial analysts refer to Walmart as a "bear market stock," since it tends to outperform the market during periods of economic contraction. When times are hard, people are more likely to spend more of their money at places like Walmart that promise the lowest prices around. As a commentator from *Slate* put it, "In a pinched economy, consumers are embracing their inner skinflint. And Walmart is a penny pincher's paradise."[13] For similar reasons,

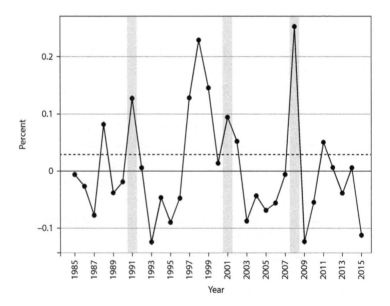

FIGURE 3.2 Average annual abnormal returns at Walmart. Shaded areas represent recessions, dashed line represents average abnormal returns across the entire period.

analysts have suggested that Walmart may underperform during periods of economic prosperity.[14] One of the arguments that Walmart makes is that poor people depend on the company's low prices. True. They also depend on the company for jobs. And one of the reasons that they are poor is that they are not paid enough for the work that they do. The poor people depending on low prices at Walmart are like the people who work at Walmart.

Walmart has always had an easy response to demands for higher wages: it can't change much without raising prices, and if it did that, then Walmart customers would lose out. Walmart frames the customer and the employee as antagonists, competing over the same piece of the same pie. The company has often pointed out that it has operated on a slim 3 percent profit margin for the last 20 years, that its prodigious profits are a result of its massive scale. In response to widespread criticism about a range of different issues, one of the largest companies in the world goes micro, portraying itself as an advocate for the "average working family," a lifeline, a way to survive.[15] The economics of this argument are contested and shaky,[16] but that is beside the point. If Walmart acts as though the interests of its workforce are antagonistic to the interests of its customers, this goes a long way toward making it be so.

Rebecca Sanaith felt as though customers *knew* that the low prices they enjoyed were a direct result of her and her coworkers' poor working conditions. Rebecca believes the same story too. The customers "know we don't get paid right and we get treated wrong. They're just like, 'But it's cheap . . . This place is ghetto but it's cheap. I know they don't pay their associates right, but it's better for my pocket.'" In her mind, customers believe that the low prices they are paying depend on the low wages that Walmart is paying. This is probably not actually the case. Most customers don't really think about the mechanisms by which low prices confront them. Still, in the minds of some associates, customers and workers meet on the shop floor thinking that they are structural adversaries. The reality is different. Decomposing the sources of low prices is complex, but wages are not the sole drivers of price at Walmart.

Across the service sector, customers do not interact with managers or executives; they interact with those serving them: cashiers, customer service representatives, bartenders, concierges. And in most service settings, part of the service workers' product is the experience he or she creates for the customer.[17] In fancy hotels or boutique clothing stores or expensive health-care facilities, this is the experience of luxury. A central part of the worker's job is to be cheerful, caring, and helpful, to anticipate the customer's needs, to establish rapport, to make the customer feel seen and understood. The luxury worker's job is in part to make the customer like him or her and, by association, like the business and spend money there. This feels good for the customer. When workers can believe that the service they offer is important or the place they work is providing something useful, it can feel good for the workers too.[18] Workers want to feel that they work at the best place as well, that their building really is special, that their clothes are really well designed, that their sports club is best at whatever it tries to be (a fitness center, a spa, a place to have health food), that their garage really is good at fixing cars, and so on. Absent those beliefs, the manufacturing of emotional responses can alienate the worker from his or her own emotional life.[19]

The problem at Walmart is that what the organization says it is the best at—low prices—is seen by some customers and some workers to be partially secured by workers' mistreatment. It doesn't need to be. Walmart could attribute its capacity for consistently delivering low prices to the incredible economies of scale it achieves, to its unusually effective operations research guys who model the transportation networks that get materials from farms and ports and factories onto trucks, to the fact that its associates work harder and smarter than everyone else. But until recently, Walmart's opposition to even modest increases in the minimum wage, its fierce resistance to any form of collective bargaining, its massive investments in defending itself against class action suits, in short, its public face, simply strengthens the perceived alignment of low wages and low prices.

The fact that in some places workers are able to develop a unique store identity, link their imagined futures to "a great company," or still believe in the wisdom of Sam Walton is a remarkable testament to how important finding dignity at work is, in whatever little corner one can build it. But where it seems Walmart really doesn't care, where the customers think the workers are garbage, where the workers think the customers are scum, where everyone thinks the stuff that is sold there is junk, where the whole scene is totally "ghetto," where no one has a reason to invest in an imaginary community linking customers and workers, the antagonism between customers and workers is fueled and refueled through countless everyday encounters. And the perception that there is an inherent antagonism between the interests of workers and the interests of customers is reinforced by the organization of work at Walmart.

CUSTOMERS THINK THEY ARE THE VICTIMS OF ASSOCIATES

At Walmart, workers are not given the luxury to make the experience of shopping luxurious. In truth, a "luxurious" Walmart would probably look like a Walmart that wasn't doing everything to make prices lower. And so Walmart *can't* look too good. Pallets of stock on the floor communicate the idea that no effort is being wasted in making sure that prices are absolutely rock bottom. The associates can't be seen as doing nothing, because otherwise customers might start to think that some of the hourly wage that is going to the idle worker could go into an even lower price on the shelf.

Associates at Walmart are busy. They have boxes to unpack, pallets to unload, long lines of customers to get through. One associate wrote in frustration: *Have y'all ever been told you were going overboard with customer service?* Despite Sam Walton's famous "10-foot rule," whereby associates were to smile, greet, and offer to help any customer who came within a 10-foot radius of them, in practice it is impossible for associates to use the 10-foot rule and complete all the tasks they are asked to do: *If you're busting your butt trying to stock, it's kinda hard to do the 10 foot rule. You'd probably get fired for not doing your job stocking.*

The weird thing is that amid the massive field of "we cut all costs" signifiers, customers have the idea that the associates should take care of them. There emerges a sense of dissonance between the customer's and the associate's understandings of "service." One associate writes about a grumpy old man who complained that the *workers are always in the way putting stuff away*, to which another responds, *You know they'd be griping more if we didn't have it out.* The associate sees her "service" as consisting of moving the goods—making sure that things are stocked and in place, shelves are full and appealing, aisles are clear. The customer, unable to find something, is seeking interactive service, emotional labor, information delivered with a smile. The customer, assuming that service workers are there to serve them, feels entitled to interrupt the worker's stocking work, because it does not appear to them as work related to their needs. The worker feels interrupted. Walmart workers from all kinds of different regions and backgrounds seem irrationally irritated by one specific question they get from customers: "Do you work here?" They assert it's a stupid question, and they have a point: Why ask someone wearing a Walmart uniform whether they work at Walmart? But the wrath for what is likely almost always a rhetorical question may be related to the fact that this is a question that customers ask as a way of trying to interrupt whatever the worker was doing before.

Customers may not get the smiles to which they feel entitled. The structural sources of workers' stress are invisible to them—the disrespect they get from managers, the inconsistent scheduling, and of course, the low pay. Instead, they experience the worker's stress directly as the worker failing to serve them. A long line may well be related to understaffing, but the customer does not see staffing decisions get made; the customer sees a "lazy" cashier who ought to do more to speed up the process.[20] And because customers are interested in themselves they actually think that they are the victims of the long line.

Jamal Green was one of the fastest cashiers in the business, but it was still hard to keep customers happy: "So, you will have a lot of angry customers, and a lot of this stuff was out of our control, where it was due to understaffing, or something like that, where it's the wrong price, or long lines, or something like that." It is frustrating to be working your hardest and still feel as though you are the target of customer ire. Karen Ford, the cake decorator from Cincinnati, could understand customer frustration:

> You know, you come in there, and there's nobody to wait on you. Have you ever went in Walmart and had to stand in a long line, or went to get some food from the deli, and there was nobody behind the counter to wait on you? This is going on all the time.

According to workers like Karen, customers' attributions were off: "The people look at you like you're doing something wrong, but it ain't us, it's the company not having enough workers." Carlos Sánchez, from a store in Orlando, Florida [#1084], said that due to low staffing the "customers are getting on your case, and it's not your fault." Asked how that made him feel, he answered, "Horrible! You feel like you're being attacked. And it's not your fault." Michael King, who wound up leaving his store in Elgin, Illinois [#1814], because of the stress, remembers how depressed everyone seemed who worked there:

> They would just sit there and kind of have their head down, complaining about having to cover, like, three departments, and their department being such a mess, and yet, you know, they would have to spend time helping out another department because there's just—there's just nobody working there.

The perception that there is nobody working at Walmart arises because no matter when you are there, the company has sought to minimize the number of people in the store—a number calculated previously from all the microlevel sales and flow data in that store for that time of year. Workers often feel, rightly, that they are blamed by customers for decisions made much farther up the chain of command. And customers get unhappy with workers even for things that don't have anything to do with Walmart. When California passed a law charging a small fee for plastic bags, customers got mad at associates for it: *People are being really rude about it . . . I'm getting berated over something I had no control over. . . . Granted in retail/cashier position to them it's always our fault.*

THE CUSTOMER IS ALWAYS RIGHT

Sam Walton didn't invent the idea that the customer was always right, but he did help diffuse it. Here's another of his famous aphorisms: "There is only one boss—the customer. And he can fire everybody in the company from the chairman on down, simply by spending his money somewhere else." Everyone knows that the customer is not always right, that the customer is not literally the boss, but it doesn't matter. The idea that one should act as if the customer is always right, that the customer has more authority than the worker, makes good business sense. The marginal cost of replacing a product—which for anything that actually costs anything is driven back to the supplier or easily written off as loss—is never worth the potential diffusion of negative sentiment through interpersonal networks. In communities where such networks are dense and intact—like the communities Walmart came out of, in small towns in rural areas of the country—arguing with customers is a guaranteed way to send your business into the ground.

But having the customer be "boss" is also a management tool, a way to offload an element of performance reviews, to subject the employee to constant supervision without spending a dime. There are exponentially more customer "bosses" than salaried staff. Think of the disciplining power of tipping systems at restaurants, the ways in which "comment cards" at hotels or "brief surveys" after calls with customer service representatives or even Yelp reviews might allow managers to watch their employees more carefully. These are all strategies of making the customer a part of management.[21] Sam Walton must have realized that all of this customer supervision is free. He also must have realized that if managers, particularly those hourly "managers" at the lower levels of the store who still have routine customer contact, treat all customer complaints as legitimate, they would not waste associate time or their own time trying to get to the substantive reality of the situation. By giving a small gift or taking the price off or apologizing; by disciplining the associate; in short, by acting like the customer is right even when the customer is obviously wrong, one could send the customer out the door, satisfied quickly, without a scene. Surely some managers are able to play front and backstage simultaneously, satisfying customers while simultaneously confirming through a subtle conspiratorial look or sign or follow-up conversation that they know the associate is right. But surely others are not, and surely some come to believe as a result of their acting that the customer really is always right and the associate is always wrong.

Here too there is unevenness in the control that customers can exert over associates. In communities where Walmart workers and customers overlap and are close-knit, customer complaints may risk tearing the social fabric in which they are embedded. Consequently, complaints (and control) from customers are probably reduced. In contrast, in the communities broken apart by poverty, customers may have more incentive to complain (what is known is that if you complain you get things) and they pay none of the costs, because they do not pay a relational price for getting free stuff.

Leilani Griffin, who worked at a Walmart in Cincinnati, remembered, "If a customer complained that you didn't help put her bags in the car, knowing that you did . . . she'll tell your manager that, and the manager will believe [the customer]." She continued, "I believe the customer's always right, but . . . the customer could be always wrong, too." Dawn Mills, from the Walmart in Franklin, Ohio, said, "Walmart lets customers, lets rude people like that, get by with anything and everything. They reward them with giving

them a gift card if they complain enough. That kind of thing."
Jason Matthews, from the Walmart in Glenwood, Illinois [#5404],
said, "Due to the fact that Walmart [thinks the] customer is always
right you have some customers that will come in there mad at the
world and will literally take it out on you verbally and physically.
Walmart will not do anything to protect you." Patricia Bowman,
who worked as a cashier at a Walmart in Merritt Island, Florida
[#771], reported, "We have customers cuss us out constantly." But
what made it worse was that managers "take the customer's side
90 percent of the time." She continued: "And when you're being
cussed out because you're not selling alcohol because they're
underage and don't have an ID, you don't need that and you don't
need management apologizing to the customer. You need them to
back you on that." Vickie Allard, from the Walmart in Rosemead,
California, referred to one of her supervisors as the "Queen of
Hearts," because "if a customer spoke out against you. . . . It was off
with your head."

Customers played another negative role for many of those who
worked at Walmart: as the audience for the abuse to which they
were subjected by management. The presence of customers added
to the humiliation they felt at the hands of their supervisors. Ann
Regnerus, the former gravestone cutter, described how management at her store would "chastise you, right in front of the customers." She continued,

> And they'd call you up on the intercom and they'd say stuff like, "And
> you will be held accountable!" And I was just thinking, man, this is,
> like, right out of 1984, you know? It's, like, Orwellian. And it was just
> abusive, really.

In stores where associates know their customers, such public
admonishment would be embarrassing and degrading. Losing face
is uncomfortable. Losing face in front of friends is something one
hopes to avoid as an adult.

WALMARTISM

In the late nineteenth century, as modern industry increasingly displaced old patterns of work in the United States, the Knights of Labor—a radical predecessor to the better-known and more conservative American Federation of Labor—expressed concern about whether political freedom was possible among a class of permanent wage earners. These early labor activists thought wage labor was a form of domination not only because of laborers' dependence on employers for a wage but also because of the employer's everyday authority over the labor process.[22]

Labor's attention to interactive domination during this time arose naturally from the changing organization of firms during this period. As documented by Richard Edwards, quickly expanding companies like McCormick Harvesting Machine Company and Pabst Brewing turned to what Edwards calls "hierarchical control" to convert labor power—workers' time—into actual labor. When companies had been smaller, owners' personal ties with their workers helped to blur class lines and inspire workers' loyalty to the boss.[23] But as the sheer size of firms prevented such personalistic ties between workers and owners, companies hired foremen and managers to serve the same control functions previously served by the owner himself, now without the boss's charisma: "The result was arbitrary command rule by foremen and managers, who became company despots encumbered by few restrictions on their power over workers."[24]

It was these forms of arbitrary control, as much as concerns about wages and benefits, that provoked the first concerted wave of labor agitation in the United States. In 1894, the Pullman Palace Car Company, on the South Side of Chicago, just across the street from the Pullman Walmart where Anthony and Beth met for their interview, had been the epicenter of one of the most militant labor actions in American history. Eugene Debs, the head of the nascent

American Railway Union, and later the most successful Socialist Party presidential candidate in history, led a strike at the plant and an associated rail boycott that froze the movement of merchandise from Chicago to the Pacific Ocean. For both the workers at Palace Car Company and the railway workers who supported the boycott, foremen's despotism, brutality, and arbitrary exercise of authority were central grievances.[25]

Edwards goes on to argue that many of the changes to the structure of the industrial firm over the course of the twentieth century—from technical innovations like the assembly line, which reduced the discretion of management by encoding control in impersonal machinery, to later organizational innovations like bureaucratic roles, rules, incentives, and job ladders, which reduced management discretion by articulating standard operating procedures according to which supervisors could punish unproductive and reward productive behavior—were responses to workers' outrage at and resistance to the despotism of their immediate supervisors. This is what Edwards described as bureaucratic control; it suffused the "core" of the U.S. economy. Simple, despotic control remained, but only on the periphery.

What is surprising about the centrality of Walmart and other massive low-wage service-sector companies in the contemporary U.S. economy is that, with respect to the exercise of arbitrary authority, they represent a return to a form of workplace control that seemed, in an earlier historical era, to have spawned such intense resistance.[26] But a closer look reveals a more complex control system, one that draws on old systems but is nevertheless something new. This is Walmartism.

The arbitrary authority of managers here is tightly coupled with a penetrative system of observation, measurement, and feedback that constrains both workers and managers—a system assembled from technological innovations unavailable to Walmart's nineteenth-century counterparts, an array of different kinds of cameras and counters and scanners; and from social innovations emerging from the relations of production in the service sector, the most important of which is the deployment of customers as indirect agents of control. Likewise, Walmart draws on elements of "flexible specialization" in the organization of its workplace—departmental cross-training; just-in-time delivery of goods and schedules; a rhetoric of horizontalism, teamwork, and "open-door" problem-solving—but does so without the investments in human capital or power-sharing with which this term has traditionally been associated.[27] And without all that much flexibility either: despite the uncertainty introduced by unpredictable customer traffic and tastes, and the resulting managerial discretion, the set of services delivered by Walmart associates—as a whole—is quite routine.[28] Where Walmart as an employer is most "flexible" is in its scheduling practices. But this flexibility is, in reality, merely a strategy by which the company forces employees to absorb fluctuations in consumer demand.[29] It also serves as a strategy for labor control in other ways: unstable schedules reduce the extent to which workers form relationships with one another, reducing their likelihood of recognizing common interests; and since workers are often underemployed and those who are able to work across multiple departments have a higher chance of getting more hours, the company incentivizes associates to enhance their skills at no cost to the company itself.

Even simple control is not so simple at Walmart. Managers still watch workers and give them orders, tell them where to go and what to do. But the stress of subordination is heightened by the cross-talk of different layers of supervision—from above (store managers, comanagers, assistant managers, zone managers, department managers) and below (customers)—who issue contradictory and therefore impossible to resolve orders and thus create double binds for associates. It is also heightened by the absence of any machinery through which workers can structure their tasks and thereby limit the legitimate demands of those who have authority over them.[30] Meanwhile, associates are watched constantly: by cameras, customers, scanners, and supervisors. Even peer pressure—which at one point was a resource for the labor movement, both to set the pace of work and to maintain a union shop—is reconfigured by management as an element of control.[31] Recall, for example, that collective incentives tied to injury create pressures for workers to work hurt so as not to reduce their friends' quarterly bonuses. Residual elements of bureaucratic control tied to the invention of internal labor markets remain as well—"There's opportunity here!"—but this is more rhetoric than reality, and the job ladder narrows quickly. Walmart expects and counts on the fact that most of its workers will leave soon after they begin.[32]

As we have seen in previous chapters, this form of control relies on a series of broader social, political, and economic changes that have eroded workers' power in the low-wage labor market by increasing their dependence on it, and—in a closely related development—have thus allowed employers to break down previously sacrosanct boundaries between work and home, primarily through unpredictable schedules, which interrupt any stable notion of family time; but also through instruments that reach beyond the workplace, like personality tests, drug tests, credit checks, health screenings after injury, and so on.[33] Meanwhile, Walmart remains the employer, and retailer, of last resort. Those who work at Walmart cannot afford to shop anywhere but Walmart or places like it.[34]

THOSE LEFT BEHIND WANT RESPECT

Spending time in the aisles of Walmart, it is easy to convince oneself that the good life is something purchasable: that it consists of a microwave ($35), a fishing rod ($18.31), and a 50" flatscreen television ($269.99). Material security is, of course, important to everyone. But for many of those who work in the low-wage service sector, these material goals are secondary to something more basic: a feeling of respect and recognition at work. This should not come as a shock. Historically, as Elizabeth Anderson notes, the most powerful social movements for equality have conceived of inequality as referring "not so much to distributions of goods as to relations between superior and inferior persons."[35] That understanding is what gave energy to the early American labor movement.

The desire for respect at work may be important for everyone, but it is likely particularly pronounced in the service sector. Where fixed capital investments are high, where employers rely on what Edwards calls technical control, workers' experiences of authority are likely mediated by the machinery of production: power is expressed through the speed of the line rather than through the direct encounter with middle management. Even without such technical control, where individuals work independently on machines as operatives, "control processes are simplified," because "machines are easier to control than human beings" and because workers become socially integrated with their machines.[36] This integration induces a process in which the machine and the operator interact in an established manner defined by the machine, which soaks up the avenues for discretion that were once negotiable between the craftsperson and the supervisor.

Once the machine becomes the principal point of interaction for the worker, other social relations in the workplace change as well. While technical control can give workers new sorts of structural power vis-à-vis their employers, workers' interactions with machines may also limit possibilities for interacting with other workers. More critically, supervisors no longer have to be skilled operators; rather, they need only be the supervisors of the behaviors of workers now circumscribed by their machines. Freed from the requirements of technical know-how in a specific industry, middle-level management can appear on the shop floor as specialists in supervising sets of human-machine interactions. Distance between management and workers increases (no longer can workers imagine that they will be able to take their technical skills to management, since those skills are irrelevant), and increasing distance may also decrease the arbitrary exercise of authority. This is not to say that disrespect is uncommon in manufacturing, only that it is likely experienced as more structural and thus less interactive and, hence, less arbitrary.

The situation at Walmart and many other low-wage service-sector employers is unlike the industrial factory. There are fewer machines that pace or coordinate workers' tasks. The machines that remain—like the cash register and the MC40 scanner—measure individual activity more than they manage it. In the meantime, managers have few skills outside the technical know-how they have garnered from working on the floor; managers, at multiple levels, confront the uncertainty of customer traffic and tastes by giving orders to associates, who must navigate different managerial requests at the same time they confront customers who want more help than Walmart has been organized to give. This often leads, among associates, to a feeling of being at the mercy of others' arbitrary whims, even (perhaps particularly) at a place as meticulously programmed as Walmart.

For the reasons outlined above, workers in such settings today seem to care more intensely about dignity than wages, more about voice than benefits, more about community than hours. The labor movement once knew this: recall the motivations behind the Pullman strike and the leaders of the Knights of Labor. For complex reasons, which we discuss in chapter 4, the movement forgot this element of its collective history until relatively recently. The leaders of OUR Walmart recognized it. But to turn this recognition into action, to reorganize around respect, they would have to overcome obstacles posed both by Walmart—one of the most vicious anti-union employers around—and, equally problematic, by what was left of the labor movement itself.

4

MAKING CONTACT

BOUNCING BALLS

Kevin, the Summer for Respect participant with the *polytropōs* tattoo, walked into the Walmart in Franklin, Ohio, for the first time on June 11, 2014, like any other shopper. His strategy when he was getting a feel for a new store—one he had learned from Robert, his supervisor at OUR Walmart, the organization we were working alongside—was, at first, to interact with workers in ways that preserved some ambiguity. He wanted it to seem like he could be just a shopper, or someone looking for work, until it was clear that he might have a sympathetic reception when he broached the topic of organizing.[1] One tactic was to ask an employee for something that Kevin knew Walmart didn't carry, which would give him time both to observe the worker and develop some basis for further discussion. In electronics, for example, he'd ask if they had a copy of Stanley Kubrick's *Eyes Wide Shut*. They never did.

On that first day at the Franklin store, Kevin met Matt in the electronics department, and asked him for movie recommendations. According to Kevin, Matt *displayed his expertise about such products by meticulously going through what he thought of each movie on the shelf I had pointed to (it appeared as if he'd seen them all).* Matt seemed like a movie expert, which gave Kevin an idea for how to move the conversation forward: *"Man, you really know what you're talking about,"* Kevin remembers saying, *"I hope Walmart pays you enough for the great service you're providing here."* When Kevin asked Matt what he thought of his job, Matt answered that he generally liked it *but that there were a lot of people in the store who didn't.* The conversation ended quickly, and Kevin left for the day.

Four days later, Kevin came back. Kevin thought that Matt seemed a little suspicious of him this time, although this seems unlikely given how many people the average worker interacts with on the average day. Either way, though, Kevin *merely gave a friendly wave and walked on by.* Instead, he began to talk to Jenny, another worker in electronics. This time he cut to the chase more quickly, explaining his role as an intern with OUR Walmart. *She had evidently been very confused as to why I was asking so many questions about what it was like working at Walmart, so to hear that I was an organizer made a lot of sense for her. There was almost a sense of relief on both of our parts: for her, she knew I wasn't some weirdo and that I was asking her such questions as part of my job, and for me, I knew that she wouldn't snitch on me and that she was down with the cause.* Jenny was frustrated by many things about her work: they never had enough staff; her schedule was unpredictable; she had job responsibilities that did not match her pay.

While Kevin was speaking with Jenny, Matt came over, *this time complaining about his exhaustion from having had to push carts in the parking lot.* The three talked briefly. Talking in a group of three had its advantages and risks. On the one hand, problems that might be experienced as individual could now be recognized as collective. And a triad is a group in a way that a dyad isn't, so talking in a small group can create an experience consonant with the organizer's argument about the benefits of solidarity. As Harmony, another participant on the Ohio team, put it, "I personally liked it when I could talk to workers together, because they would feed off each other.

And it felt more like I wasn't talking at them and they were talking to each other." Those were the advantages.

On the other hand, a group was more conspicuous to managers—while customers would interact with individual workers all the time, it was uncommon for a customer to interact with more than one worker at the same time. So Kevin kept the interaction brief, asking Jenny about her next shift so he could touch base with her again. Before the interaction ended, Jenny mentioned that Kevin ought to speak with Gerald in the photo lab, *a suggestion that Matt chuckled at. Evidently, Gerald was quite opinionated about Walmart and wasn't afraid to run his mouth about the store. When Jenny described Gerald*, Kevin recalls, *she spoke with both an air of amusement and pride, as if he were the voice of their store.*

Bob Moses, the civil rights leader who helped to spearhead Freedom Summer, was once asked how to organize a community. He replied:

> By bouncing a ball. . . . You stand on a street and bounce a ball. Soon all the children come around. You keep on bouncing the ball. Before long, it runs under someone's porch and then you meet the adults.[2]

This imagery is profound in its simplicity. Bob Moses's suggestion was that processes of social interaction and relationship formation are central to processes of collective action. This is different, in important ways, from saying that existing relationships and networks are important to social movement success—a point that is also important but is more widely recognized in social movement scholarship. For Moses, organizing was about embedding oneself strategically within existing social networks to help reshape these networks around collective goals. This is what the organizers in Mississippi tried to achieve in 1964. And this is what doesn't happen when one just "makes contact." To build organization, one needs to identify existing networks, work within them, and turn them. People are embedded in all sorts of quasi-groups, latent pieces of social structure that might be activated to achieve collective ends.[3] The ball running under the porch might allow one access to a quasi-group of conversation and meal sharing. And embedding in such quasi-groups may lead one to those more formal organizations that bind people together. By the time we visited Kevin and his teammates in Ohio in late July, Kevin could often be found sitting next to Gerald and his coworkers while they took their breaks at the Subway in the Franklin store, Gerald leading informal meetings on various workplace (and non-workplace) issues, with Kevin taking notes alongside.

Kevin had been trained by Robert, a tall, gangly, tattooed white guy in his early 30s, with a long hair and a beard, who had more than a passing resemblance to the gigantic statue of Jesus that dominated I-75. Robert, in turn, had been trained by the leaders of OUR Walmart. Kevin would find out through his interactions on the shop floor what these other leaders already knew, something we discussed earlier: among those who work in low-wage service jobs today, wages and benefits are often concerns secondary to the sense of disrespect they feel from those who wield authority over them.

The Organization United for Respect was not just a catchy acronym. Before OUR Walmart's founding in 2010, the organization's leaders had undertaken their own research process to better understand the concerns and hopes of Walmart workers. Through focus groups, online surveys, and one-on-one conversations with workers around the country, they landed on "respect" as a unifying theme.[4] Indeed, the language of respect has been shown to be effective across many of today's organizing campaigns.[5]

The problem was that, even as some of today's labor leaders—like those at the helm of OUR Walmart—understood the importance of organizing the unorganized and recognized the importance of respect as central to this organizing vision, they did so within bureaucracies that (with a few exceptions) did not easily create the social conditions within which workers could experience the respect and sense of community that they felt was missing from the job.[6]

UNIONS ARE JUST CORPORATIONS TOO

Rather than making a pitch or delivering a message, Kevin was quietly familiarizing himself with the social networks of the Walmart in Franklin, Ohio. Eventually, though, he would have to discuss OUR Walmart and what it stood for, which meant he would have to frame the organization's program in a way that aligned with the concerns he saw percolating up from the shop floor. It's important to get the message right, that is, to align the organizational vision with what is happening on the ground. And as a consequence, something is often lost in an organization's attempt to control the message.

One day, the members of the Chicago team—and others associated with OUR Walmart at the site—watched aghast as staff from the UFCW handed prewritten speeches to Walmart workers to deliver as their own for a rally. According to June, "You say you're a worker-centered movement. But then you're writing speeches for them . . . I didn't like watching that at all."[7] Beth felt like "an organizer should be there to bring out the power in the workers." Instead, she thought, "A lot of times I think an organizer acts in a lot of other ways [like] the bosses act that are problematic." She went on, "Talking it out with my teammates, [I realized that] unions are businesses." Jordan went even further: "[A union is] just a fucking corporation, basically. It's very business-oriented. You know what I'm saying? It's about efficiency, and numbers, and blah blah blah."

The idea that unions are just corporations—that they just care about their own bottom lines, their member numbers, and the salaries of their staffs—is not uncommon. It's a false equivalency that employers have been touting for decades, but it resonates well enough with some workers' experiences of unions to have an impact. And this image, fair or not, is at least partly responsible for labor's precipitous decline.

Of course this is not the whole story. The decline of manufacturing and rise of service-sector employment in the United States has transformed the labor market, and this transformation is also partially

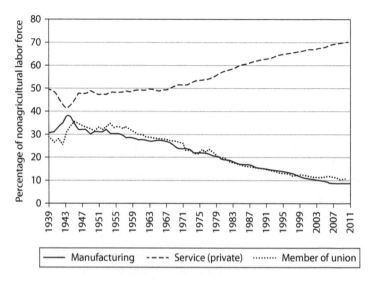

FIGURE 4.1 Employment by industry and unionization rate.

responsible for declining rates of unionization, since unions have traditionally been most prevalent in manufacturing. Figure 4.1 shows the percentage of workers in manufacturing and service-sector jobs between 1939 and 2014, as well as the percentage of workers who are members of unions. The declining percentage of union members closely tracks the decline of U.S. manufacturing.

Yet neither is the decline of manufacturing in the United States a sufficient explanation for declining unionization. Other countries have experienced declines in manufacturing while sustaining high rates of unionization.[8] Moreover there are no really good reasons that rates of unionization in the service sector remain so low. Many aspects of the service sector would actually suggest the opportunity for greater, not lesser, union penetration. On the surface, service-sector workers have some sources of structural power that are absent in traditional manufacturing contexts. Consider, for example, that service-sector industries—from health care to retail businesses to hotels—cannot outsource production abroad very easily, nor can they as easily replace workers with machines.[9] While the changing structure of the economy explains why it may be harder to unionize in manufacturing industries, and while the "union premium" in these industries has declined over time, it does not tell us much about the failure of unions to break into or re-unionize industries like health care, education, and retail.

Ever since President Reagan broke the air traffic controllers' strike in 1981 by summarily firing more than 11,000 workers, there has been the sense that one of the reasons for declining unionization is increased employer opposition buttressed by an anti-union state (though in the case of the air traffic controllers' strike, the employer was the state). There is certainly a temporal correlation, and the rise of the anti-union industry in the past 50 years has undoubtedly played an important role in undermining organizing attempts.[10] A recent study of over 1,000 union election campaigns found that employers regularly fire union supporters (in 34 percent of union election campaigns); threaten to close the business (57 percent); threaten to reduce wages and benefits (47 percent); use mandatory one-on-one meetings with employees to interrogate them about the union (63 percent); and threaten union supporters with disciplinary action (54 percent).[11] In contrast to the situation in other Western industrialized countries, many of these strategies are actually legal under U.S. labor law.[12] From this perspective, U.S. employers may not be any more anti-union in their attitudes than employers from other countries; they just have more legal flexibility.

But these strategies and worse have been around for decades, and employers' advantages under U.S. law go back far earlier than the recent upsurge of employer anti-unionism that began in the late 1970s and early 1980s. The whole of American history overflows with moments in which the state has sided with employers over workers.[13] During the Pullman Palace Car Company struggle, for example, the national railroad strike was crushed when a powerful employers' association convinced President Grover Cleveland to call in federal troops.[14] The history of Pullman and other key battles in early American labor history—Homestead, Cripple Creek,

Haymarket, the Ludlow Massacre—help to put contemporary anti-unionism in perspective.

One doesn't even have to travel back to the late nineteenth century for examples. In 1929, striking textile workers in Gastonia, North Carolina, were assaulted by mobs of masked men who escaped prosecution; in 1934, more than a thousand National Guard members with machine guns broke the Auto-Lite Strike in Toledo, Ohio; a decade later, in 1946, the U.S. government seized hundreds of refineries, railroads, and mines to break strikes by miners and oil workers; in 1970, the army took over post offices in New York City to break a postal strike. In short, we have experienced more than 150 years of state-supported opposition to labor organization. So it is hard to see how contemporary employer coercion uniquely accounts for the decline of unionization when increased unionization—albeit less than what would be expected absent such violence—was observed in periods when violent opposition was the most intense. And what about the temporal correlation? Well, just because things happen at the same time doesn't mean that one causes the other. Think about minivans and autism. Prevalence increased for both at about the same time, but the idea that minivans cause autism is absurd.

But if employers' exceptional power in the United States is not new, it may nevertheless help to explain the decline of labor—though not, or not only, for the reasons we often think. It is not just that powerful employers have prevented labor unions from forming; it is that powerful employers have impacted the development of labor's organizational cultures and structures. U.S. employers' exceptional degree of power, not just on the shop floor but in the halls of government, has repeatedly helped to strip the labor movement of its movement.

In the late nineteenth century, the Knights of Labor had as broad a social and political vision as any labor organizations in Europe. As a result, they inspired employers—with the aid of the state—to organize, often violently, against them.[15] Such an assault would be repeated in response to the syndicalism of the late 1910s, and in response to the radical industrial organizing of the CIO in the 1930s.

Labor's expansive and inclusive vision was almost literally beaten out of it. And so by 1955, the height of labor union membership as a percentage of the workforce and the year when the CIO merged with the AFL, what was left was a much narrower organizational form: a bureaucratic system of collective bargaining at the employer level, confined to a limited set of manufacturing industries. Those labor leaders with communist sympathies, who had been so central to the militance of the 1930s, had been purged. Political mobilization, strikes, women's auxiliaries, and other forms of collective action had given way to armies of lawyers and union staffers negotiating and administering thousands of firm-specific contracts, all with the result that "what may have begun as a spark of collective action for workers on the shop floor" is today "quickly extinguished by the soporific of bureaucratic procedure and legal interpretation."[16]

What remained, then, was by and large a set of leaders and organizations who made the idea of a labor "movement" seem like a contradiction in terms. As labor's horizons contracted, moreover, many union leaders prioritized representing their own members at the expense of those outside their rather narrow niche of manufacturing industries. The wages of unionized workers in industries like steel and auto rose dramatically, propelling them into the middle class, while millions of workers in agriculture, domestic service, retail, and elsewhere were left out. Unions also negotiated with individual employers for an array of selective incentives that, in other countries, became entitlements through processes of political struggle—health insurance, mortgage assistance, tuition benefits. This U.S. exceptionalism widened the gulf between unionized workers and everyone else, not to mention that it inflated the ranks of those union bureaucracies necessary for providing the unique array of services promised to its members.[17]

The irony is that as some trade unionists became wealthier and more established, their interests diverged from those of other workers and they became more conservative. By the late 1960s the typical union member, while still a Democrat, was increasingly likely to be socially conservative. A trace of that conservatism is revealed by labor's decreasing centrality in social protest over the period from 1961 to 1968.[18] More obvious, perhaps, is the fact that hard hats became the iconic opponents of the student, feminist, and anti-war movements.[19]

It is hardly surprising that these unions started to articulate messages that conformed to their members' fears and desires. They were, in fact, representing their members. Labor unions behaved like those charismatic church sects that, having once served the needs of the dispossessed by directly addressing the problem of theodicy (why bad things happen to good people), morphed—as their congregations became more established—into established churches with increasingly abstract, esoteric rituals and messages drained of emotionality. If a hostile external environment first compelled unions to abandon broad solidarity for a more narrow protectionist stance, the growing chasm between unionized workers and everyone else only reinforced this conservatism. Unions came to protect existing jobs and existing members, winning the preservation of the status quo for their members at the expense of new hires or the unorganized, and doing little to address new generations of workers who saw—often correctly—that the unions were not speaking to or for them.[20]

As time went by, a demographic wave eroded the size of the unionized base as their membership slid into retirement. And so, when the bottom fell out and unions came under a new wave of attack, they had a much smaller, older, and more conservative base with which to resist.[21] They could not easily speak to or for workers as a whole. Meanwhile, to the extent that union leaders had insulated themselves from any accountability to membership, they were able to continue to collect paychecks even as their organizations shriveled. Not surprisingly, challenges from the movement side— typically cast as critiques of corruption, when the more pressing problem was routinization—were often brutally suppressed by union officials. In the meantime, the economy was in a period of rapid transformation to which union leaders initially paid little attention.[22]

It is, admittedly, difficult to sort out the relative importance of external political and economic changes and internal organizational failures to the decline of the labor movement in the United States.[23] These explanations are mutually constitutive. A history of employer and state opposition to those elements of the labor movement with the most expansive visions—from the Knights of the 1880s to the radicals of the 1930s—helped structure labor unions into the sclerotic bureaucracies they became, organizations that have been unable to respond adeptly to the economic changes and political assaults of the last 30 years.

Historically, the UFCW, which financed OUR Walmart at its inception in 2010, had been a pretty good case study in such union bureaucratization and inflexibility. It was founded in 1979 as a result of a merger between the Amalgamated Meat Cutters and Butcher Workers of North America and the Retail Clerks International Union, and since then has been the only large union in the retail industry. Since its founding, unionization rates in retail have declined from just under 9 percent to just over 3 percent, a drop of nearly two-thirds.[24] And yet many in the union did not seem to think this was much of a problem. In a study of union revitalization, Kim Voss and Rachel Sherman seemed to cast the UFCW as a foil as they reported the responses from UFCW leaders who, "despite having lost almost all their power in the retail sector, still spoke of 'not having to worry about market share' because they had simply decided to think of themselves as representing only grocery workers."[25] Faced with crisis, the UFCW tended to look away.

But the UFCW could not ignore Walmart forever. Walmart was and continues to be, as Kim Moody puts it, "the 800-pound gorilla" in the labor movement.[26] The point may have been driven home to the UFCW after it led a massive, unsuccessful strike in Southern California in 2003–2004, during which 59,000 unionized grocery workers struck or were locked out of more than 850 grocery stores at Vons, Safeway, Ralphs, and Albertsons. After nearly four months, at a cost of approximately $1 million per day, the union accepted a contract that reduced wages and health insurance coverage for new employees, a concession that Ruth Milkman suggests was seen by "friend and foe alike . . . as labor's greatest defeat since the 1981 air traffic controllers' strike."[27] What made these employers so aggressive after a quarter century of labor peace in Southern California? Nelson Lichtenstein writes, "The strike was convulsive because the most important player was not at the negotiating table. Supermarket executives, in Southern California and elsewhere, were taking a hard line against their employees because Wal-Mart was ready, willing, and anxious to eat their lunch."[28]

REORGANIZING AROUND RESPECT

In the late 1980s and early 1990s—more than 30 years after union-ization rates had peaked—a few unions began to make large invest-ments in organizing the service sector, a move that surprised labor and organizational scholars, many of whom had by this point left the American labor movement for dead.[29] In Southern California, while the UFCW was losing its power in the grocery industry, work-ers in the building services were gaining power with the SEIU's Justice for Janitors campaign.[30] Beyond Southern California there were scattered successes too: home-care workers across California, hotel workers in Las Vegas, and clerical workers at Harvard, to name a few.

The irony of the labor movement's effort to organize service workers today, one that is recognized by organizations like OUR Walmart, is that it may need to return to the older, evangelical sect strategies of the 1930s, of 1919, of the late 1800s, to return to the idea that the essence of workplace organization is positive solidar-ity, a sense of belonging.[31]

Fostering this sense of positive solidarity, of collective identity, on Walmart's shop floor is difficult, though. Community can sometimes arise on the retail floor, but it is irregular, always at risk of being interrupted by the capricious demands of supervisors and customers. And the sources of structural power that likely facilitated workers' sense of collective efficacy in the factory, like the assembly line, are absent. While production at Walmart can be metaphorically described as an assembly line, it is more accurately a disaggregated set of tens of thousands of lines, each product moving at a different (average) pace from the truck to the shopping cart and out. Small groups of workers here do not have the same potential for disruption as they do in a plant; it would take a bigger group to bring operations to a stop.[32] Against this background, note that because it is a global treatment, working to rule is one of the most powerful weapons available to service workers. But while effective against airlines and railroads, where there is a built-in distance between customers and, say, the pilots and engineers, working to rule is interactively enormously costly to workers at Walmart, who have to directly bear the brunt of dissatisfied customers—sometimes friends and neighbors—who would be unable to park, find products they want, and, if so fortunate as to find things, would be stuck in endless lines.

In America, the peculiarity of the contemporary labor movement is that it is dominated by organizations that, while still oriented around the collective good, seem ill-suited to respond to the underlying meanings and motivations of the collectivities that need it most. Unions might give individuals more money, but money is not usually what drives people to organize—community is. And where the conditions of production don't naturally induce and sustain community, organizing around bread-and-butter issues is going to have a rough ride. Even in a context of crushing poverty, the movement needs to offer something other than a promised wage increase to be successful in the retail sector.

All this was understood by OUR Walmart. But putting understanding into practice would ultimately mean challenging many of the norms and rules and understandings of those who lead what is left of organized labor today.

ORGANIZING IS ABOUT MAKING
A BUNCH OF LINKS

During Freedom Summer, in 1964, organizing meant embedding oneself within existing social networks to reshape those networks around collective goals. Rewiring social relationships—forming new ties where none existed before or helping to change the emphasis of a tie from one of friendship (or church membership or classmate) to one of solidarity—was an important strategy organizers used to help individuals and loosely connected networks coalesce into collective actors.

Fifty years later, in the summer of 2014, it is what the participants in the Summer for Respect program set out to achieve as well. The students didn't invent this idea. It was a central premise of OUR Walmart and has been a central premise of organizing at least since Alexis de Tocqueville, who wrote in *Democracy in America* that "[i]n democratic countries, knowledge of how to combine is the mother of all other forms of knowledge; on its progress depends that of all the others."[33] It's an idea that has since been memorialized in books like Saul Alinsky's *Rules for Radicals* and revived in more contemporary work like Hahrie Han's *How Organizations Develop Activists* and Jane McAlevey's *No Shortcuts*.[34] And it contrasts in important ways with the "frame theory" that predominates in social movement studies, in which language itself is given the power to shape participation through persuasive cognitive frames or metaphors or emotional appeals, as if language has power outside the social relationships that make language possible and influence how it is understood.

Consequently, it didn't surprise us that, when Kevin was asked in an interview what he thought made a successful organizer, he responded, "An effective organizer is someone who doesn't just go from one person to another person but kind of embeds themselves within a group and becomes almost part of that group, in a way." This idea was echoed across many of the interviews with the students when they were asked what it is that organizers do.

They described themselves as network entrepreneurs—at once figuring out the social networks of the stores (several were taught to diagram these networks on paper)—and changing them, building ties strategically so as to enhance the density and connectivity of the community of union support. Michelle, from the Los Angeles team, said that organizing was about "trying to make a lot of links," linking workers to information, workers to one another, workers to the OUR Walmart organization.

AMBIGUITY OF INTENTION AND POSITION CAN FACILITATE CONTACTS, UP TO A POINT

After hearing about Gerald in the photo lab, Kevin returned to the Franklin store the following week, and set out straight away to find him. While Gerald helped another customer, Kevin killed time by looking at a GoPro camera display. When Gerald finished, Kevin introduced himself as a friend of Jenny and told Gerald that Jenny had told him Gerald was unhappy with the store. Gerald thought it was high time they had a union at Walmart. Jenny came over to listen. Kevin jotted in his phone, *Speaks his mind like no other. Could be a great leader.*

In retrospect, Kevin realized that Gerald—"labor-stealing motherfuckers"—was already a leader in the store, an *"old head" whose lived experiences gave some perspective to what it was like working at Walmart.* Jeff, another participant from the Ohio team, thought being able to identify existing leaders like Gerald, "specific people in a department that people look to for certain things," was what made great organizers.

Gerald also knew just about everyone, could give Kevin guidance on whom to speak with and whom to avoid. He told Kevin that the clothing section of the store would probably be supportive of OUR Walmart—Virginia, in particular, was a good candidate. She also had past experience as a union representative. Finding former shop stewards at Walmart was a bit of good fortune. It also was much more likely to happen in southeastern Ohio than it was in Dallas or central Florida. While labor unions had more or less collapsed across the Rust Belt, people there were still carrying around memories of what labor organizations had done and could do. One important implication is that, following this logic, we are living in a relatively narrow period of time in which the memory of what unions do (or might do) is still alive in people who once were—but are no longer—members of them. Presumably the closing of this window will make the resurgence of labor even more difficult.

Gerald also told Kevin that he would help lay the groundwork among the women who worked in the clothing section of the Franklin store. So Kevin approached the clothing aisles *with an air of confidence.* The unusual thing about the clothing section was that the women there worked in groups, and so initially Kevin was stymied, since he worried that talking with more than one person at a time would increase the risk that one of them would report him to management. He set out to *"pick off" certain employees, luring them into some far recess of their department where I could ask them questions.* And that was how he met Judy—he asked her for help finding 7 for All Mankind jeans, a brand that he knew Walmart didn't carry. Gerald had already spoken to her; she was prepared for Kevin's approach. Kevin was not prepared for the fact that the organic group that formed around the women in the clothing section was the key to successful organizing. All that needed to happen was for the conversations to turn to collective topics.

Over the course of the summer, Kevin became a network entrepreneur. He would find these organic work groups and seed them with something different to talk about. He discovered and developed a social network of 18 workers at the Franklin store. Ten of these would go on to become members of OUR Walmart.

Many of the other participants in the Summer for Respect project also discussed using the ambiguity of their positions in the store—shopper? job seeker? advocate? interviewer?—to identify and connect with workers supportive of OUR Walmart and connect those supporters to one another. Harmony would often buy a pack of gum and talk to the cashiers. Greta, who often spoke to workers at bus stations, would use her smoking habit to her advantage: *I told myself I was going to quit smoking on this summer vacation, but I realized that, when we started doing bus stops, I was like, it's too good of an organizing tool.* When she saw a Walmart worker, she would just "casually walk up" with her cigarette: *They're like, "Oh, can I bum a cigarette?" That's perfect. It's a perfect excuse. They already feel like they owe you something because you already gave them a cigarette.*

Routine, role-ambiguous interaction within the store made an organizer seem less like an outsider. As Rebecca from Chicago put it, "making your face known" was important. Rebecca suggested, "It's the mundane conversations that are the important ones, because that's what establishes you as a presence." Harmony, from the Ohio team, said she learned from Evelyn, the organizer who trained her, that "organizing is all about building relationships that strengthen over time." Evelyn told Harmony, "I just hang out [in the store] and get to know people, and eventually, when people ask me why I'm always here and who I am, I tell them." According to Harmony, Evelyn would "shoot the shit with people and hang out for months at a time before she tells people what she's doing there." Harmony's first reaction was that this seemed "like a weird thing to do . . . When it's an issue that you're committed to, what's the point of doing that when you can be more direct?" But over time she appreciated the strategy and wished that she could have been in the field for more than two months. A longer stay would have allowed her, like Evelyn, to "hang out with people and get people to trust you as a person before you talk about other things." Importantly, the goal wasn't to become friends. It was to gain trust.

The strategy several participants described, then, was to use local action—not to reveal their intentions, but not to say anything that was inconsistent with the ultimate organizing conversation they were hoping to have. As Kevin put it, "I don't think our deception ever led to me pretending to be someone that I wasn't." And it didn't. After all, they were just doing what Bob Moses suggested, bouncing a ball until they could meet some adults, and then hanging around in their networks sufficiently often to change the conversation.

SCALING UP

One can imagine that if it were possible to scale up the process in which Kevin and other students were engaged and stretch it out temporally—the conversations organizers were having with workers and workers were having with one another, the recognition of common concerns and the equally startling recognition that, together, you might actually be able to do something about them— one could build a social movement, or at least make the conditions more fertile for one when it came along.

This was, and in some sense still is, a central premise of OUR Walmart. And it seemed to bear fruit. On Black Friday, November 23, 2012—the day after Thanksgiving—Walmart workers across the country walked off their jobs in the biggest one-day strike in the employer's history. A *New York Times* article reported protests at over 1,000 stores and in 46 states, "ranging from a couple of community supporters' asking to talk with store managers about raising wages to raucous demonstrations in the Los Angeles, New York and Washington areas that each attracted hundreds of people."[35] Was this the birth of a new labor movement among those who work at low-wage jobs? Many labor scholars were optimistic. Soon after the protests, Kate Bronfenbrenner, one of the foremost authorities on labor organizing and employer anti-union campaigns, said, "I feel hopeful . . . and I haven't felt hopeful about Walmart workers ever before."[36]

That early optimism was premature. First, it assumed that the UFCW and other unions would act on the opportunity that others saw in OUR Walmart and pour resources into building on the momentum of the strikes. Instead, as some in OUR Walmart reported, leaders at the UFCW seemed unaware of the strike and unappreciative of the potential of the moment. Labor has Stockholm syndrome, one put it. Second, unsurprisingly, OUR Walmart's action provoked a strong reaction from Walmart. Even before the 2012 Black Friday protests, it would later be revealed, Walmart had hired Lockheed Martin, the large defense contractor, to help the company spy on OUR Walmart supporters within its workforce; contacted the FBI; tagged particular stores as dangerous hot spots; and increased its already large investment in monitoring its workforce for signs of dissension.[37] And so, finally, by the summer of 2014, relatively few members of Walmart's massive workforce had signed up formally as members of OUR Walmart. And there was little evidence that the marginal cost of recruitment was declining: if anything, new members were becoming harder, not easier, to recruit.

PMS

To see the opportunities and challenges faced by OUR Walmart, we need to return to the early days of OUR Walmart and to the lessons learned at one of the organization's most active stores: the Pico Rivera Walmart Supercenter in Los Angeles. What happened at Pico—and in a few other stores—is that workers reclaimed the dignity that they felt Walmart had taken from them by adopting a new, collective identity. At Pico, this was about what it meant to be a woman. In Dallas, it was about being in an army of the just, like David battling Goliath. In Chicago, it was about race and the legacy of civil rights. The irony here is that the workers acted collectively as Walmart workers, as people whose new identities (as empowered women, as David, as freedom fighters) were centered on Walmart. From that standpoint they could and did make moral claims on their coworkers, on the public, and ultimately on Walmart executives hunkered down in Arkansas. So what happened at Pico?

Discussing the motivations that led to their organizing, Dora Avila, the key associate leader at the Pico store said, "Walmart has been advertising that they are a family-oriented company. And if this is how family is treated, then I would rather not have a family at all."[38] Dora dates her "radicalization" to being transferred to a Walmart in nearby Hemet [#1853] where she was confronted with blatant racism from the mostly white management there. She had never been treated so badly, she says, and she started to feel that

> no associate needs to be disrespected, no associate needs to be mistreated. Like, everybody works at different speeds, everybody works differently. It literally opened my eyes . . . And until you experience it yourself, then you know what your associates are talking about.

Even after her "eyes had been opened," though, it would take what for her was experienced as a serendipitous encounter[39] before she became an active member of OUR Walmart. An organizer for the organization was dating Dora's ex-brother-in-law, and Dora agreed to meet her at a local Starbucks: "She told me what it was about. I was, like, 'Oh, sign me up.' She was like, 'For reals?' So I was, like, 'Yes. I got it, I understood it. Sign me up.' " Dora became the fourth member of OUR Walmart at the Pico store, on January 13, 2011. With Dora, the organizer had found the Pico Rivera equivalent to Gerald in the Franklin store—someone who was already a leader among her peers, who could connect other workers to the organization and to one another. Michelle Rogers was one of the first new recruits Dora brought into the fold.

Michelle had been a regular shopper at the Pico store and became friends with an inventory management specialist named Pat, who suggested she apply for a job there. Because she had a friend when she started, Michelle says her job "was kind of nice at first." But she soon started getting chided by management—first because she wasn't able to speak Spanish to the largely Latino clientele, and then because she was working the registers too slowly: "They really humiliated me and they always made you feel that you weren't worthy. And that was the hard part working there. Always." As she started talking to others at the store, she realized that managers were making *everyone* feel bad, targeting the Spanish-speaking employees for their bad English as much as they were targeting her for her bad Spanish.

Michelle describes the small, arbitrary indignities from management that began to get under her skin. During the holidays one year, the "lines [were] going crazy" when Michelle got kicked off her register for her lunch break. An assistant manager came by and told her that she couldn't take lunch just yet because of the crowds. Michelle was worried that she'd be in violation of company policy, but the manager said that he would take care of it, and "put in his code on the register to have me stay." A few days later she was disciplined for violating the policy, just as she had feared. When she told her managers that she had been told to stay, they said, "It doesn't matter. You should have just walked away." It left her feeling as though she were "damned if you do, damned if you don't."

Michelle heard about OUR Walmart from "Crazy Dora Avila," she remembers. "She was always asking me, 'Hey, mama, how's things going?' And I would tell her, 'Not good,' you know. . . . And she would say, 'You know, when we get a chance, let's talk.' " They met at a Del Taco, a nearby fast-food joint, where Dora introduced Michelle to some of the organizers from OUR Walmart. Then Michelle went home and "looked it all up to find out what was going on." She concluded that "if I was going to have to be here for a few more years, no matter what," then she would have to "either make change or just take the beatings." She joined the organization on February 12, 2011.

Sandra Lopez provided the crucial third leg. In contrast to Dora and Michelle, Lopez had some prior political experience; she had previously volunteered with an immigrant rights organization called Vecinos Unidos (Neighbors United): "It was a way to help people and talk to people, just not be at home, because by then my son was in school full time and I just needed to keep busy, because I think you go crazy at home." Her early political activity was as much about finding connection with others as it was about commitment to particular issues. Sandra stopped doing this volunteer work when she got her job as a cashier at the Walmart in 2004.

Early on at Pico she found herself on the short side of the favoritism game. Her experience resisting and still surviving gave her some confidence. It helped that she had less to lose than the other two:

she says, "I've never been quiet. I'm scared, but I don't think I'm as scared as everybody else, because I do have a choice, and that takes a lot of the fear away." Sandra was supported by her "complication" at home and like a lot of other women had started working at Walmart because she was "bored at home." Sandra explicitly references the fact that she has more flexibility, more "choice," than other workers at Walmart, and that this helped take away her fear. Losing her job would be okay.

These three women—Dora, Michelle, and Sandra—became the backbone of the organizing effort at the Pico Rivera store. They decided to call themselves Pico Mighty Strikers, or PMS. Michelle explains, "One, because most of us were women and, you know, the whole thing, we all know generally in medical terms what PMS stands for. But at any rate, *don't mess with PMS*."

Early in their organizing, both Michelle and Dora faced retaliation from store managers. Dora was called in repeatedly for infractions like not completing forms correctly or being a minute late back from her break (managers have admitted to targeting OUR Walmart supporters in these ways). Her first response was fury—she remembers telling her manager, "I'm not going to sign [the disciplinary warnings]. . . . You could kiss my fat ass before you would ever get a statement from me!" In consultation with OUR Walmart, though, she channeled that outrage into filing an unfair labor practice charge against the store. Ultimately she was able to clear her record entirely—and, through this success, demonstrate to herself and her coworkers that one could successfully challenge the higher-ups. Michelle also had to fight back when her managers charged her with fabricated absences. She took advice from Dora and told them: " 'This is retaliation.' And I told them that and they backed off." But the experience of getting over her fear and standing up to her managers "reminded me how big they are not."

Each step in the store's escalating campaign was both frightening and exhilarating. Dora remembers being terrified during their first one-day strike: "I kept on thinking, 'Oh my God, oh my God, oh my God, we just went on strike!' " But she had to hold it together for

Michelle: "My friend was next to me. She was, like, 'Are you okay?' And, like, I snapped out of it." She continued: "Like, I had to get into that mode of, like, you cannot show your fear, because you're going to show it to everyone else, and they see you as their leader and you can't. But I do remember that moment that I was, like, 'Oh, shit. We're on strike.' " Michelle, in turn, remembers how Dora helped her through her own fears: "I was getting sick. I was shaking and I kept telling myself, 'What am I doing?' " But Dora helped her persist: "I eventually did it. I eventually walked with Dora."

Because of the leadership of Dora, Michelle, and Sandra, the Pico Mighty Strikers grew quickly over the course of 2011. In under six months, over 50 workers had signed up for OUR Walmart within the Pico store. Eventually more than 120 would sign up there. A core group of committed leaders soon snowballed into a critical mass of activists. We can recreate this snowball in another way by turning to notes taken by OUR Walmart organizers in the early months of the Pico campaign, which document the unfolding of a store-level organizing network. Examining the network at yearly intervals lets us see the registration drive as it unfolded. Dora, Michelle, and Sandra were each at the center of a different subnetwork of workers. They were reaching out to different sets of workers (figure 4.2).

Yet even here, even with more than one-third of store employees as members of OUR Walmart, the organization never really posed much of a threat to the store's operations. On its last Black Friday strike, in November of 2014, Pico posted the highest number of one-day strikers of any store in the country: 19. If Pico were an assembly line, then it is possible that less than one-tenth of the workforce might be able to shut down production. At Walmart, though, 19 workers can go on strike and—aside from the effect on customers who might have to cross a picket line—it is difficult to notice. Lines might be a little longer and bathrooms a little less clean and shelves a little more disorganized and products a little more scattered. But the essential aspect of the store—the fact that things are cheap and that people are buying the things that they want for less than they can get them anywhere else—well, that stays pretty much the same.

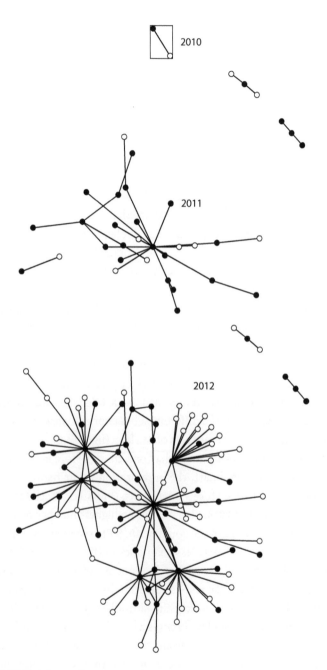

FIGURE 4.2 Cumulative OUR Walmart conversation network at Pico Rivera, 2010–2014. Workers are represented by circles, and conversations between workers are represented by lines. Circles are black when they represent members of OUR Walmart, and white when they represent nonmembers. Each panel displays cumulative network at the end of the year indicated.

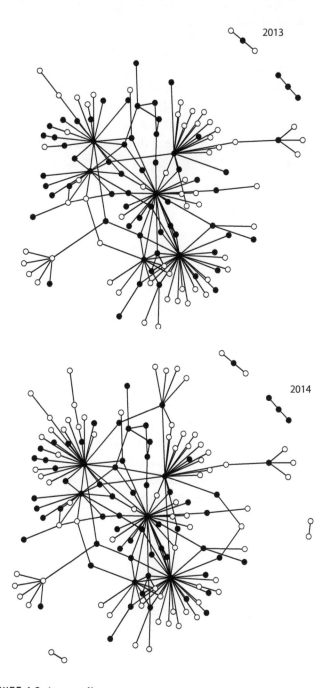

FIGURE 4.2 (*Continued*)

More significantly, a funny thing happened at Pico in April of 2015. The store developed some kind of plumbing problem. Walmart had to shut it down and lay off all the workers; the 120 who joined PMS and the 180 or so who didn't. Six months later, Walmart had a grand reopening at Pico. Not one of the women affiliated with PMS was rehired.

TIES THAT BIND

Given the macrostructural, organizational, and historical obstacles to labor mobilization in the contemporary period reviewed earlier, it is unsurprising that OUR Walmart has not yet reached scale. In fact, perhaps the explanandum should not be the absence of large-scale mobilization but rather the presence of *any* such resistance. What had inspired Dora, Michelle, Sandra, and others at Pico to become so committed to such a seemingly Sisyphean struggle? And what can this teach us? For them, taking part in OUR Walmart felt like an obvious and necessary response to the injustices they experienced at the company. Dora's immediate enthusiasm about the organization—"Sign me up!"—makes it seem like a no-brainer.

But while many feel a sense of injustice at the way they are treated by their managers at Walmart, feeling injustice is generally insufficient for standing up to it. In his classic book *Exit, Voice, and Loyalty*, Albert Hirschman describes, in a simple yet brilliant formulation, the two possible responses to organizational problems: exit and voice.[40] (We will return to loyalty in a moment.) Exit, he argued, was the market response: You don't like a product? Stop buying it. You don't like an organization? Leave! If Dora, Michelle, and Sandra disliked working at Walmart so much, surely they could find other jobs that they would like better.

In the context of a labor market (or any market, for that matter), exit is the option that is most familiar, and many workers at Walmart take advantage of it. By January of 2015, you will remember, Anthony Thompson—from the commercial—had left Walmart for a job at Enterprise Rent-A-Car. Anthony was hardly the only one: even workers with long tenures like Eric Jackson, who had spent five years as a cart pusher at the store in Forest Park, was also ready to call it quits. At one time it had been a relaxing place to work, back when his friend Ray was there too. But Ray had quit for a job at the temp agency Kelly Services, and Eric was thinking of doing the same thing.[41]

Isn't exit the sensible option? In terms of the raw economics, it makes almost no sense why any individual—one of 1.4 million Walmart employees in the United States—would invest any time trying to make such a massive corporation better. That time could be invested in doing any number of other things, like searching for a better job, taking night classes to qualify for a higher-paying job, or watching television while others try to make the company better. In the classic formulation of the "collective-action problem," Mancur Olson showed that—under most circumstances—it is economically irrational for an individual to participate in collective action to secure public goods when he or she can "free ride" on the efforts of others.[42] Of course, there are many exceptions that center around the provision of selective and solidary incentives, the structure of social relations, and so on. Still, all things considered, it takes a leap of faith to imagine that one's contribution to the provision of a collective good will actually result in that good being provided.

High turnover rates in the low-wage service sector are more evidence that, at least here, employer intimidation may not be the primary obstacle to labor organization. As Stuart Tannock writes, "If workers are planning to quit their jobs in the near future in any event, then the risk of being fired for standing up for their rights may not seem so daunting."[43] Of course, under these conditions, the reasons for staying and standing up for one's rights may feel absent too. The problem, that is, may not be the extent of employers' opposition to unionization so much as the seemingly low costs of exit (and therefore low incentives for voice).[44]

But while exit may be sensible from the perspective of the individual worker, it is likely detrimental to those who work in low-wage jobs as a whole. The problem with exit is that it can only lead to organizational changes ("recuperation" in Hirschman's terms) when there is some elasticity in the demand for the good (or the job) the organization offers. If there is a large group of equally capable workers ready to take the spot of any Walmart worker who quits, it is unlikely that the organization will feel any pressure to change as a result of such turnover. If anything, the company will be happy to have the disgruntled worker disappear. Furthermore, if other options are just as bad, individual workers might not actually be better off using exit either—they might repeatedly exit bad jobs with the (false) hope that the next one will be better, wasting energy they might otherwise have spent working to improve any one of those earlier situations.[45] Despite the costs of turnover, the churn might help low-wage employers collectively avoid any claims on them. So the most sensible choices from the perspective of any individual worker—keeping one's mouth shut or leaving the company—are also the choices likely to leave the distribution of jobs unchanged.

The formal economic irrationality of collective action begs the question why people like Dora, Michelle, Sandra, and thousands of others decided to use voice instead, to take on the company rather than take off from it. OUR Walmart was not proposing to unionize the company. The potential collective payoffs to participation in the organization were highly uncertain in time and scope, and so the impact of the marginal contribution of an individual worker was also difficult for anyone to understand. So what explains participation and what can this teach us more generally about the possibilities for labor mobilization among those who work in low-wage jobs?

The answer, in short, is that people participated because of the ties they had with other participants—ties that acted both as channels for information and influence and as tethers that kept them from leaving the company altogether. Moreover, these ties gave rise to a new sense of self, and as a consequence, the activists became other people, like the people engaged in PMS. In Hirschman's formulation, one key determinant of a person's or group's likelihood for using voice over exit is loyalty, by which he means not an unquestioning allegiance to an organization but rather a "special attachment" that makes an actor "willing to trade off the certainty of exit against the uncertainties of an improvement in the deteriorated product." Loyalty is not people doing nothing. Loyalty forces us to turn away from the easy exit and "thereby pushes men into the alternative, creativity-requiring course of action from which they would normally recoil."[46]

For many workers at Walmart it was connection to and loyalty to one another that encouraged them to get involved in the organizing to begin with. This is, on its face, somewhat counterintuitive. It was the best parts of the job—people's connections with one another, their codependencies at work, their sharing advice, their helping one another out—that provided both the motivation to fight against the company's unjust practices and provided the avenues through which this participation occurred. What is counterintuitive is also part of the labor organizer's common sense. Isolated, estranged workers rarely participate in labor organizing. Rather, it is those who are already in some kind of instrumental, task-oriented relationship with one another who are likely to take part. That is why the production line, which can induce such task-oriented collaborative relationships, often provides an immediate foundation for joint action in pursuit of a common good.

The importance of such networks is affirmed across the interviews we conducted with workers. When discussing how they got involved in OUR Walmart, most of our interviewees discussed it in the context of their existing relationships in the store. The most common account, related by 17 workers, was that one of their coworkers introduced them to an organizer who, in collaboration with the coworker, recruited them to participate; or, in a similar but distinct process, the worker was recruited by an organizer alongside a coworker, and the two joined together. Another common account, related by 10 people, was that one or more coworkers recruited them to participate in the organization without the involvement of any organizer at all. In all accounts of this type, workers discussed the respect they had for the coworkers who were a part of their recruitment. Julie Soto, who worked at a Walmart in Orlando, Florida [#908], got involved through her "best friend at work." Julie continued, "We discussed about favoritism, sick time, cutting hours. At that time, I was really upset, so she asked me if I wanted to join the organization. So, I told her yes."

For other workers, it was not that coworkers introduced them to the organization but rather that organizers began speaking with them along with their peers. Here, organizers engaged in the kind of process that Kevin described in the previous chapter, embedding themselves in the existing social structure of the store. Sue Rogers, who had found a sense of community among her coworkers over Friday-night dinners at the local Applebee's, learned about OUR Walmart when organizers invited her and her coworkers to a meeting at the same restaurant: "I went to that first meeting there at Applebee's, and they gave me all those booklets to read. And I started reading up on it, and I listened to the other people's stories, and what results that they got from them, and it made me think, 'Well, if enough people got together, and enough people voiced their opinions and voiced what they feel, maybe things will change eventually, in the long run.' "

At the Walmart Supercenter in Rosemead, California, Vickie Allard and her coworkers had begun to meet outside work over the summer of 2010. This was shortly after Vickie had been ordered to change her name tag from "Vickie" to "Victoria." She invited a group of cashiers over to her house one Friday night. It evolved into a weekly event over the summer of 2010:

> Some of the cashiers would come down to my house and would bring chips and drinks, and we would sit there and literally have what I would call a "bitch session" because we would sit there and bitch about everything [the management] would do to us.

Sitting outside, eating barbecue, they shared their common concerns. In the midst of these meetings, Vickie said, her sister reminded her that they had a relative who worked for the UFCW.

One day the relative showed up at her door, with another UFCW organizer in tow, and told her about a new association of Walmart workers getting off the ground called OUR Walmart. "You wanna call your other friends?" she asked. Vickie called some of her cashier colleagues—those she trusted—to come to the house, and the organizers told them about OUR Walmart. Vickie remembers, "And I go, 'What does OUR stand for?' And they said, 'Organization United for Respect.' And I said, 'Hell yes, give me a pen.' And so did the other girls that were there with me, were right there with me signing it." Here, again, relationships forged in the store served as the fabric into which the OUR Walmart organization was woven. In each case, a small group of coworkers gave new meaning to their existing relationships, becoming a core of the organizing effort.[47]

THE HOW, WHEN, AND WHERE OF WORKER SIGNING

A wide variety of network processes got workers involved with OUR Walmart. But becoming a member of the organization was always—or almost always—about being alongside people who also joined. In only seven cases out of the 43 accounts of joining did we hear a worker report being recruited alone by a paid staff organizer. And there were only two cases of workers signing up online without first being in touch with anyone. Signing was a decision made in relationship to others.

We know when each member in each store signed up for the organization, which allows us to see the order in which members signed up, broken out by store. One way of testing which relationships mattered for signing is to see how similar consecutive signers are along different relational dimensions. For example, if people tend to discuss the organization with others of the same gender, we would expect people of the same gender to sign consecutively more often than if signing occurred randomly by gender within a store. We ran 50 simulations in which we held constant the distribution of signers by category by store (e.g., we held constant the number of men and women who signed in a particular store) but randomized the order of these signers, and then compared the results of these simulations with the observed pattern of signing.

This sort of analysis is revealing of the types of ties that matter most for recruitment. Not counting family ties, which are powerful predictors of joint joining, workers are significantly more likely to work in the same department as the previous card signer than we would expect by chance. In contrast, the characteristics of workers that predict friendship play no role in motivating signing. For example, a worker was only 3 percent more likely to be of the same gender as the previous card signer than we would expect by chance, and tended to live in only a slightly more demographically similar neighborhood as the previous signer (4 percent more racially similar and 3 percent more similar by mean income). So while work department is a powerful source of social influence in card signing, demographic similarity—which tends to undergird friendship[48]—does not play an important role.

Processes of social influence can help to explain why individuals sign up for OUR Walmart; they can also help to explain how OUR Walmart gained momentum within particular stores. Key to seeing this momentum is the time between card signings within stores. Restricting our sample to those stores with a lot of members (defined in this case as those stores with over 50 signers), we investigated the average time between card signings (see figure 4.3). Here again, we can see evidence of a contagion effect in early card-signing uptake: the time between signings diminishes as group size increases. While the average time between the first and second card signing was just over 147 days, the average time between the ninth and tenth card signing was just under 6 days.[49]

These observations are consistent with the network dynamics we have described so far. In deciding whether to participate in collective action or join an organization like OUR Walmart, people take into consideration how much other people in their immediate work environment have already contributed or are likely to contribute.[50]

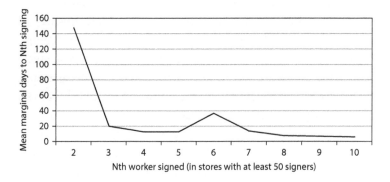

FIGURE 4.3 Marginal time to card signing.

So we know that processes of social influence are important for the development of OUR Walmart chapters within particular stores, and we know that traditional predictors of friendship are less important for this recruitment process than ties based on shared workplace department. We can also explore whether there are certain positions or store attributes that make people more or less likely to sign up.

To examine these individual attributes and store characteristics, though, we have to compare those who sign up for OUR Walmart with workers with whom the organization was in contact but who did not sign up. Restricting our analysis to the well over 8,000 workers for whom we have department information, we see that some departments are much more likely to sign up for the organization than others. For example, the most likely positions to sign, in descending order, are those who work in the fitting room, cart pushers, and cashiers. Those least likely to sign are those who work in the back of the store, either in inventory or in shipping and receiving.

The most obvious difference across these positions involves the interactions workers are likely to have with one another and with organizers. Those working in the back of the store are isolated from the rest of the workplace and are difficult for organizers to reach.[51] In contrast, cashiers and cart pushers are easy for organizers to find and engage in conversation. The same is true for fitting-room associates, who also serve as bridges across multiple departments and groups of workers, since the fitting-room desk serves as the "control tower" for the store, often responsible for answering outside phone calls to the store and directing them to the appropriate departments.

What is surprising about the three positions most likely to yield signers is that the selection process into those positions, should it matter, seems likely to be very different. Cart pushers, if they want to be cart pushers, seem likely to select that job because it has little customer interaction and is outside the view of managers. Fitting-room associates, on the other hand, have to spend a lot of time with customers, and they are constantly interacting with managers. Cashiers are essentially public facing. The fact that these positions demand such contradictory things suggests that their commonality—ease of contact for organizers—is what drives their overrepresentation among members.[52]

Our data also let us ask which kinds of stores were most likely to have people sign up for OUR Walmart, after controlling for the contacts that OUR Walmart made in a store. Here we see that stores in poorer and more heavily African American neighborhoods were more likely to elicit signatures. More interestingly, we see that bad Yelp ratings are strongly related to card signing. There are three ways to understand this relationship: first, whatever store-level factor is making workers unhappy is also making customers unhappy; and/or second, workers' unhappiness, which expresses itself in signing up for OUR Walmart, is itself making customers unhappy; and/or third, unhappy customers make for unhappy workers.[53] All three are probably self-reinforcing.

We also see that if a store experienced an Occupational Safety and Health Administration (OSHA) violation anytime in the years before OUR Walmart's founding (i.e., pre-2010), it is more likely to experience card signatures. Again, it is somewhat difficult to interpret this relationship. On the one hand, an OSHA violation could signify a mismanaged store, which leads to more OUR Walmart members. On the other hand, an OSHA violation could indicate something different: that there is at least one worker at the store who is conscious enough of his or her rights and engaged enough to file an OSHA violation. In this case it is an indicator of leadership potential rather than store mismanagement.

These relationships are significant even after we control for the region of the country (three-digit zip code) in which the store is based. Once we drop this control, we can see a final store-level variable that helps to explain card signatures: the distance between the store and Walmart headquarters in Bentonville, Arkansas. Why does distance matter? It turns out that the distance between a store and Bentonville is a relatively good proxy for the age of the store, since Walmart's strategy between 1962 and 1995 was to expand slowly outward from home.[54] Newer stores tend also to be more receptive to organizing, probably because, all else being equal, older stores have a higher percentage of people who have worked for Walmart for a long time, a factor which is associated with being less interested in OUR Walmart (likely a result of people who are happier in their jobs selecting into staying). It is also true that Walmart's corporate culture, developed in the Ozarks, may be less convincing to workers far away from headquarters.

Why have we spent so much time reviewing these data? For one thing, they show how a labor organization like OUR Walmart might use multiple sources of data to identify particular kinds of stores and particular sorts of employees within these stores to target. Whatever the causal relationship underlying the associations, it seems that labor organizations might use Yelp and administrative data like OSHA violations to find those stores in which organizing attempts are the most likely to get off of the ground.[55] Furthermore, these data provide marching orders for how an organizer, or a customer ally, might most productively conduct a store visit: start in the parking lot with the cart pushers, go visit the fitting-room desk, and chat up a cashier as one buys a pack of gum on one's way out.

With this said, all the analysis in the world can't get past the one central fact. As a self-sustaining membership organization, OUR Walmart did not succeed between 2010 and 2015. Few people signed up. Still, that doesn't mean that it failed. The Black Friday strikes and OUR Walmart's other actions contributed to the sense that there was too much inequality in America, helping to fuel successful drives for increases in state minimum wages and, ultimately, increases in the minimum wages paid by the company. As importantly, for the people who did get involved, their involvement could be, though was not always, transformative.

THE PEOPLE WILL RISE UP, AND THIS GREAT EVIL WILL FALL

Much of the language that we have for talking about personal transformation is religious. It is not accidental that we describe radical transformations of self as being "born again." One is born into existing social relations. Being born again implies that one enters into radically new relations with others. And our most intense personal experiences are usually relational at their core. Perhaps this is why religious imagery suffuses so many accounts of participation in OUR Walmart. Among the Pico Mighty Strikers, Michelle Rogers said,

> Everybody wants to find their purpose on this earth, you know . . . And I find my purpose in that area, being able to speak for others who can't speak for themselves, to be able to stand up to management who think they were God. You know, I love it. . . . It drives me. It's my passion and sense, my purpose on this earth.

Sally Novak, from a Walmart in Glenwood, Illinois, used very similar language to describe why she participated in the organization. "I'd be filling the shelves and putting stock up on there and I'm talking to myself as I'm doing this, 'Why am I fighting this? Why am I doing this? Why don't I just quit?' " And yet, she says, "I just have that fight in me that doesn't want to quit and I just can't back down. That's my purpose. It's my purpose in life and I think I finally heard the calling. Maybe I haven't been listening to it, but that is—seems to be my purpose." When Sally gets the urge to quit, she feels a "nudge or that little voice behind me [that] says, 'No, you don't want to do that.' " She continues, "Honestly, I really don't know if it's my conscience talking to me or it's really—is it God talking to me saying, 'No, this is what you need to do'?" Rose Robinson, from a Chicago store, said she felt that God put her in the store "for all the scared babies up in there" who refused to outwardly support the organization.

In June 2013, Juan Meza joined a delegation of coworkers attending Walmart's shareholders' convention in Bentonville, Arkansas. He recalls a night when he was sitting in his hotel room with some of his coworkers. He says that he "never read[s] the Bible," but that night, because "I got a feeling in me," he picked up the hotel Bible and opened it to a random page where he read: *The people will rise up, and this great evil will fall, when the people finally rise up together.*

> Man, my skin got all goosebumpy and everything, you know? I stopped and repeated that to everybody. I told them what I had just went through, and they're like, "Read that thing out loud." I read it out loud to everybody, and it's just the moment, the trippy vibe of just, wow. This spiritual moment in the room. That kind of changed my life in a way.

There is an otherworldly character to these experiences. Walmart is revealed to be a false God. Don, an organizer from Dallas says:

> Here is this giant laughing at this whole army and mocking the one, true God. Here is David, a little boy, who brings into remembrance that God is with him, who remembers that he killed the bear and he killed the lion. . . . He has enough courage to know that what Goliath is doing is mocking his God. So, he steps up to him and says basically, "I'm going to defeat you this day, but it's going to be with the power of the Lord on my side". . . . People think of Walmart as a giant they can't beat. . . . That's what Walmart wants you to think, but the truth is, yes, you can, and all you need is a few smooth stones to bring him down.

David made history. The religious imagery makes possible linkages from past struggles to imagined futures. Richard Walker, a worker in the produce department at the Walmart in Lancaster, Texas, connected others' hesitations about being involved to examples from the civil rights movement: "What if Rosa Parks . . . would have hesitated? Malcolm X would have hesitated?" Dorian Jenkins, from a Walmart in Chicago, also responded to a counterfactual question about worker hesitancy with lessons from history:

> Now I asked a young lady, "Do you want to sit there and let them talk to you like that?" The first thing that comes out of [her] mouth is, "I need my job." I said, "I understand that, sweetheart, but you also need your pride and your dignity too. You just can't let nobody run over you like this. What did Mama told us when we was coming up? 'Do not let no one run over you there. You stand up for yourself.' If they wasn't out here marching Civil Rights, back in the '60s, the late '50s and '60s, man, we'd really be in a situation now."

At the same time he looked to the past for inspiration, he also looked to the future, imagining that people might understand the work that he and others were doing in the same way that he looks back at the sacrifices made by his parents.

> We got other little young kids that's coming up. I may not be here long . . . but they're going to be here. Walmart's going to be here, and if they happen to can't get no other job and they might have to work at Walmart. . . . Maybe, down the line, they'll say—I'll say in 2031, they're going to see a poster of everybody from OUR Walmart sitting up there like this is the movement that changed everything in here.

Campaigning for God is deeper than just trying to increase wages. Campaigning for God is about changing everything. Mobilizing workers into a movement that connects them with history, that lets them imagine a new history they are actively writing, requires that people are really able to be embedded in new social relations, in a new community.

The idealized community represented by OUR Walmart wasn't that different from the things that Walmart employees wanted out of their jobs at Walmart in the first place. They wanted, at once, a sense of community and a feeling of recognition. They wanted freedom from power relationships that felt exploitative—an abusive husband, an abusive boss. Religious experience propels the real communities that people search for into an imagined world. Insofar as churches can provide a relational underpinning for that imagined world, people can and do feel as though they belong to something greater than themselves, that they are therefore greater than themselves. But membership organizations have trouble sustaining this kind of relational energy. The desire for a community where community is absent is inexhaustible. It spills beyond the boundaries of any organization. It easily falls prey to other forms of religious content—that is, other contents in which the real problems of the world we live in are solved in imaginary futures. The trick is to build a community that works for people in such a manner that they can come to act collectively without requiring that the participants be born again—a this-worldly calling.

5

SOCIAL TIES AND SOCIAL CHANGE

We started many chapters ago with the students who volunteered to work on the Summer for Respect project. In this chapter we turn back to them, to see what we can learn about labor organizing, social solidarity, and collective action from their experiences.

Drawing on interviews, social network data, and brain scans, we show that the nature of collective identification among students changed over the course of the summer and that this evolution may have implications for labor organizing more generally. Because the brain scan data is difficult to introduce quickly—after all, it requires some understanding of a whole new field, cognitive social neuroscience—we discuss the results of the scans in the appendix. Interested readers can turn to it, yet those hoping to avoid reading about different brain regions, voxels, vectors, the amygdala, and so on can feel comfortable skipping it. The one thing to say here is that many of the conclusions we reach in this chapter arise from our thinking about the common elements that link the scan data with more conventional interviews and ethnographic observation.

The students tried, and often succeeded, in developing a sense of community—with one another, with Walmart workers, and with their supervisors in the OUR Walmart organization. When they did so, they were able to remain resilient and creative, committed to the project, the ideals it represented, and one another even in the face of external uncertainty, injustice, and hardship. When they failed at establishing this community, external pressures refracted into internal crises, and the students returned feeling demoralized and defeated. As we see here, "social movement unionism"—often described in the literature as a common set of orientations and practices[1]—can take many different forms.

And this, in microcosm, captures the same dynamic we have seen in stores: in some stores associates worked hard and succeeded in building communities with one another, communities in which they were able to feel a sense of mutual respect and, occasionally, were able to develop a sense of collective power. In other stores they did not work hard at this, or worked hard and failed. The micropolitics of community, then, emerge as a central theme in this and the subsequent chapter—these are the politics that shape how people make sense of their work, and how they make sense of the organizations that might give them a voice at work.

THEY LOOKED LIKE HELL

The 20 participants in the Summer for Respect returned to New York City in early August after 9 weeks in the field. Collectively they looked like hell, which by itself is an accomplishment for a group of 19- to 24-year-olds. Two of the participants on the Los Angeles team were not speaking with each other. Over 2 full days, in the small, sweltering basement office at Columbia where INCITE is located, the assembled group criticized us; criticized the UFCW; criticized OUR Walmart; criticized the Summer for Respect program; criticized the racism and sexism and homophobia they encountered in the field. But they also talked about the moving and hopeful and funny and ridiculous things that had happened; they sang freedom songs; they taught one another the cheers they had learned at their sites; they broke up and hooked up and sought and sometimes found the silver lining to the whole thing. Most are still in touch with us and one another today.

By most measurable indices, our project was a failure. Over 9 weeks, the 20 volunteers reported signing up only 22 members for OUR Walmart—an average of 1.1 new members per person. Most did worse. The Ohio team alone signed up 15 of those 22. Kevin alone signed up 9. Some of the students didn't sign anyone up. More significantly for the UFCW, the union that had sponsored the project, the students had collectively gotten into 5 (albeit minor) car accidents over the summer while driving rental cars leased on the union account. The union's insurance company was threatening to raise its rates as a result.

It is tempting to account for the students' failure by attributing it to their backgrounds: these privileged kids, dropped into unfamiliar circumstances, were unable to connect with the workers they found at Walmart and so were unable to become a part of these workers' networks. This account may have some face validity, but the truth is that many of the students did not come from privileged backgrounds. And Kevin, the student who had the *most* success (and the least prior experience), came from a background more elite than most of the others. In the Ohio team, Kevin's teammates had more in common with the Walmart workers they were encountering than he did. Max could relate on an experiential level to poverty and powerlessness, and had been politically involved since high school. Harmony, who had grown up in a rural part of Massachusetts, felt at home among workers who hailed from rural Ohio; she liked that she was "able to talk the way I used to talk with people back home" and felt "so much more comfortable talking to people at Walmart than I ever have talking in campus group meetings and stuff." And Jeff had grown up in a working-class neighborhood of Los Angeles surrounded by lefty longshoremen; his mother's family was filled with "longeys."

What explains Kevin's relative success? Kevin might have had more social skill than the others, he might have just been better able to talk to and listen to strangers, get them to trust him, and connect them to one another. This trait, this gregariousness, could have just been his personality or—ironically—might have actually been a product of his class privilege, of a formal and informal education that defined membership in the elite as indexed by the ability to capaciously consume culture and experience. These new omnivorous elite, in contrast to their parents, no longer sequester themselves in privileged hamlets but rather navigate all spaces with ease; they can appreciate rap music and country music and opera.[2] Kevin's tattoo, *polytropōs*, "many turns," might as well be the cultural omnivore's motto. The new elite can chat up a brick wall in the name of experience.

It could also be that, in southeastern Ohio, Walmart associates were far more open to a white male labor organizer than they were to a black transgender labor organizer or even a white woman. More subtly, perhaps Kevin's white maleness allowed him interactive space that wasn't available to some of the others. When Max tried to perform the same role ambiguity that Kevin had mastered ("Where's the Kubrick?"), Max was sometimes regarded as a shoplifter. When Harmony tried it, many male associates would assume she was hitting on them:

> I got numbers all the time from Walmart workers, and texted them with the hope of having follow-up conversations about what change they wanted to see in their stores. Most of the workers who actually texted me back were men who ignored that question; instead, they'd respond late on Saturday nights asking me if I was out partying. Or they'd tell me that they saw cute photos of me on Facebook.

In any event, Kevin's relative success challenges the assumption that it was these students' privilege that prevented their success. If anything, perhaps we should have found kids who were more unambiguously elite to participate in the project. Of course, those elites were not beating down the door to join us. Being "omnivorous" seems difficult to reconcile with the political commitments that led people to the project: omnivores are more likely to go to a rave in Brooklyn than risk spending the summer driving around Dallas.

EYES IN THE BACK OF THEIR HEADS

OUR Walmart's membership growth was slow during the summer of 2014.[3] Ohio was the only site that was growing quickly relative to its past; Chicago and Dallas were growing slowly; Los Angeles and Florida almost not at all. It is not entirely surprising, then, that the Ohio team had more success than the others and that none of the teams had much success at all.

The company's vehement opposition to OUR Walmart had a lot to do with this slow growth. There was a long history here. When nine meat cutters managed to win a National Labor Relations Board election in 2000 at a Supercenter in Palestine, Texas, the company announced that it would no longer have meat cutters in Palestine, Texas—or anywhere else in the country. Instead, the company would sell only prepackaged meat.[4] When workers at the Walmart in Jonquiere, Quebec, voted to join the UFCW in 2004, Walmart responded by shuttering the store for good, in violation of Canadian labor law.[5] This was the same fate as befell the Pico Rivera Walmart when it was closed in April of 2015, ostensibly for plumbing problems.

Since the turn of the twentieth century, U.S. corporations have tried to defeat every local organizing success by the same basic strategy: lift the conflict to the next level, where unionization is more difficult or irrelevant.[6] A problem with the butchers? No problem, eliminating fresh meat makes meat cutters irrelevant. An active store? No worries, closing a store forces organizers to operate at a regional level. But given the importance of ties at the store level for organizing, elevating the conflict out of the store almost guarantees labor quiescence. That is what Walmart does when it feels it may be losing, but it rarely has to go this far. Most of the time Walmart nips organizing attempts in the bud before they have a chance to pose a threat. As documented by Nelson Lichtenstein and others, the company has used the results of employee morale surveys to identify the stores most vulnerable to unionization and thus focus executive attention; it has developed extensive manuals to train managers in dissuading employees from unionization without crossing too far across the line into illegality; and it has developed a "labor team" that is flown at a moment's notice to a store in the midst of an organizing attempt.[7] Walmart also fires people if they are thought to be leaning toward or traveling with the labor movement. In this effort they are aided by the constant video surveillance of the store, which enables them to claim that they saw a work violation without any obligation to show what they "found" to the associate in question.[8]

Associates do get to watch some videos, however. New hires at the company are routinely subjected to videos that promote the company's "open door" policy and warn against the evils of unionization. In 2015, one of these videos—which had been shown to new associates between 2009 and 2014—was leaked online.[9] The nine-minute spot features four actors of different races, ages, and genders—a young Latina, a young white man, a young black woman, and an older black man—outlining how a union would take workers' money ("just like taxes"), prevent individual workers from advancing in the company, undermine profitability, and interfere with the "open and direct communication" that the company has with its associates. The video paints unions as parasites, "multi-million dollar businesses that make their money by convincing people like you and me to give them a part of our paychecks." The video finishes by asking workers not only to think of themselves but of their coworkers: "Signing a union card isn't just about you. You could also be affecting people who have worked here for years and enjoy Walmart for the same reasons we do." Don't mess it up for us.[10] Walmart was invoking a form of solidarity in order to prevent associates from thinking about joining the union. Walmart understood what mattered to their associates—the sense of community, a sense of shared history.

And when the Walmart family and community rhetoric collided with reality, the kind of reality that makes one think "if this is a family it's not a family I want to be a part of," intimidation could almost always seal the deal.

Once managers knew that organizers had entered a store, they would do everything they could do to eliminate the threat. On one afternoon at the Walmart in Dayton, Ohio, we were able to experience this firsthand. Robert, an experienced organizer from southeastern Ohio, wanted to make sure that Kevin and Max had the opportunity to speak with workers at the store. Management knew Robert well—according to him, his picture had been circulated among managers at several local stores, and his car was tracked by store surveillance as well, so as to anticipate his approach.

Robert "sacrificed himself" and was the perfect decoy. As Max and Kevin surreptitiously spoke to workers, we walked into the store with Robert, and within five minutes a store manager was following us. The manager, a clean-shaven, crew-cut white guy with glasses, did not confront us directly. After all, we were not doing anything improper. Rather, he stayed an aisle or two over, walking in parallel, keeping us within his sights. Robert began to have fun. "Okay, you go left and I'll go right," he told us. We began walking in opposite directions. The manager paused for a moment, said something into his walkie-talkie, and then followed Robert rather than us.

In Los Angeles, where the OUR Walmart campaign was more established, managers were even more attuned to, and aggressive toward, the Summer for Respect participants. Michelle, from the Los Angeles team, often wound up feeling like the "Walmart store is like a war zone, where you are worried that at every turn there might be a manager or that you might be presented with a difficult situation." She discussed this as having a negative impact not only on workers but also on herself. As a result of the "cat-and-mouse game" with management it was easy to forget that "organizing is a lot of developing friendships with people and trust and getting to know people." She would try to convince herself to forget about the managers tracking her: "You sort of have to forget about the game of it, and just try to have conversations." But her fear would return—it was always in the back of her mind, because managers seemed to have eyes in the back of their heads. Which they did, in the form of cameras. And those cameras were always on.

It's a testament to the intensity and severity of Walmart's system of intimidation that it worked so effectively on our students. Our students' jobs, after all, were not in the hands of Walmart's managers. Managers had no formal authority over them. Nevertheless, it takes a lot of interior strength to go to work each day knowing that you will be constantly observed and that at any moment you might be confronted by hostile store managers. By the end of the summer, faced with day after day of managers following her, and workers too scared to speak, Kollette—another participant on the Los Angeles team—was beginning to come apart: "I've just grown really weary, I think." She would often cry before the workday began. One of the store managers began putting her down, telling her, " 'I'm here doing a real job' . . . implying that we're not doing anything [real] there." Kollette had been trained to write down what the managers said to her while she was in a store. When the manager saw Kollette writing, she said, "Oh, are you writing a book report? That's adorable." Kollette felt belittled, condescended to, and the manager was not even her boss: "I can't even imagine what workers go through. Because, like, I am there, because I want to be there, you know. There is no necessity driving me to be there. And just taking that kind of crap is just so, I'm not used to it." Which was true for most of the participants. They really were not used to it.

TEAM SPIRIT

It is easy to forget that social influence operates on both sides of an interaction. At the same time an organizer is hoping to identify potential members and encourage them to join the organization, nonjoiners can demobilize organizers (and other workers) by a process of reverse influence.[11] Day after day of hostility from Walmart managers and relative indifference from the Walmart associates they were trying to enroll took a toll on the Los Angeles team. Rather than organizing workers, they were unorganizing themselves, turning energies initially devoted to recruitment inward, against one another.

But if the external environment were entirely determinative of the teams' experiences, then the Florida team would have been equally as frustrated as Los Angeles, and Dallas and Chicago would have been only slightly less so. Even Ohio, while successful relative to the other teams, had little to write home about in absolute terms. Just thinking about the Ohio team's yield—where things went the best—tells you how frustrating the whole experience was: 15 new members for 4 organizers over 9 weeks, assuming 40 hours of work per week, amounts to just under 100 hours of work for each new member.[12] Nearly all of the teams faced nasty Walmart managers, long hours, and regular rejection or downright hostility from workers who did not want to have anything to do with the organization. Some teams were forced to confront the police on a regular basis. The managers at the Red Bank Walmart in Cincinnati [#2250], for example, would regularly call the police on Jeff and Harmony—according to Jeff, the "cops are very cozy with the managers" in that particular store because of the police station near the back of the store's parking lot.

Consequently, we cannot account for the despair of the Los Angeles team members based solely on their reception in the stores. The teams reacted differently to similar pressures. Incredibly, in retrospect, the teams from Florida, Dallas, and Ohio all returned with a sense of solidarity: feelings of connection to one another and feelings of collective accomplishment with regard to the work. The team from Chicago came back feeling friendly with one another, but disillusioned with the labor movement. The team from Los Angeles felt alienated from one another and from the work. Failure was, by and large, a universal treatment across the five sites. So what explains the different spirits in which they returned?

The Los Angeles team, it turned out, was dealing not only with nasty Walmart managers but also with difficult UFCW supervisors. Home to the Pico Rivera store and PMS, the Los Angeles site had at one point been the most vibrant corner of the OUR Walmart campaign. But those successes were in the past, and by the time the students arrived the site had settled into a sort of holding pattern while it waited for the rest of the country to catch up. The site's leadership could be cliquish; the site's program could feel rote and repetitive.

Like the members of the Ohio team, members of the Los Angeles team were assigned their own stores to organize. But in Ohio the students felt treated respectfully by their supervisors. They would brainstorm together in staff meetings; they would all go out for ice cream or drinks at the end of a long week. And the supervisors would allow the students room to experiment, fail, adjust. For example, Kevin and Max spent a few weeks visiting a store where they were unable to make any progress, a fact they ultimately attributed to the composition of employees there (mostly college kids and the semiretired). They made the decision, in consultation with their supervisors, to drop the store and focus their energies on the places where they were having more luck.

The OUR Walmart supervisors in Ohio were creating small pockets of autonomy for the students, who could then see the work that they were doing as expressive of their creative instincts. The work felt different in Ohio than it did in Los Angeles. There, the students felt as though they were of markedly lower status than those supervising them. Michelle observed, "We have the same work schedules and the same responsibilities as everyone else. But it feels like they kind of understand us as interns, even though three of us have already graduated college." Jackie echoed this point: "We're essentially working as organizers independently and reporting to them. We have all of the responsibilities as the next full-time organizer who's working at the other store down the street. We have the same responsibilities as he does. But I feel like we have a bit of a lower status." It probably didn't help that the members of the Los Angeles team were, on average, slightly older than the members of the other teams: three of the four Los Angeles team members had already graduated from college. It may have been easier to transition from being a student to an "intern" than to transition from being an Ivy League graduate to an "intern."

In our exit interviews with them, Michelle and Kollette each separately discussed a detail indicative, to them, of their lower status. Every Monday, organizers would gather to discuss their results from the previous week, results that would be posted on a large chart on the wall. While all of the organizers had their names listed on the wall, the students were unnamed. According to Kollette, "We're just named after our store"—that is, rather than Kollette and Nicole, the row would read "Long Beach." This may indeed have been an indication of their low status, but there are other ways to read this too. Maybe the simplest is that the supervisors, knowing that our students had not been able to get any traction, settled on using the store names so as to not embarrass them individually.

But the students' interpretation was different, and so it is no wonder that the difficulties of the work took on a different valence for the Los Angeles team. It did not feel as though they were bound together with OUR Walmart in a noble and difficult undertaking. Instead they felt isolated. They felt like failures. It was as though the experience of working at Walmart was becoming their experience too—the disrespect that workers experienced mirrored in the lack of respect they felt they were receiving. Kollette said,

> I can't divorce the fact that I believe in it so much and then not being able to get anything rolling at the store. It just kind of really makes me really sad, you know. . . . Not being able to develop anything, it just makes me really, like, depressed.

The Dallas and central Florida teams confronted external environments that were in many ways more difficult than Los Angeles, though the teams' experiences were by and large much better. In Texas and Florida, OUR Walmart was legally prohibited from stepping foot on Walmart property—these were two of the five states nationally in which the company had successfully pursued legal injunctions that made store visits impossible. Greta, from the Florida team, recalled how the boundaries of the company parking lot would be clearly demarcated from the surrounding asphalt so as to make it clear where they were not allowed. The student participants were warned by their supervisors to not even cross the stores' parking lots, "because you might be tempted to talk to somebody," as Michael—another Florida participant—put it. On one particularly hot day, though, he crossed the parking lot to get to the bus station. The experience of being so close to workers, when they were so difficult to find elsewhere, was hard to bear: "I just saw all these workers getting in their cars, and I was like, 'Wow, I will never talk to you. There's no way.' But, like, dang, you're literally right there."

Los Angeles may have confronted hostile managers, but participants from Dallas and Florida were not even able to get their feet in the door. In Florida, the students spent weeks trying to find workers at places other than work—knocking on random doors in nearby housing complexes,[13] stalking the bus station, hanging out in the fast-food chains next to the stores, driving around central Florida to follow up with workers who had been in contact with the organization at some point in the past.

Even these strategies were imperfect given the geography of central Florida. To the four members of the Florida team it seemed as though everyone in the area lived in a gated community—even the house the organizing team shared for the summer was in a development ensconced in iron. This made knocking on doors, that most basic of organizing strategies, a herculean task. As Valerie put it, "Every neighborhood has a gate. I don't care if it's the projects or a mansion. They have a gate at the beginning of the thing, which ended up being a problem a lot of times." According to her, the team would have to "chill out and wait for somebody to come up behind." When someone approached, they would say something like "Oh my god! I can't get in. Can you help me?" And most of the time people just let them in. Greta said, "We always had to hop gates if we wanted to door-knock. We would find some way to get into a gated community." But these strategies could also lead to trouble: "We got kicked out of two developments for soliciting," she continued. Gated communities may not have had a formal injunction against OUR Walmart organizers, but they were not exactly welcoming to outsiders either. At the workplace and at workers' homes, the message was clear: Do Not Disturb. And really, if an organizer hopped a fence to knock on your door, how receptive would you be to the message?

If the gated communities were one obstacle in Florida, the distance between gated communities was another. Much of the team's time was spent on the road. According to Greta, "We drove at least 35 minutes to get anywhere." Valerie said, "We would drive easily two hours commuting every day." It took forever to knock on doors where Walmart workers might be living, given that the kinds of poor communities where workers might seem to be were scattered across the region. Moreover, the fact that everything was so spread out, coupled with an almost complete absence of public transportation, meant that almost everyone drove a car, again limiting organizers' opportunities to speak with workers in spaces where they might be found in small groups—for example, bus stops—and able as a consequence to see how their experiences were shared by others. Elsewhere the bus stop might have been a good bet, but the chance of finding a Walmart worker at one in Florida was way too low. As Greta said, "It's particularly hard in Florida, because everything is so car dependent." Michael added, "In Florida, not a lot of people use public transportation because it sucks so much."

But despite the hours and hours of driving, the frustrations of being simultaneously so close and so far from Walmart workers, the gated communities, and the lack of local organizational allies, the Florida team returned from the experience deeply committed to the work—three have continued to work in the labor movement since. And this, again, seems at least partially to do with the structure of the work down there. The students on the Florida team worked closely with three organizers, two of whom were relatively new to organizing themselves and all three of whom were former Walmart employees. Together they brainstormed strategies, checked in, and provided emotional support to one another as relative equals. The leader of the Florida team, Stacy Krier, offered optimism and energy and the space for team members to experiment and fail. Michael said, "I think some of the other teams that maybe had a larger, more established organizing team, had less autonomy than we did. Which I think served a lot to our benefit, both for personal growth and for our eventual effect in this organization." Michael continued, "We just had to be really creative and really think about where we were going to spend our time and how to structure our days." It was also a smaller operation in central Florida than it was elsewhere, which made the members of the Florida team feel like "they needed us," as one put it. "When we left, it was like, they don't know what they're going to do."

The Dallas site was more established than the Florida site, insofar as there was already a cadre of strong worker leaders involved in the campaign. In Dallas, somewhat paradoxically, the injunction against the union seemed to have an unexpected benefit, in that it forced organizers to develop strong worker-leaders who could run the campaign from inside the stores. While the students on the Chicago team felt as though the organizers treated workers condescendingly, as instruments for OUR Walmart's designs, those in Dallas saw workers leading the campaign. Louisa explained how workers would take on specific leadership roles at their stores: "One person was on health and safety for his store. One person was on community outreach. One person was on membership fees. It was empowering and well delegated. . . . They weren't being used as props." Alexis, from Dallas, thought that the disconnection between organizers and workers described by members of the Chicago team would have been "somewhat impossible" in Texas because of the injunction: "You had to be team players with the workers, because otherwise you wouldn't have any connection to them. You wouldn't have any way to access them, because the organizers can't go into the stores." When staff organizers wanted to meet with workers, they had to go through existing worker networks—so, for example, they would work with an existing worker-leader to organize a barbecue with the worker's friends from work.

Instead of visiting stores, the organizers in Dallas would spend time thinking about how to build a self-sustaining community of worker-leaders outside the workplace. Alexis remembers how, after a one-day strike, the lead organizer in Dallas planned a roller-skating night with workers so that they could continue to feel the sense of community they had felt during the action. He would assign the students responsibility for organizing similar kinds of community events—a trip to the local water park, maybe, or a bowling expedition. The students on the Texas team were incorporated thoughtfully into a well-functioning local organization, their particular skills put to use. It was here that the students put into practice one of the ideas we had thought would motivate their work: using the oral histories as a deliberate part of the organizing strategy—they would set up interviews with unsigned workers, which would slide seamlessly into conversations about joining OUR Walmart.

But there seemed little room for this kind of community, or creativity, in Los Angeles. At one point over the summer, Kollette had heard about another local internship in which the staff took the interns out every Friday in order to unwind, debrief, and build camaraderie. Kollette brought up the idea to her own leads, who "just laughed at the idea of coming together and talking about our feelings."

TIES ARE MORE IMPORTANT THAN FRAMES

The Chicago team's frustration with their supervisors was not restricted to the condescending ways that they approached Walmart workers. They also reacted to what they perceived as rampant sexism among their supervisors, many of whom had been shop stewards in meatpacking plants for the UFCW before being assigned to the OUR Walmart campaign. This came to a head for Brittany one day when she was driving around with the lead of the Chicago team, Sean, and he asked her if she had a boyfriend and then followed up with, "Oh, what would you say if I asked you on a date?" While "nothing bad happened," she continued, "I lost a lot of respect for him." This incident in particular, combined with what she felt was the casual sexism of many of the full-time organizers at the site, made Brittany feel as though the labor movement was myopic in its concern for workers' rights without caring about other kinds of inequality: "They all do it—transphobic comments and homophobic comments and stuff . . . I don't really know what to do with [it] and [it] definitely makes me uncomfortable."

At the beginning of the project, Brittany said, she felt as though she and her teammates should be able to transcend the differences in background between them, their supervisors, and workers from Walmart. But by the end, Brittany's initial commitment to transcend their differences in the name of "solidarity to fight the same thing" had dissolved: "I think [the differences] are way too harmful to just ignore and to stand in solidarity. . . . The way we would get there is too different and the way that people are getting there right now is causing too much harm in the process for it to be worth it to just ignore." Brittany's experience in the car with Sean became a totem for the students on the Chicago team, an emblem of the misogyny plaguing the labor movement.

But just as organizing failure was a common outcome across the five sites, and so cannot uniquely explain the dissolution of the Los Angeles team, it is also the case that the students on almost every team encountered some degree of misogyny, homophobia, or racism, and so these encounters cannot uniquely explain the Chicago team's disillusionment with their leads. One of the supervisors in Dallas commented on Alexis's breasts and (on another occasion) on the length of her dress. Another supervisor in Texas told Diana, a queer white woman, that he went by "scripture literally" and that he believed "homosexuality is an abomination as the Bible says." In Ohio, a supervisor asked Max, a transperson of color on the Ohio team, for Max's "God-given name." And Harmony, another member of the Ohio team, would often feel silenced and overlooked by her white male supervisors. And this is to say nothing of the array of unpleasant experiences that the students had with workers and other members of the public—getting hit on, ogled, ignored, or followed menacingly around an outdoor shopping plaza.

Yet here, again, the relational context seemed to matter as much as the linguistic content of interactions for the team's experience—the frames were less important than the ties. In some cases, the relationships that the students had forged with their supervisors and with one another provided the trust necessary to cope with, contextualize, and challenge the kinds of interactional disrespect that arose in the field. Brittany may have gotten the causal order backward. It was not that the Chicago team's sense of solidarity couldn't withstand misogyny, but rather that there was no solidarity within which to understand and challenge the site's misogyny.

In Chicago, Sean became a focal point around which the team's broader disillusionment with the project came to be understood. He became emblematic of the misogyny of labor, its blindness to issues of gender and sexuality (despite the fact that OUR Walmart's female director had responded swiftly and decisively in response to the incident).

In Dallas, on the other hand, members of the team returned to New York City enthusiastic about OUR Walmart despite even more extreme experiences of harassment. But there was a different relational context to the work in Dallas. Alexis did not experience her supervisor's ogling as particularly threatening because of the openness she had with him and the support she found in her teammates in relationship to him: "We have a really informal relationship," she said of her supervisor. "But also things need boundaries. It's just weird. I'm like, 'Don't speak to me like that.' . . . But also I laughed." In the staff meeting at which the supervisor made the comment on Alexis's dress, Louisa stood up for her: "If he's going to single her out in front of everybody in the middle of debrief, then I have the right to single him out in front of everybody in the middle of debrief. And so I was like, 'OK. Maybe you should have said that to her individually, or not even at all.' " Yes, Diana was deeply hurt by the deterioration of her relationship with the organizer with whom she had been working, but even here she was able to discuss the situation with her supervisor and reach a (albeit unsatisfactory) détente.

It was not that the misogyny or homophobia was accepted or swept under the rug in Dallas; rather, it was addressed publicly and openly in ways that allowed people to remain committed to the work and to one another. Likewise, in Ohio, participants described themselves as being close with their supervisors despite simmering tensions around race and gender. Max discussed weekly meetings with their supervisors as being "good for reframing and rebasing ourselves." Max went on to say that the supervisors were "very present at the meetings. And very interested in the work and interested in our lives. . . . They were good to us." Harmony felt like there was "a lot of support" from their supervisors, and mentioned particularly her connection with a staff organizer named Melinda: "She felt like my mom. There's some mom thing going on. Her maternal organizing was rubbing off."

The students' attention to issues of race, gender, and sexuality may have been unfamiliar to longtime UFCW organizers, whose experience and training directed them to believe that class cleavages are more salient than other social divisions. That is, after all, one of the reasons that they are labor organizers. That other cleavages are often seen as epiphenomenal means that there is a tendency to appear indifferent to the understandings of self and other that the students—immersed in an academic culture that tends to make sense of the structures of inequality in terms of intersectionality[14]— brought to the table.

Not one of the students excused the microaggressions they experienced in the field. But in some places these aggressions were experienced within a context in which the bosses were "interested in our lives," in which these supervisors gave logistical and emotional support, in which the students' contributions were acknowledged and appreciated. In short, the difference between the teams that worked (Dallas, Ohio, and Florida) and those that didn't (Los Angeles and Chicago) was that where things worked, OUR Walmart was able to foster a sense of community among the students involved in the project and between the students and the staff.

The students' experiences are instructive for thinking about what works and what doesn't work in organizing more generally. Whether we are talking about work at Walmart, workers' organizing with OUR Walmart, or students' experiences in the Summer for Respect, the most salient parts of people's experiences were not reducible to the resources that people had (or did not have); their material struggles or aspirations. The most salient parts of people's experiences were their experiences with other people. The community in the store—the camaraderie among associates and between customers and associates; shared celebrations of anniversaries with the company and in-store memorials when associates died; and the pockets of autonomy one could find and social recognition one could receive for what one made of them—these were as important in people's daily experiences as wages and hours and schedules.

Low pay did not feel unfair until it was connected, in workers' minds, to the sense of disrespect they felt in their relationships with unjust authority. Likewise, the students didn't mind working hard for very little gain when they felt they were part of a community. The deprivations that the students faced—the long hours, the cramped living quarters, the daily improbability of having any real success—seemed less important to the way they made sense of the experience than the relationships they forged (or didn't) with their supervisors and with one another.[15]

Where OUR Walmart was most successful it was a communal experience; people were bound together not only by shared material circumstances, but by a shared orientation to these experiences, a collective myth in which they considered the present from the perspective of the past and future, their joint efforts the climax of a story the moral of which was still indeterminate.

RELATIONSHIPS AMONG THE SUMMER FOR RESPECT STUDENTS

The relationships among the Summer for Respect students evolved over time. At the start of the program, in the first few days when students were just meeting one another, some students were simply much more popular than others. These people attracted others and served as the central glue for the group as a whole.

Over time, though, this fascination with a few students declined and came to account for a much smaller percentage of people's individual liking. In other words, relationships became more idiosyncratic, more individuated, determined less by group status and more by the specifics of people's experiences with one another.

At the beginning of the summer, the students were attuned to one another in ways that seemed likely to reproduce inequality among them. But this is not where they wound up. Instead, they built a new kind of community—one based on reciprocal dyads rather than on common, group-level orientations. The students became a horizontal community rather than a vertical one; or, rather, their horizontal ties with one another made the remaining hierarchies less salient. From a structural perspective, the students developed a supple form of social solidarity, one that may have made group action in pursuit of common goods easier to achieve. In their own development as a group, the students replicated the experiences of other groups put into positions in which collective action is required to make change.

To see this, we have to revisit the famous Milgram experiment—and challenges to that experiment. Milgram demonstrated that isolated individuals subjected to unjust authority would follow orders even if those orders meant that they would harm others.[16] But a follow-up study, conducted by Gamson and his colleagues, which socialized the Milgram context by putting individuals into groups and subjecting them to unjust authority, came to very different, though less well-publicized, conclusions. This study—*Encounters with Unjust Authority*—is important for us, because it socialized the

Milgram experiment, and by doing so provided a better foundation from which one can make inference to the real settings in which people find themselves.[17]

Isolated people are sometimes confronted unjustly by authorities, but more often such encounters occur when we are with others. Gamson and his colleagues were interested in understanding why in such contexts some groups acquiesce to authority when others do not. What they found is that two conditions need to be met before a group refuses to acquiesce. The first is that the group needs to believe that all the members share similar standpoints. The second is that, while a single dissident cannot carry the day, having more than one such dissident can induce a cascade to full rebellion.

The emergence of affective dyadic reciprocity, insofar as it limits the generation of hierarchy and hence creates the context for a shared standpoint, solves the first problem. Such affective reciprocity provides a building block to overcome the second problem as well, since the emergence of reciprocal ties of the sort that we observed among our students is required for transitive closure, the induction of balanced triads that undergird group identity. The sorts of reciprocal ties that the students had been forming were perhaps the sorts of relationships that could allow them more effectively to stand up to injustice themselves.

ORGANIZING IS MORE ABOUT COOPERATION THAN FRIENDSHIP

Of course, "liking" isn't the only relationship we have with others. Focusing on "liking" alone, at the exclusion of other types of relations, threatens to obscure the myriad ways in which people are in relationship with one another. Sure, we like people (in different ways); we also trust them, are influenced by them, are helped by them, shoot the breeze with them, and so on. One way to distinguish among our different relations with others is according to whether or not these relations are instrumental or affective. Influence, help, trust—these are relations in which people cooperate to accomplish some purpose, and so we can identify them as instrumental. In contrast, hanging out, gossiping, and getting along are less tied to the instrumental achievement of an end; in a way they are ends in themselves and, consequently, tend also to be affective—oriented toward the relationship rather than some goal external to it.

One of the things we saw with our students was that trust in their supervisors was much more important to their success than whether or not they liked them. This was also true about their relations to other members of their teams. Associates at Walmart also spoke of trust more often than friendship when they described their organizing experiences. Recall that the Pico Mighty Strikers all felt that their other team members had their backs.

It is far less important for the organizer to be a "friend" of those he or she organizes than to be trusted by them. Indeed, the process of inducing cooperation may in some important ways be orthogonal to the process of getting people to want to hang out. The organizer's role is one of agitation. There are plenty of perfectly rational reasons people have for inaction, and plenty of understandable feelings that inhibit the formation of collective identities and collective organizations—fear, apathy, indifference, exhaustion, resentment. If an organizer merely listened to workers' stories, it is unlikely that anything would ever change. Like a friend or a coworker or family member, the organizer would be another receptacle for others' complaints, frustrations, and naturalizations of experience, by which we mean accounts that make sense of our experiences and the structures in which we are embedded as just the way they are, because they are "natural."

The organizer's dilemmas—becoming embedded in a network of social relations while working subtly to rewire them; becoming versed in a network of cultural beliefs and expectations while working to reconfigure them; staying inside the "experiences of your people" while pushing them outside their comfort zones—may have a basic solution: become someone that others trust but don't necessarily become their friend.

With this distinction between affective and instrumental relations in mind, if we turn back to the smaller groups, we can clearly see what worked and what didn't. Everything went wrong in Los Angeles. The students couldn't cooperate and they didn't trust one another at the end of the summer. In Los Angeles, influence ran in the wrong direction—student interactions with workers, managers, and the OUR Walmart supervisors convinced them that collective action was impossible, futile, risky. Their interactions with one another made things worse. Neither friendship nor cooperation was discovered.

In Chicago, the students became friends but never really learned how to cooperate—with one another, with workers, or with OUR Walmart. One indication of the superficiality of the Chicago team's relationships with one another is the number of times that they mentioned one another's names in the interviews we conducted with them at the end of the summer. On average, each of the other teams mentioned teammates 100 times—Florida and Ohio slightly more, Los Angeles and Dallas slightly less. The members of the Chicago team mentioned one another's names only 20 times across all of their exit interviews (less than the average number of times each individual on the other teams spoke of her or his teammates). The Chicago team got along—they were friends—but they never really got to work. Not surprisingly, the three teams that came back to New York most committed to the project (Dallas, Ohio, and Florida) were not the teams that liked one another the most, but they were the groups that trusted one another the most and, because of that, seemed to come back with one another on their minds.

LOOKING FORWARD

The variety of microcultures that arose among the separate teams dissolved to some extent on their collective return to New York City. While some students were frustrated, most were energized. They would take their experiences back into the field working on a variety of issues at school—sexual assault, police violence, mass incarceration—which were coming to the fore at Columbia and other college campuses in the fall of 2014; many would take them into social justice work after graduation as well.

OUR Walmart, meanwhile, would face a new, unexpected challenge, as the UFCW withdrew its support from the organization. This came, paradoxically, at a moment when OUR Walmart was earning accolades for driving increases in minimum wages at the company. With its funding and staff support stripped away, OUR Walmart was nevertheless able to survive as a result of the community that it had built in a somewhat surprising place for a labor organization: online. There, the organization continued to try to build the kinds of communities characterized by mutual trust and commitment that the students—and workers like the Pico Mighty Strikers—had sometimes achieved. Their attempts to do so, and the possibilities and perils of the online world, is the topic of chapter 6.

6

OUR WALMART ON THE LINE

Doug McMillon—the youthful-looking CEO of Walmart—faces the camera. It is February 9, 2015, about six months after the students have returned from the field. He is seated in a collared shirt and sweater behind a large desk in the Bentonville office once occupied by Sam Walton. Behind him hangs a painting of tractor trailers lined up into the distance along a stretch of highway. On each side of the painting, bookshelves are stacked with various titles, including, somewhat surprisingly, *Wal-Mart: The Face of Twenty-First Century Capitalism*, a collection of mostly critical essays edited by the preeminent Walmart scholar Nelson Lichtenstein.[1] McMillon pledges to increase entry wages at the store to $10 by April of 2016, to raise the wages of department manager to the symbolically significant $15 an hour, and to make changes in scheduling policy that will alleviate stress on the company's associates. "It's clear to me that one of the highest priorities today must be an investment in you, our associates," he says.[2] In remarks on *CBS This Morning*, McMillon would go on to tell Charlie Rose, "In the world there is a debate over inequity, and sometimes we get caught up in that." He seemed to be admitting the impact of

OUR Walmart's campaign, a rare moment for the CEO of a company like Walmart.

Nevertheless, the cause of such a change at Walmart was and continues to be hotly contested. Paul Krugman wrote in a *New York Times* op-ed that the change was evidence that "low wages are a political choice, and that we can and should choose differently." According to him, the company was responding to "political pressure over wages so low that a substantial number of employees are on food stamps and Medicaid."[3] But others suggested that the company's move was driven by increasing labor demand in the retail sector—across the retail industry, they observed, wages had been increasing faster than in the labor market as a whole, and quits were higher.[4] Still others suggested that the policy changes were a result of the company's recognition that compensating workers more would make them more productive—and might turn around the company's sagging customer service.[5] Was this a political concession, a sensible response to a changing labor market environment, an implicit recognition of efficiency wage theory, or a bit of all three?

Under normal circumstances, the changes would have been framed and celebrated by OUR Walmart and its allies as a significant victory. Regardless of the relative impact of political or economic calculations, the company seemed cognizant of the need to make some concrete changes in relationship to its workforce. The efforts of thousands of workers and hundreds of organizers were bearing fruit.

But at the time, OUR Walmart was facing a crisis that made it difficult to capitalize on the win. In December of 2014, a few months after participants in the Summer for Respect project had returned home, the UFCW—the fiscal sponsors of OUR Walmart—elected new leadership. The incoming president, Marc Perrone, had campaigned in part on a promise to rein in spending on the Walmart campaign. According to Perrone and others within the union, too many resources had been spent on Walmart without it leading to a single new union member—and without any clear plan to get any (an OUR Walmart "member" was not a unionized worker). Many in OUR Walmart felt that Perrone and his allies represented old-school, traditional unionism rearing its head and that the UFCW was protecting an aging membership at the expense of the unorganized. But from the perspective of many in the union, Perrone was merely expressing one side of a long debate about union strategy—the membership's short-term versus long-term interests, the labor union's relative obligations to its current membership versus the "working class" as a whole.

By April of 2015, an article in the *Washington Post* reported that the UFCW had slashed funding for OUR Walmart by over 50 percent.[6] Then, in May of 2015, the UFCW fired OUR Walmart's two directors after they had begun independent fundraising.[7] It was during this period of public commendation for the company—between headlines like "Walmart Ups Pay Well Above Minimum Wage"[8] and "Walmart Is Raising Its Minimum Wage for More Than 100,000 U.S. Workers"[9]— that the Pico Rivera store suddenly developed its plumbing problems.

But the challenges for OUR Walmart ran deeper than the withdrawal of support by the UFCW. The organization had found pockets of leadership in certain stores and in certain communities, but it had not yet found the smooth stones to take down Goliath. The largest wave of strikes in Walmart history was still small in relationship to the size of the Walmart corporation. Even if "hundreds of [workers] did not report to work"[10] in November of 2012, it was unlikely that this number exceeded one-twentieth of 1 percent of the company's U.S. workforce. Granted, even at the height of CIO organizing in the 1930s, a relatively small percentage of industrial workers were actively involved in the movement.[11] But there is a difference between a relatively small percentage and 0.0005.

There are real limits to the leverage that such a small percentage of workers can have. It can raise visibility for issues facing Walmart workers and can serve as a cadre of spokespeople for media inquiries into company changes. What it can't do is impact the company's production process. Since the birth of labor unions in the late nineteenth century, the power of the union has derived—at its root—from the employer's dependence on its workforce as a collective actor. While one worker may be replaceable, the workforce of an entire

factory or industry is much less so. OUR Walmart had symbolic leverage but not yet structural leverage. It succeeded in creating a public relations problem for Walmart that the company answered with
policy changes that were just big enough to change the narrative.

SMALL VICTORIES MAY NOT CUMULATE INTO LARGER MOVEMENTS

A traditional model of organizing imagines that small victories arising from small local actions cumulate into larger movements. Saul
Alinsky argues that if "people feel they don't have the power to
change a bad situation, *then they do not think about it.*"[12] So the organizer has to create experiences of small victories within people's
experiences to prove to people the possibility of bigger ones; only
then, he says, will people reflect creatively and intelligently on their
own situations. The most critical small victory is the first experience
of solidarity. At some places at some times, OUR Walmart was able to
induce this solidarity. Even in the field sites where the students were
working there were signs of success. Consider, for example, two of
the most effective organizers for OUR Walmart—the Rev in Chicago,
and Don in Dallas.

By the early summer of 2014, the Rev—the organizer who had
told Anthony Thompson point blank: "If you're not satisfied with
your check at the end of the week and you don't think you're going
to be able to make it, you need to be part of OUR Walmart"—had
the reputation as being the most successful organizer in Chicago.
The Rev was "the Rev" because he was a Reverend—he often wore a
black T-shirt advertising his *Change You Can Believe in Church* in white,
Comic Sans font. According to Rebecca, he *made you feel like he had
been born for spiritual leadership.* And he had followers. Most organizers would do what Kevin did—walk into stores as "customers" and
chat surreptitiously in the aisles. The Rev had enough charisma that
workers came to him. At the Chatham store he would walk in only
long enough to make his presence known, then *walk back outside and*

sit on the concrete plant bed where workers took their breaks. Workers would then join him there on their breaks, all together, *wearing their blue-collared shirts and smoking cigarettes in the hot Chicago sun.*

Don, the most successful organizer in Dallas and a former used-car salesman, was an older white man who built the organization's membership in the area within a mostly young, mostly African American workforce. Don had faith in OUR Walmart's message, but he understood that the message was just a start—a way of getting one's foot in the door. For Don, like for the Rev, his was a message rooted in religious faith.

For Don, workers needed "time to hear the message." Workers didn't just need to hear the message; they needed time with the message, by which he meant time with one another, time in which they could feel the truth of what Don was saying about the power of solidarity, because they were hearing it together and feeling its truth, a self-fulfilling prophecy of the power of solidarity that would become real as a result of people's collective beliefs in it and collective actions in its name. Investment follows action; it doesn't precede it. Jane McAlevey likewise inverts more standard social movement accounts when she suggests that experiences of solidarity lead to an appreciation of the benefits of collective action rather than the other way around.[13] Kneel down, move your lips in prayer, and you will believe.[14]

THE CHALLENGE FOR OUR WALMART WAS AND REMAINS ONE OF SCALE

But these successes and the theory of action that precipitated them never managed to spill beyond the boundaries of the small, strongly solidaristic groups that the Rev, Don, and some others were able to organize. The analogy to David and Goliath sounds good, but it isn't quite accurate. Goliath was just a really big person. Walmart is a company with over one million employees, thousands of stores, and an army of faceless operations research guys moving goods across the entire globe. It has almost unlimited state support to ensure that the little pockets of resistance that may emerge remain isolated and weak. For movements to succeed, one has to match scale, and while building an organization one member at a time at the point of production—in the parking lot while smoking a cigarette—may theoretically be possible, it isn't likely to happen.

One store visit at a time, one local context at a time, OUR Walmart could not scale up to a size that would have an impact on the company's production process. With thousands of stores, many open 24 hours a day, sparse numbers of workers at any given moment, and no consistent shift schedule around which solidarity could easily be built, Walmart is simply too big for these traditional strategies alone. In those few places where they succeeded, the stores were immediately shut down or those most active workers lost their jobs.

OUR Walmart was always thinking creatively about how to address this problem. Our project was just one indication of that. And in some ways the split between the UFCW and OUR Walmart provided new space for OUR Walmart to confront the scale problem more directly than it had before—to think outside traditional strategies and traditional organizational frameworks about how it might scale up. The split had brought to light the kind of internal crisis that scholars suggest can (though do not always) spark leaders' imaginations.[15]

One ongoing challenge to any contemporary labor organization is figuring out how to embed itself within and transform the relational networks that already exist among workers, their families, and their communities. As Don puts it, people do not just need to hear the message, they need time with the message. And they need to hear messages not just from outsiders but from people they trust. This is a point that Alinsky makes too. He writes, "One of the factors that changes what you can and can't communicate is relationships. There are sensitive areas that one does not touch until there is a strong personal relationship based on common involvements."[16] But how does an organization find and form and foster these trust relationships?

The workplace is a difficult place for the organizer to develop these relationships, even more today than in the past. Because both employers and labor organizations recognize the importance of social interaction to the reception of a message, the rules governing the microinteractions among organizers, employers, and workers have been subject to intense regulation and legal contestation over time. Baked into the legalese of labor law are rules that make it easier or harder for people to hear different messages. For instance, in the years just after the passage of the National Labor Relations Act of 1935, any employer speech regarding unionization was considered inherently coercive. Given that the employer had so much power over the worker, the logic went, he would inevitably and unfairly influence the worker if he expressed opposition to unionization.[17] But the rules would soon change. The Taft-Hartley Act of 1947 granted "free-speech" rights to employers.[18]

Since then, with minimal constraints, it's perfectly legal for employers to express themselves on the subject of unionization. In turn, at the same time that employer "free speech" has been affirmed, a series of Supreme Court decisions has placed limits on the times when, places where, and manners by which nonemployee organizers are permitted to interact with employees.[19] Employer-employee interactions initially defined by law as coercion had been redefined as free expression; in turn, organizer-employee interactions once defined as free expression were redefined as trespass. The injunctions against OUR Walmart from entering Walmart property— now in seven different states—follow directly from these decisions.

That said, in recent years, the largest and most concerted organizing efforts in the private sector have taken place in service industries like hospitals, hotels, restaurants, casinos, and retailers— industries in which many employees come into contact with members of the public everyday, all day, as a part of their jobs.[20] Under these circumstances, it is more difficult for employers to constrain organizers' access to employees at the workplace. The customer— or, more precisely, customer role—gives outsiders opportunities to ally themselves with workers as workers begin to advocate for themselves. If Kevin could buy a pack of gum and talk to workers about the conditions of their work, so can we, and so can you. And so, at the same time it is more difficult than ever before for an organizer to enter a store repeatedly without getting the police called on him or her, it is easier than ever before for a volunteer to casually discuss a worker organization in the midst of shopping. This is the reverse boycott—instead of using economic power through exit, the customer might use political power to exert voice, to seed conversations about worker organization while going about his or her shopping.[21] There is a long and illustrious history of "salts," surreptitious labor advocates who took jobs in places of employment they hoped to organize.[22] The customer salt may not have the same access as the traditional salt, but if the customer is always right, then perhaps the customer might be right about worker power too.

It follows that one potentially productive new strategy for labor organizations may be to treat shop-floor interactions more like insurgent warfare—short, dispersed interactions among customer volunteers that are difficult to attribute to a single legal entity. And then the long game, the deeper relationship development, would take place elsewhere: at home, at church, or even online.

ONLINE AND OFFLINE AND BACK

Back in 2010, before the Arab Spring and Occupy Wall Street and Black Lives Matter and Russia's online interference with the 2016 elections and #MeToo, the leaders of OUR Walmart used Facebook to conduct an online survey of those who identified as working at Walmart. It was out of this survey, in part, that the organizers identified the centrality of "respect" to those working at the company and came up with the name of the organization that has stuck to this day.

Since its inception, then, the organization has been thinking about how it might use social media in new ways to learn from workers and to enhance their collective power. In the beginning this strategy was fairly unsophisticated. Social media was merely another platform for messaging, for framing, for broadcasting links and messages about the Waltons' wealth and the kinds of indignities faced by workers in their jobs.

Tanya Bowman, a former Walmart worker turned organizer, would get these messages and feel like she was on the receiving end of a sales pitch. A leader of OUR Walmart remembers Tanya telling her, "You don't sound like us; you're not connecting." Tanya argued that she and others who worked at Walmart did not want news articles or "third-party-sounding stuff," but rather wanted to see themselves "reflected back." People did not want to be talked at online; they wanted to connect with one another.

Tanya was more agile than the rest of the OUR Walmart staff with new online technologies and helped the organization develop a series of "closed," or private, discussion groups for associates; spaces in which they could share their experiences, get support from one another, and strategize about what to do together. Soon OUR Walmart began hiring staff who could both facilitate the conversations going on in the online groups and work to translate the online discussions into collective practices in the stores.[23]

It was through this process, in fact, that the Florida site was seeded—the site where Greta, Wendy, Michael, and Valerie would spend the summer. Stacy Krier, who had once worked in the deli at the Walmart in Gulf Breeze, Florida [#2533], was living in southeastern Texas, where she had been hired as an online-to-offline organizer with OUR Walmart. Through her online communities she began to find a cluster of promising leaders in and around Tampa and Orlando. She would start conversations with these workers online and visit sporadically: once a month, then twice a month, then weekly. By the time our team arrived, Stacy was living most of the week in Florida, traveling back to Texas to be with her husband on weekends.

Beyond her ongoing work in Florida, Stacy also became the primary organizer and moderator of a large online discussion group of other current and former Walmart associates. The group is not formally associated with OUR Walmart at all—Stacy, who helps to select other moderators, tries to make sure that even the moderation is shared across members and nonmembers so "no one can say it is only for OUR Walmart." This group has grown exponentially over the course of its four years in existence. As of this writing it has almost 50,000 members, current and former associates who discuss anything and everything having to do with Walmart and a lot of other stuff as well. The group is a beehive of activity, vibrant to the point of being overwhelming, a deluge of conversations and questions and answers, gripes and expressions of gratitude. You can find people in the group who love Walmart and people who hate Walmart and people who feel every shade in between. The group provides a sense of what can happen online, good and bad, and the evolution of this group has been instructive for OUR Walmart as it works to more fully flesh out the potential of the relationship between online and offline organizing. If, as we argued earlier, the challenge for traditional unions is to return to those "evangelical sect" strategies that appreciated the value of positive solidarity and belonging, the challenge for such an online community is to channel belonging into a sense of common purpose sufficient for collective power.

To be able to begin to think about this question concretely, though, we have to develop a method for understanding what the online conversation is all about.

THE MEANINGS OF WORDS ARISE FROM THEIR POSITIONS IN A SEMANTIC NETWORK

Our data in this case are posts, comments, and replies within one large discussion group open to current and former Walmart associates. There were 661,335 such posts and comments and replies in response to comments contributed by 23,020 different users between 2011 and early 2017. Just over half of the members of the group have ever contributed—which for boards of this size and kind is a remarkable level of engagement. On most discussion boards the vast majority of "members" are just lurkers.[24] They may be influenced by what they read, but one never sees any sign of that. Here, though, there are more actual participants than lurkers. And that tells you something about the importance of the discussion board for those who have signed up. Our units of analysis are the posts, and all of the comments that are linked to them. As is often the case with discussion boards, people post images, sometimes with text but often without—shelfies and selfies and pictures of memorials to deceased employees are the most common. But here we just focus on the text, leaving aside these visuals.

To make sense of hundreds of thousands of contributions on such a board requires that we adopt some strategy for distant reading. This strategy needs to accomplish two things simultaneously. First, it needs to be able to identify words that are roughly equivalent with respect to meaning. Second, it needs to arrange text into clusters of similar content and map these clusters' relationships to one another, with the idea that such a mapping serves the same general function as key words, or subheadings, or chapters in a book—a way to organize a narrative or description into its constituent elements.

With respect to the identification of equivalent meanings, let's say we encounter a word—"ghoul"—that we are not sure about. The dictionary entry tells us that a ghoul is "a legendary evil being that robs graves and feeds on corpses" (as an aside, this is something about ghouls that neither of us knew). Obviously, ghouls are things that one should avoid, especially when dead, but we would need a thesaurus to tell us what other things are in the class of ghouls that might also be better kept at a distance. Here, the thesaurus tells us that a ghoul is similar to a *cacodemon, devil, fiend, ghost, demon, imp, hag, lamia, vampire, incubus, genie, bogey, bugbear, familiar, shadow, specter, spirit, spook, gnome, goblin, gremlin, kobold, troll, monster, ogre*, and a bunch of other things. We don't know what a lamia or a kobold is, but if they are similar to ghouls we know to avoid them because, like trolls, monsters, ogres, and fiends, they must be scary. Notice that in this list are things that we cannot avoid, like shadows, unless we are dead. Shadows are only scary sometimes. Most of the time they are innocent things that are very near to us.

We know to distinguish the not-scary shadows from the scary shadows by identifying the other words around shadow that make them scary, like "dark," "alley," "looming," and so on. Our understanding of the things similar to ghouls as scary invokes the idea of structural equivalence, that is, the idea that all those things are essentially the same, from any point of view. They are things to be avoided.

We can identify which words are similarly positioned in a text relative to other words—and therefore likely to have equivalent meanings—using a model called word2vec.

In such a model, the proximity of words to one another represents the extent to which one word can be substituted for another. From the 600,000 + posts, then, we can see, for example, that there is a rich vocabulary of conceptually interchangeable words among Walmart associates related to how one is or is not permitted to appear at work: "vest," "tattoo," "blue jeans," "khaki," "hat," "offensive," "piercings," "leggings." The ghouls and ghosts and goblins of the dress code at Walmart are piercings and tattoos and colors like "purple" and "pink."

We also learn that people in the online discussion tend to talk about Walmart "greeters" in the same way they talk about "asset protection" and "security." Earlier we discussed how Walmart figured out that greeters would deter shoplifting; reading what associates post tells us that they too can see behind the "customer service" function of the greeter. The greeters are there to protect stuff as much as to provide service. They are security.

As another example, people tend to discuss how their jobs are boring in the same ways that they discuss how their jobs are stressful—"stressful," "easy," "boring," and "bored" are nestled together. This demonstrates something that is a bit counterintuitive about work at Walmart and many other service-sector jobs: that stress and boredom are equivalently constitutive of the experience of work.[25] On reflection we can see that these experiences are constituted by the same underlying process, which is characteristic of all server systems. The flow of customers into the store is unpredictable; or rather, there is always an error term, even if the flow can be predicted with some level of precision. The operations researchers who design the algorithms that design the work schedules for Walmart workers are aiming—for any given minute of the day—to match staffing resources with customer traffic in order to provide a consistent level of customer service (which, as we have seen, may be different depending on the market power that the company has in a particular neighborhood). But this matching process is imperfect. In actuality, in relationship to the predicted level of staffing needed for a particular period of time, some periods will be characterized by congestion, and some by idleness. There are hours in the day when the lines at checkout may be 20 deep, and hours when there are no lines at all. The bunching of demand is difficult to avoid, because arrivals in the form of customers come on their own schedules—and this leads, alternately, to stress and to boredom, though presumably Walmart as a company would rather have workers stressed than bored (whereas a luxury hotel might rather have workers bored than stressed, prepared to handle an influx of demand at any moment). Our text analysis confirms the equivalence of these experiences among workers at Walmart.

A final example: Across the discussion group, words related to being sick or otherwise facing an emergency ("sick," "flu," and "emergency") are in close proximity to words having to do with absences ("absence," "miss," and "excused") and words having to do with getting disciplined or fired ("points," "occurrence," "coaching," and "termination"). What this analysis tells us is that these words are transposable; getting sick is similar to getting disciplined, which is similar to getting fired. Just as the analysis reveals that boredom and stress are two sides of the same coin, it also reveals that getting sick and getting fired are two similar concepts at Walmart, like ghouls and goblins.

With respect to mapping texts so as to induce clusters of similar content, we need to focus on the co-occurrence of words. When we read, we infer what a text is about by the network of words that are linked together in paragraphs or chapters. Of course, we don't do this in any conscious way, but it is what is happening in the background. Take this book. It is about a program inspired by the Freedom Summer project, organizing, Walmart, workers, respect, creativity, autonomy, and low-wage work in America today. The book has the word "car" in it, and also "track," and "race," and "fast," and "red," and "number," but it is not a book about race cars, or cats, or golf, or personal hygiene, or a gazillion other things, and we know that because the likelihood of a book being about, say, race cars, is very low when the words related to race cars (for example, "car," "track," "race," "fast," "red," "number") are not related, or close, to one another. Our minds treat the fact that words co-occur within a unit of text (like a paragraph) as a network tie, and we learn what a text is about by mapping (mentally) the things that it talks about. Sounds easy enough, except that with more than 600,000 units of text written over long periods of time by more than 20,000 different people, we need an algorithm to represent the whole corpus as a network on which we can run community detection methods to reveal the topics that people discuss and represent them as a map. Here we will skip the details of how these kinds of algorithms work. Interested readers can look at recent papers of ours that make use of these methods.[26]

THE GLOBAL STRUCTURE OF CONVERSATION

The global map of the discussion board (figure 6.1) generates 15 clusters. We can consider these as separate conversations, so the map induces 15 conversation topics. These topics are overlapping and connected to one another.

To see how this works, consider the simplest case, for example, the very small cluster on the far right of the graph, labeled "police." It is connected to the large cluster to its left that is anchored by discussions about customers—but also cashing out, greeting, discounts, and the like—by a single word: "cameras." Inside the police cluster there are just a few unique terms.

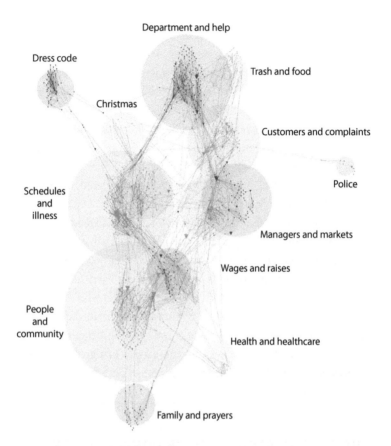

Department and help

Dress code

Trash and food

Christmas

Customers and complaints

Police

Schedules
and
illness

Managers and markets

Wages and raises

People
and
community

Health and healthcare

Family and prayers

FIGURE 6.1 The structure of the global conversation at Walmart.

Here (figure 6.2) we can see that when there is a discussion about police, it is often a conversation about how the police (or cops or police officers) arrest someone, a weird or strange guy or female.

The board is sometimes used to narrate events that happen in the store—"today a weird guy was arrested by the police"—and sometimes to discuss practical issues facing workers who may have questions about the ways in which policies work, their coverage, and so on. Focusing on what is discussed in these conversations also tells us what members of the discussion board are not thinking or talking

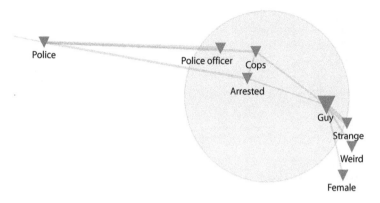

FIGURE 6.2 The police arrest weird people at Walmart.

about spontaneously. For example, linking cameras to the police makes sense; but throughout Walmart there are cameras meant both to deter shoplifting and to supervise and monitor workers. When cameras come up in the discussion, no one seems to mention how associates are being monitored as well.

There is a conversation related to schedules and illness and the likelihood of termination located on the left central side of the global graph, surrounded by a complex discussion focusing on doctors, overtime, holiday work, and pay (figure 6.3). In this conversation, we see the central role that the management team plays in coaching, and ultimately termination, an outcome linked to illness, doctors, injuries, and attendance. In the experiences of Walmart workers, getting sick and getting fired are quite closely related. Where we might see a link between this conversation about illness and doctors and the conversation about the health care provided by Walmart (indexed by the conversation about health and health-care at the bottom right), we do not see one. So the conversations about illness are stories about individuals who experience negative outcomes from illness, but these stories tend not to be linked to the macrostructures of policy or the specific characteristics of the job that lead to injury. In the spontaneous accounts of Walmart

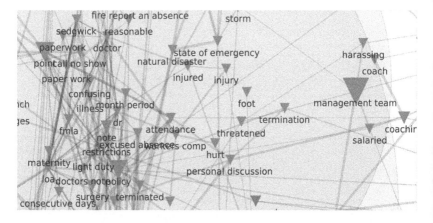

FIGURE 6.3 Getting sick and getting terminated are pretty much the same thing.

workers, then, people's individual experiences with illnesses are not systematically linked to Walmart policy.

In the global map, one can detect a strong partition between the top half of the graph and the bottom half. At the top is the world of work: the activities that one engages in, the clothes one wears or is not allowed to wear (dress code, on the left), the departments and tasks that organize the store (department and health, trash and food, on the right), the schedules and days that people work (on the left). In the center right lies the management team (managers and markets). They bridge between customers and associates. Below this middle level are conversations about the character of work at Walmart (on the left) and compensation (on the right). In the large cluster towards the bottom left (people and community) are all of the descriptions of the nature of work at Walmart. It is "great," a "good job," but also "horrible" and "unfair." Here we see the pride that workers take in their jobs, the efforts to make their work meaningful, and the frustrations they experience when their struggles to bring dignity to their jobs are blocked. This sense of identity as a worker is tied directly to the cluster on the far bottom (family and prayers) that is composed of family: husbands, wives, parents, children, and other Walmart associates.

CHANGE OVER TIME IN THE STRUCTURE OF CONVERSATION

So far we have considered the global map over the entire life course of the discussion board. But there are good reasons to suspect that it might have changed over time. The most obvious reason for change is selection into participation. In any voluntary organization, those who join first are more committed to the mission of an organization than those who join subsequently. In general, this fact leads to all sorts of suboptimal outcomes for organizations that take the form of the "small exploiting the great." In these situations, those with the greatest interest (the great) have a vision for the things that they might do. They expend their energy building the framework for those activities and for recruiting new members. Thinking that the new members are (or will be) as committed as they are, they anticipate great things for themselves. But if the new members were as committed, they would have been in the founding group already. So each wave of new members is more and more disinterested in the vision of the founders. Consider Girl Scouts. Founding parents want them to do good deeds like plant flowers in median strips or visit old people in their homes. They form a troop. The next group of parents to join care less about those goals and more about just having a place for their daughters to go once a week after school. They happily consume what the founders have provided (a troop) without contributing anything but a daughter.[27]

As the Walmart discussion board grew, the people recruited to participate became necessarily more distant from the core workers who led it. These other workers did not necessarily want a place where they could think about Walmart as a site of potential struggle;

they may have just wanted a place where they could share. If that is their project, that is what they will do. They will share about the things they care about: their kids, their successes, their anniversaries. We can assess the extent to which the discussion board loses its focus on Walmart and the opportunities for organizing there as it becomes larger and more heterogeneous.

To get a sense of change over time, we partition the posts into three equal periods. There are obvious continuities over time. Posts across all three periods discuss Walmart. They discuss the things that people do there, and they discuss the experiences that workers have there. They also focus on policies and rules and pay and managers and customers. In the main, and not surprisingly, given the nature of the board, there is significant consistency over time. At the same time, there are major structural changes.

In the first period, the dominant structural feature is a strong split between conversations that focus on dynamics inside Walmart and those that focus on life outside and the things that Walmart provides (or doesn't) to its workers. All of the things that Walmart provides to workers—bonuses, benefits, and pay—along with all of the anxieties of workers related to absences, illnesses, and termination are structurally decoupled from the world of managers and customers. OUR Walmart figures prominently in this "outside" Walmart box, which suggests that at this stage of the discussion board the organization is seen as taking up bread-and-butter issues rather than solidaristic issues that arise from within Walmart. The structure of conversation changes dramatically by the second period. An entirely new set of conversations emerges, focused on associates and their families, the things that happen to them (both bad—deaths, injuries, accidents, which give rise to condolences; and good—anniversaries, promotions, feelings of accomplishment, which give rise to congratulations and emoticons). OUR Walmart, organizing, social change—in short, the ideas that were integral to those who developed the board in the first place—are no longer present. By the third period, the structure has stabilized. The conversation clustered around family, associates, children, pride, and stress is now anchored by a self-reflexive conversation about the board itself. The dominant theme is support. The changes over time suggest that the conversations move from the instrumental to the affective realms as the group expands.

MUTUAL AID AND COLLECTIVE PURPOSE

The capacity of a labor organization to effect change at the point of production is associated with whether it can control the production line. If workers can withhold effort by working to rule or striking, they can bring a factory (or a store) to a halt and force employers to make concessions. To be able to act collectively at the point of production—to be able to ensure that collective action slows down or stops the line—workers need to be able to trust one another, to be confident that everyone will contribute equally to the collective action and not free ride on the efforts of others.

Trust arises from shared experiences, observations over long periods of time, and the capacity of organizations to provide selective incentives for participation and disincentives for free riding. We know already that the brain appears to organize relations of trust, influence, and hence the bases for collective instrumental action in pursuit of a shared goal differently than relations associated with friendship (or pure affect), and so it isn't surprising to learn that successful action at the point of production doesn't require that workers be friends with one another. Friendship and trust often overlap, but there are some reasons to think that friendship might sometimes make it more difficult to organize collectively, since it can lead to subgroup formation, and may cut across the collective commitment needed to prosecute something like a strike.

Returning to our survey of Walmart workers, we asked a series of questions about the relationships associates had with their coworkers and about their support for OUR Walmart. As we saw in chapter 2, being connected to one's customers and coworkers tends to be positively associated with how one feels about one's job. That said, different kinds of relationships with one's coworkers seem to correspond with different sorts of feelings about OUR Walmart. In general, those who reported having more friends at work tended to be less supportive of the organization; but those who reported asking their coworkers for help more often tended to be more supportive of the organization—even after controlling for things like how workers felt about their job or the kinds of hardships they faced outside of work. Now it could be that joining the organization leads workers to ask their coworkers for help. But one of the advantages of our survey is that we are able to reach workers from parts of the country that OUR Walmart has not sought to organize; and the effects hold even after controlling for whether or not one is (or has ever been) a member of the organization. These results are also supportive of the idea that workers' instrumental ties ("help") with one another are more conducive to organizing than their affective ties ("friendship").

But without active moderation, the risk of an online group is that it becomes a place of friendship at the exclusion of help, advice, and trust; that people come to the group to share funny and moving and banal things about their lives but not to cooperate. This tendency may also be facilitated by the proprietary algorithms undergirding the discussion group itself, which likely bump posts and comments that receive "likes" to the top of the group feed and downplay topics that are "downers"—like most of the difficult problems people face. In her study of Facebook and the Black Lives Matter movement, for example, Zeynep Tufekci shows how the algorithm undergirding Facebook's news feed tended to downplay early protests against the killing of Michael Brown in Ferguson and, instead, highlighted things like their friends participating in the "ice bucket challenge," the benefit for amyotrophic lateral sclerosis.[28]

The intuition behind the idea that one can use an online board to build community and induce social change is driven by the empirical evidence that such technologies allowed otherwise inchoate movements to cohere and change a national conversation (Occupy Wall

Street), or topple existing regimes (Arab Spring). And the logic of building an online movement is also impeccable. Labor struggles are most successful when labor is able exercise its structural power. The typical response of capital to large-scale movements is to elevate the struggle to a point where it has a competitive advantage. The online world provides opportunities for labor to connect across multiple stores simultaneously, invoke customer support, and broadcast ill treatment widely and quickly. In the same way that Black Lives Matter was able to use images and videos of police murder to initiate a conversation about police violence, one could imagine that similar media could change how people see Walmart management, and hence erode their confidence in the belief that the company is just a big version of a quaint little store with American values grown in rural Arkansas by a nice guy named Sam.

But as this large discussion group grew over time—as it became more heterogeneous with respect to support for OUR Walmart and as it consequently became more representative of the community of Walmart workers as a whole—the content of the discussion changed, becoming more and more about expressions of affinity or identity and less and less about purposive solidarity. Using simpler text-analytic techniques, the results of the structural analysis of topics considered earlier hold. Expressions like "we should," which connote collective projects; discussions of injustice (words like "unfair," "not fair," and "injustice"); and explicit mentions of OUR Walmart or UFCW or labor organizations in general all declined notably over time, linearly, as the number of people in the discussion group increased. Meanwhile, a whole host of other conversation topics, from pets ("my dog," "my cat") to anniversaries to birthdays to deaths increased in frequency over time. After a while, a casual glance at the board gives the impression that the participants have built a community in which they share their accomplishments and their losses and funny things that have happened at their stores and in their lives.

People left to their own devices build relational communities that are rich and supportive. We are like plants in a hothouse. But when we get all intertwined with others' emotions and aspirations, we sometimes stop wondering as much about the glass that keeps us in. The natural tendency of the group as it grew was to become a support group rather than a framework for change. As a support group, it did what support groups do, which is to make people feel good. That is easy for accomplishments like having ones' twentieth anniversary at Walmart, or getting a promotion, or passing a certification exam, or having a child, or having a relative hired by Walmart, or making a beautiful display and taking a shelfie of it. And support is also natural and appropriate when workers or stores experience losses: a worker whose relative dies of cancer or in a car accident, a worker whose home is destroyed by fire, a worker who faces an eviction that will leave her homeless.

There is, of course, potential for collective purpose to arise out of mutual aid. What this demands, though, is that someone, or some process, helps to connect the patterns in people's biographical experiences to the social structures that produced them—to help people recognize that the similarities in their experiences are not natural, not a result of unchangeable forces, but rather a result of common structural positions that, with organization, might become leverage for structural change. Take, for example, the many cases where the board is used to raise money that associates need because something went seriously wrong. The financial targets—for new furniture following a fire, for money to repair a car so someone can get to work, for someone to help a child in need—are small: $100, $300, and so on. The generosity of workers at Walmart to associates and managers from their own stores is remarkable, and this kind of mutual aid seems akin to the helping relationships that are associated with interest in becoming part of OUR Walmart.[29] But without interpretation, the crises that precipitate the need for generosity tend not to be seen in the context of the larger system of social inequality and exclusion that make them so severe, and might even reproduce them by preventing the kind of collective understanding that can surface into collective action.

EVERYTHING IN MODERATION

What OUR Walmart has learned through this process is the importance of moderation—of organizing—within such online spaces, both through the interventions of individual organizers and through the structures and rules that govern the spaces themselves.

The large, open discussion group has only one main rule, strictly enforced by the group's administrators: *Associates do not need others telling them, "if you don't like it quit," when they are venting about issues they may have at and with Walmart. This will get you removed from the group.* Outside of trolling and harassment, one can say pretty much anything in the group. But one can't use market reasoning—"It's your choice to work at Walmart, you should leave if you have problems"—to shut down others' grievances; one can't use the possibility of exit to shut down voice. The importance of this rule is affirmed by the frequency with which people violate it, trying to shut down criticisms of Walmart with some version of the banned statement.

To see the importance of moderation, we can look at the differences in the kinds of language used and conversations engaged in by OUR Walmart's online organizers within the group. Take Stacy, for example. In her posts and comments, Stacy uses very different language than the average discussion board member—she is far more likely to use injustice words and to talk about the importance of organizations like OUR Walmart. She is also far more likely than the average user to use collective action phrases like "we could" or "we should." Tagging those conversations of which she is a part, we can see that, even excluding Stacy's own comments, the conversations tend to use injustice words, organization words, and collective action phrases far more often than the discussion group as a whole. Likewise, if we look specifically at the set of users with whom Stacy is most often in conversation, these users are also using language more like hers: more injustice words, organization words, collective action phrases. These patterns are similar for several of the OUR Walmart leaders who are most central in the conversation network. Yet aside from Stacy, most of the other formal moderators of the group—those with the power to let people in and kick them out—seem less inclined or less able to organize in the online space.

Just as Terry, or the Rev, or the Pico Mighty Strikers would work within their stores to find and build subnetworks of solidarity, so, it seems, organizers like Stacy and her allies in the group were able to identify and develop people who were interested in deepening their engagement with the organization. Likewise, just as an organizer in the store might try to find a place to meet with members outside—at someone's house or at a nearby restaurant—OUR Walmart online organizers have developed a series of different, smaller discussion boards for different subnetworks of people: affinity groups (like women, veterans, people of faith); groups for people with different levels of commitment to OUR Walmart; groups divided by geographic region. Such cross-cutting groups allow associates to be in touch with one another across a range of different identities and focal concerns.

Moreover, offline and online can combine in all sorts of ways that organizers are only beginning to explore. The trick may be to find ways of mixing and matching strategies across physical and virtual space. This gives rise to a wholly new way of thinking about what mixed methods means. And it turns out that such a mixed-methods strategy works. In stores where OUR Walmart has organizational presence, the conversation online is different than in stores where OUR Walmart has been shut out. Among those workers from stores in which there is at least one member, workers are more likely to discuss injustice, more likely to discuss OUR Walmart, and more likely to discuss other associates. Workers in these stores are also more likely to discuss "friends," suggesting that affective ties may be a necessary if not sufficient condition for organization. If we look at the posts according to the number of signers in a store (rather than a simple dichotomy), we see that the more people have signed up in a store, the more likely someone is to use the phrase "we should"— a simple, though seemingly clear, signal of collective instrumental intention. Among those in stores with no organizational presence, workers are more likely to use words like "prayers," "condolences," and "for your loss"; more likely to talk about "pictures"; and more likely to say "I love my job."

This sort of analysis, of course, cannot tell us whether there is a causal relationship between organizing at the store level and the discursive patterns we find among workers from these stores. But the association is interesting either way. If there is a causal relationship (i.e., store-level organizing changes the discussion), then this suggests the importance of store-level actions in tandem with the development of the online community. Just as Occupy Wall Street and Black Lives Matter use social media to amplify and extend the reach of their offline actions, so might OUR Walmart use social media strategies to build ties among small groups of mobilized workers (like those Don and the Rev developed) to broaden their cohesion, reach, and impact. On the other hand, if this is a noncausal association (i.e., worker grievances lead both to signing up for the organization and to certain kinds of posts about unfairness), then the online community may serve a different purpose, helping organizers focus their offline activities on those people who express certain kinds of sentiments and on the stores where they work. It becomes useful as a sort of rolling barometer for where there might be enough tension to develop an offline community.

All of this should not minimize the challenge of threading together collective power out of unwieldy discussion groups; faced with almost 50,000 members, organizers like Stacy cannot frame all conversations all the time. The sheer intensity of posting means that conversations are lost almost as soon as they appear, replaced by some other topic or sentiment. And for those conversations that do get a lot of attention, like those involved in raising funds for an emergency, moderators cannot intervene and say, "Hey, guys, think about how this wouldn't have happened if you were paid a living wage." It's true, but it's not the right time or place, and it would risk "talking at them" rather than "speaking with them."

WORK IT

A problem that faces organizations seeking to use existing online infrastructure—Facebook, Twitter, other sorts of online groups—is that the platforms' algorithms privilege some kinds of content (cat videos, conflicts among celebrities, good news, celebrations) over others, because those kinds of content receive more "likes" or their equivalents (retweets, shares, stars, etc.). Because of this, the typical post that people see is privileged content, and consequently, participants learn what kinds of content they too should share. Depending on the algorithm, this kind of learning model can easily lead to vacuity. Against this background, OUR Walmart has started to design and implement online technology that might more directly address some of the problems faced by people working in low-wage jobs today—problems that labor unions have addressed in the past, like the problem of information.

Associates at Walmart, and others in big-box retail, work in a control regime we have called "Walmartism." They face an onslaught of contradictory requests from supervisors and customers and are shifted from one task to another across unpredictable schedules that limit their access to the kinds of support structures that might make their dependence on Walmart for employment less intense than it is. Walmart managers exert control over their associates in part through the discretion they have, putatively in the service of just-in-time supply chains.

The traditional power of a union contract is twofold. First, through collective bargaining, workers are able to limit managerial discretion by negotiating and formalizing aspects of the labor contract that otherwise remain unspecified and are controlled by the employer. Second, related but distinct, the contract renders transparent what is expected of employees and employers and spells out processes by which violations of these expectations can be remedied. In short, it both restricts managerial authority and makes its exercise contestable.

But even without collective representation, of course, there are formal rules—federal and state laws, as well as company policies—that govern and limit what managers may ask workers to do. At Walmart, however, not only do workers have no say over what the rules are, but they often do not know what these rules even cover. Associates are not given employee handbooks and, until very recently, have had only limited access to the online system through which such rules were made explicit. Without a contract, there are few limits to what managers can ask workers to do; without information about what these few limits are, they are difficult to enforce. And so it is almost impossible to challenge authority, even if it seems unjust.

Within the last year, OUR Walmart has designed a mobile application—WorkIt—that helps associates access information about the conditions of their employment. The answers to common questions are provided by employee "experts," in consultation with labor lawyers and others, who can tell associates what rights they actually have and what to do if these rights are violated.

The design is simple: associates download the WorkIt app, which allows them to ask questions about their jobs. If the question (or a similar question) has already been asked and answered, the application uses machine learning to provide the answer. If the question is new, then it is sent to the panel of experts for an answer. Associates can also easily scroll through a menu of different job-related topics ranging from compensation to harassment.

Since its release, thousands of associates have asked for advice, and what they ask about is instructive. If we partition the questions into three broad categories—compensation, work experience, and state and federal policies—we discover that the questions primarily concern the conditions of work. Only 25 percent of all questions relate to compensation, broadly construed. Less than 10 percent relate to formal policies and benefits at the state and federal level like family leave, heath insurance, and so on. More than 50 percent focus on what is happening at the point of production—on scheduling, harassment, what happens if they are called in for coaching, and processes of termination.

While there is obvious overlap across these broad categories, the lesson from WorkIt, much like the message from the associates we talked with, is that what matters for them, what they care about most, is what is happening on the shop floor. The associates at Walmart would surely like higher wages and better compensation. But what they seem to want even more is a coherent schedule that allows them to build a life outside Walmart, respect at work, and a clear definition of what they can expect to happen when they show up for their shift. In a nutshell, they would like more respect.

Currently, WorkIt is a one-way street—associates with questions raise those questions with experts and get information. But OUR Walmart recognizes that the WorkIt app—or apps like it—has the potential to be even more powerful. WorkIt might link workers to one another around common "questions" and concerns; it might facilitate mutual aid, from childcare exchanges to health insurance; it might even facilitate collective action by structuring "assurance contracts" that could help to overcome collective action problems.[30] Associates could potentially use an app like WorkIt to send photos of labor conditions they feel are unsafe, or forward recordings of unfair interactions for expert review.[31] Connected to an organizing campaign, an app might help leaders figure out, in real time, the issues of most importance to workers, and hence provide an entry point into conversations about how to impact these issues. And if customer allies had an app like WorkIt, they could use it to document unfair labor practices that they see or report on the issues of most concern to the workers with whom they speak.

WHAT IS POSSIBLE

The idea of moving online to match scale is powerful. The online environment provides a solution to the Walmart tactic of breaking up solidaristic work groups within each store by intimidation, scheduling, or store closures. The board also provided a solution to the isolation of workers. By connecting the experiences of workers in one Walmart with those in others, the board makes possible the identification of common problems and the diffusion, should they arise, of common solutions. Most critically, nothing stops the board from expanding its membership. And there is evidence that such boards can grow to remarkable size quickly. When they do, they can serve to organize protesters and topple regimes.

What kinds of relationships do online connections in a discussion group make possible? Some have suggested that such boards foster relationships that are asymmetric and ultimately unrewarding. Studies have linked Facebook use to depressive symptoms and suggested that this may be a result of people making social comparisons to the lives of their "friends" they see online.[32] One possibility worth entertaining is that when one looks at other people online, one may react to them like the students reacted to one another at the beginning of the summer: those who are the most popular online might elicit the most "likes" and "shares" and "retweets," because seeing them, witnessing them, feels rewarding. In which case the online community becomes another community in which inequalities are reproduced or even amplified. And that is depressing. Another possibility is that the content on such discussion boards tends toward vacuity or clusters into dense but segregated subnetworks that have a hard time speaking to one another. Either possibility might be explained by the difficulty of segregating audiences on a platform like Facebook.[33] Because Facebook forces us to be the same person across many different social roles (friend, coworker, parent, child, casual acquaintance), we only reveal the superficial parts of ourselves that are consistent across all of these roles—or limit our networks to those few people with whom we share everything. Think about the last cocktail party or school barbecue you attended. The choices seem to be mingling, and so sharing the things that happen to all humans—births, deaths, funny experiences, the weather—or standing in a corner with the one or two people with whom you feel you can be yourself.

And yet, the relationships people have online are not all that different from the relationships people have offline. Like our offline relationships, what happens depends a lot on infrastructure and leadership: the size of a group, the kind of moderation that takes place, the rules of engagement. There is nothing inherently revolutionary about the online world. But neither must it be as vacuous as a cocktail party. Given the severe challenges of scale, coupled with the intense disruption of everyday routine—in short, Walmartism—organizing online, because it can match scale and is time invariant, seems promising if done right.

7

OUR WALMART

THE FREEDOM SUMMER REUNION

The summer of 2014 marked the fiftieth anniversary of the Mississippi Freedom Summer. In late June, about halfway through our program, veterans of Freedom Summer returned to Jackson, Mississippi, for an anniversary event at Tougaloo College—a reunion, a celebration, an opportunity to take stock. Eight of the students from the Walmart project made the trip as well—two drove in from Texas, two from Ohio, and all four team members from Florida. As Greta from Florida put it, the few days were "like camp, except with radicalism and alcohol." The old heads would sing songs from the summer of 1964, most of which were unfamiliar to Greta and the other Summer for Respect participants. But if the particulars of 1964 Mississippi were lost on them, the significance of the event was not. Greta wrote that it felt as though the place *swelled and pulsed with meaning.* Veteran organizers like Bob Moses (*Eyes moving slowly and intelligently across the room. Not even a whisper of a smile on his face*) sat on panels and met in casual conversations with younger activists and organizers—those battling climate change, the corporatization of education, police brutality, and a range of other causes.

On the last day of the reunion, buses took reunion participants 20 miles north from Tougaloo to Canton, the site of a massive, nearly 6,000-person Nissan automobile factory. The factory, overwhelmingly African American, was nonunion, the result of a push among foreign car companies into the "right-to-work" Southern states of the United States. A group of workers there had been struggling to organize with the United Auto Workers since 2012. On this humid summer day, Wendy, Greta, Michael, Valerie, Diana, Alexis, Max, and Harmony all trudged through muddy grass alongside hundreds of other organizers and activists holding signs broadcasting the rally's theme: Labor Rights Are Civil Rights.

This may be true philosophically, or morally, but it is not true legally. The current, strange separation between employment law and labor law means that workers who are unfairly discriminated against or disciplined for engaging in collective action at work have almost none of the protections or remedies available to those who are discriminated against for their race, gender, age, or disability status.[1] Either way, this Mississippi rally failed to attract any attention, aside from a brief and sympathetic summary in the left-labor monthly *Labor Notes*.[2] Bernie Sanders, Danny Glover, and Nina Turner would return there for the March on Mississippi in March of 2017.[3] In August of 2017, an NLRB election was finally held: workers voted 2,244 to 1,307 against the union, an overwhelming defeat.[4]

Interestingly, each of the teams that sent delegations to Mississippi—Dallas, Ohio, and Florida—seemed to come back to New York City at the end of the summer with a sense of the importance of the work they had done and a commitment to remaining involved. The two teams that did not send delegations to the reunion—Los Angeles and Chicago—were the two teams that returned with palpable resignation and resentment. The Mississippi Freedom Summer reunion did not make any difference at all in the unionization drive at the Canton Nissan factory. But it did connect our students to generations of organizers and activists, made them feel part of a deeper and richer history, and may have helped them to interpret their own participation in the Summer for Respect project in ways that made them more resilient.[5]

TRAJECTORIES

What difference did the summer make for our students? It is, of course, impossible to know for sure whether the experience changed them and sent them onto new pathways or not. But many did tell us that their experiences that summer made a difference. Wendy, a rising senior at Brown when she joined our group, thought at the time that she would probably pursue a doctorate in American studies after graduation. That or law school. In the heat of central Florida, though, something clicked. She loved organizing; she was good at it: "I think that I've really been able to build relationships this summer. I think that was one of the big takeaways . . . When we first started, [someone] said workers will invite you to their house and sit down and make you coffee. And it happens."

As importantly, she formed relationships with other organizers who had dedicated their lives to social change work: "From school, the only people that I've seen as organizers are young people. The young, the idealistic, who have hope and still aren't jaded from the terrible things that the world can do." It had seemed to her like activism was something that people did before they got serious about their lives. But in central Florida she met "older people who have the same sparkle in their eye that 20-somethings have, that still think the world can change if people get together and stand up." She met Stacy Krier, the inspiring former Walmart worker and mother from Florida who had helped to develop the organization's online program. She met the director of central Florida's Jobs with Justice, a labor rights group with which OUR Walmart has partnered: "She's from Puerto Rico, has three beautiful kids, [and] a cool-ass husband. . . . Seeing her model what it means to be an organizer and a mother, I was like, 'Oh, shit.' She's a huge reason I thought this was a viable option for me career-wise."

So by the time Wendy graduated from college she was "bleeding green," as she puts it, a reference to OUR Walmart's colors. At the time, as discussed earlier, the organization had just had its funding pulled, and so did not have the money to hire her. Instead, staff at OUR Walmart helped her secure a job with the AFL-CIO. For the next two years she traveled around the country—Oregon, California, Alabama, Massachusetts—helping with various union election campaigns. But her heart was still with the OUR Walmart team. Finally, in the spring of 2017, OUR Walmart offered her a job. She now lives in Miami, where she coordinates OUR Walmart's Florida chapter, facilitates the organization's national Latino outreach, and works closely with other Florida labor leaders.

Among the students in the Summer for Respect project, those, like Wendy, from the Florida team—who had sufficient autonomy to be creative, who worked closely with a group of passionate OUR Walmart worker-organizers, who attended the Freedom Summer reunion—have remained most involved in the labor movement. Michael, for example, had just graduated from college at the time of the Summer for Respect project. After the summer, he became an organizer supporting the Coalition of Immokalee Workers, a remarkable farmworker center based in southern Florida.

Of course, it could be that the students from Florida had always been the most committed to the labor movement and that this commitment explains both their creativity and resilience in Florida and their continuing involvement since. Ideally one would want to send identical people to different sites and see if these differences launched them on different trajectories.

Beth and Greta were not identical by any means, but in our group of 20 they were as close as we can get. Both Barnard students, they had been best friends since before the Summer for Respect. They pleaded to be placed together in Chicago, but because no one wanted to be in central Florida in July and we needed someone to go, we sent Greta to Orlando, while Beth—whose story was told in the introduction—joined the Chicago team. Throughout the summer, they stayed in constant communication by text, by phone, by email. But they had radically different experiences in the field, and while their close friendship has endured, their conceptions of political action seem to have diverged.

Beth came back from the field feeling disillusioned with the labor movement. Remember, many members of the Chicago team felt like the UFCW, which staffed OUR Walmart in Chicago, was "just a corporation too," felt like the organization was using workers and their stories, felt like their supervisors were sleazy and the labor movement was insufficiently radical. Beth remembers how she and Jordan, a teammate, would reinforce one another's cynicism: *It was not easy to do the work when every time we went to a store we asked each other if the minuscule victories the organization won actually outweighed all its deep flaws. It might have felt like support at the time, in a city where I knew no one at a hotel next to an airport, but in the end I think he did more to break down my faith in organizing than he did to support me or the movement.* Her friendship with Jordan provided support, but it undermined their capacity to get anything done. On her return to campus, Beth turned her energies away from labor, and instead devoted herself to an organization called No Red Tape, which was at the time battling Columbia's administration over its response to campus sexual assault. She did not abandon social justice altogether, but her activism gravitated back toward the sort of activism she had done in high school—confronting an academic administration on its seeming hypocrisy around issues of gender and sexuality.

Greta, who had been sent to central Florida—a place she described as "no-man's-land," where "people aren't attached to that sense of place that you might find somewhere else"—was able, ironically, to find a sense of community there. Her team was given the combination of space and support to grow, experiment, and fail. Alongside their supervisors, a small group of women who had all worked at Walmart, the four members of the Florida team felt like they were part of the movement. And she was able to feel this way despite the fact that Walmart had an injunction out in Florida, making it almost impossible for the team to find workers with whom to speak.

Greta came back to Barnard in the fall in a different place from Beth. She participated in No Red Tape too, but she kept one foot in the world of labor organizing. In October of 2014 she was one of 26 people arrested for civil disobedience outside of Alice Walton's apartment in New York City.[6] During the spring of 2015 she organized a contingent of Columbia and Barnard students to march with SEIU's Fight for $15 campaign. She got involved in an effort on campus to raise student wages to $15 and helped support adjunct faculty's efforts to unionize. And in the summer of 2016 she volunteered to help conduct some field experiments at Walmart stores on Long Island, waking up several mornings at 5 A.M. (on top of her summer job) to walk the aisles. Greta and Beth talk all the time; they share many of the same critiques of organized labor. For Beth, these became reasons for exiting the labor movement; for Greta, reasons for staying involved and trying to change it. Greta and Beth each graduated from Barnard in May of 2017. Greta took a job organizing workers as part of Fast Food Justice, a new nonprofit associated with SEIU. Beth works at the New York Center for Interpersonal Development, where she focuses on issues of restorative justice. She remains committed to social justice, but is no longer interested in the labor movement.

What about the others? Many have stayed connected to issues of social justice, though few remain as directly involved in the labor movement as those from the Florida team. Rebecca, from the Chicago team, now organizes within poor and working-class Asian immigrant communities in New York City. Max, from the Ohio team, worked as a community organizer in Brooklyn for a year, and now organizes around issues of racial justice in New Haven, Connecticut.

Kevin, the participant who brought in the biggest numbers for OUR Walmart, learned over the course of the summer that he was good at organizing things and talking to people. He now manages a complex survey project at Columbia, talking to white people about their identities. A natural recruiter, he gets people to want to join his study, even if the topic—especially right now—is freighted and makes them anxious. He, too, is out of the labor movement, and like several of the other Summer for Respect students is heading off to, or is seriously thinking about, attending graduate school. Others are on paths that appear to have little to do with their experiences during the summer of 2014: freelance writing, dancing, teaching, filmmaking.

Still, more than three years after the Summer for Respect program—which lasted only nine weeks over one summer, during a period in life when careers and life goals are up for grabs—about half remain involved in social movement work, and at least three have remained involved in labor organizing. The rest have been able to translate their experience into an interpretable line on their résumés.

ONE REASON WHY UNIONS MATTER

The unionization campaign at the Nissan auto plant in Mississippi failed, dramatically, three years after the Freedom Summer reunion. Many factors contributed to the UAW's loss. The company held the standard captive audience meetings and one-on-ones with its employees and made the standard threats about plant closings and people losing their jobs should strikes take place.[7] It played anti-UAW videos on a loop in employee break rooms and promised raises and discounted rates on car purchases that would be withdrawn in the event of unionization.[8] It also accused the union of "seeking to buy support in the African-American community" through its contributions to local community organizations.[9] The local and national business communities weighed in against the union as well, as did Republican governor Phil Bryant who said, the week before the vote, "If you want to take away your job, if you want to end manufacturing as we know it in Mississippi, just start expanding unions."[10]

Still, as we argued earlier, employer coercion and intimidation were far worse in historical periods during which unions were growing more rapidly, and so Nissan's threats seem incomplete as an explanation for union failure. One union leader, trying to make sense of the Canton loss, acknowledged this implicitly when he said: "The UAW was born when 'scare tactics and intimidation' meant goon squads beating union activists, company spies infesting plants and workers being fired at any sign of supporting the union."[11]

The UAW certainly bears some responsibility for the loss. The week before the election, a former Fiat Chrysler labor relations official was indicted for allegedly diverting millions of dollars from a joint UAW-Chrysler training facility to enrich himself and another UAW official.[12] The Canton loss, at least, was less embarrassing than the UAW's loss at a Volkswagen plant in Chattannooga, Tennessee, in 2014, when Volkswagen actually encouraged workers to vote for the union and it still went down.[13]

The *Times* reporter covering the Canton story argued that, ultimately, "basic economics combined with a fear of change may have carried the day."[14] But maybe the most important factor was the absence of workers' experience with unions. Where unionization rates have always been extremely low, as they have been in the South, very few people have any experience with what being in a union means—in terms of security, wages, and having a voice at work. Few people know someone who is in a union, and so they cannot talk about that experience with the people they trust. It is no wonder, then, that Nissan officials could so successfully paint the UAW in one-dimensional terms as a parasitic organization seeking to garner dues without providing anything in return. If one has never been in a union, and if no one knows anyone in a union, understanding the benefits of unionization is just about impossible.

This situation—most intense in the South, where most people do not know someone who works in a union shop—is increasingly common nationwide. Between the founding of OUR Walmart in 2010 and today, the percentage of private-sector workers belonging to labor unions declined from 6.9 percent to 6.5 percent.[15] This ongoing decline may not seem like the most pressing of our problems, especially in light of the range of existential threats posed (at this writing) by the Trump administration, but one of the ideas we hope to have communicated throughout this book is that our current political moment may not be entirely disconnected from the current state of low-wage work and the decline of the labor movement.

Here is one way to think about it: In our survey of Walmart workers, 43 percent reported that they did not vote in the 2012 presidential election. Of those who voted, only 28.9 percent voted for Mitt Romney, while 55.5 percent voted for Obama (15.6 percent of the vote went to other candidates). For every Romney vote there were close to two workers who voted for Obama. The 2016 election was markedly different. As in 2012, the plurality of workers (39 percent) did not vote. But the majority of those who did vote (51.1 percent) cast their ballots for Trump. Clinton support was at 34.9 percent, with 14 percent voting for some other candidate.

It is worth considering that there are approximately 29,000 people who work for Walmart today in Michigan. Assuming, conservatively, a 40 percent annual turnover rate, this means that there were around 75,000 people who worked at a Walmart in Michigan at some point between 2012 and 2016. Trump won the state by a little less than 11,000 votes. If these 75,000 Michigan Walmart workers voted in 2016 the way they had voted in 2012, Clinton would have won the state by more than 20,000 votes. Using the same set of assumptions, she would have won Wisconsin and Florida too, and so would have won the election.

Among the members of OUR Walmart who took our survey, the percentage voting Republican in 2012 and 2016 was basically unchanged (and small in each year). Granted, OUR Walmart members are a self-selecting group—it would be difficult to prove that the organization influenced workers' votes. But if the organization *did* influence workers' votes, this would be consistent with accounts like that of Harold Meyerson, who analyzed exit polls after the 2010 midterm elections. He found that whites without a college degree in nonunion households voted 68–31 for Republican House candidates, while those who belonged to a union (or lived with someone who did) voted 55–43 for Democrats. He concludes, "It's not because unionized UPS drivers and nonunion FedEx drivers, say, are two different species of human. It's because the unions' political education and mobilization programs are very effective."[16] At their best, unions have been schools of democracy, in which workers become better-informed citizens and civic leaders. And so even those who do not care so much about making workers' lives better for their own sakes ought to care about these workers for the future of our country and our world.

IN SOME WAYS, EVERYTHING IS ABOUT SOCIAL TIES AND SOCIAL CHANGE

Broadly, everything we have touched on in this book has been about the relationship between social ties and social change. Making sense of when social ties reproduce the social world, and the conditions under which they help to change it, has been one of our primary concerns. But because real people in real situations make things happen, we needed to understand who was at Walmart, what they were doing there, and what working at Walmart meant to them. Thinking about the people at Walmart was the subject of chapter 1. If we had a prior idea about who worked at Walmart, it was highly stereotyped. One of the things that we learned is that there is no typical Walmart worker.

For many people, Walmart is a new home, a place where they can find friends and build community. For them, the family that they found at Walmart was, like all families, full of problems. But for many of them, the problems at Walmart were less harmful psychologically and physically than the problems that they had left behind. Others were just hanging out for the time being. When the choice was between working at Walmart and making a few bucks or sitting on a front porch watching nothing happen, Walmart looked pretty good. Different histories and motivations and orientations meant that fighting for higher wages was not necessarily at the front of everyone's mind. And so pushing forward into uncertainty is tough.

It's tough too, because people everywhere work with what they have to claim a little bit of dignity and freedom. In chapter 2 we confronted the fact that we cannot explain Walmart workers' relative silence only in relationship to lousy alternatives. There, we argued that associates at Walmart find and develop and try to nurture pockets of autonomy in which they are able to exercise a sense of creativity. And they don't do this alone. Because associates form friendships with one another and members of their community and because they are in it together, those relationships start to feel, on an everyday level, like an expression of a positive decision to stay—if not for themselves, then for their friends. These shared friendships could provide a structure for collective action, but they don't do so naturally. In chapter 5, we talked about why friendship, versus other kinds of instrumental relations, is a weak foundation upon which to build a movement.

So what does make associates feel a sense of indignity and injustice? The arbitrary authority of managers is often most salient in workers' experiences. But this arbitrary authority is only one part of the regime of shop floor control that workers at Walmart face, and which is the focus of chapter 3. What we call Walmartism combines the arbitrary authority of managers with a deeply penetrative system of observation and measurement assembled by linking cameras to scanners to customers. Other elements of Walmartism— a scheduling system that forces associates to absorb the tremendous fluctuations in consumer demand and simultaneously reduces the extent to which they can form relationships with one another; broader social changes that make it more difficult to survive outside this low-wage labor market—are also central.

It is hard to underestimate the role of customers for Walmartism. Of course, customers induce problems in any server system, which makes work less predictable and the margin for managerial discretion wider, but they also serve as proxies for managers, if only because they blame workers for organizational failures, particularly within the low-end service sector.

Collective action tends not to arise out of the ether. It demands that someone organize it. In this book we have focused on when organizing works. Most simply, we find, action is possible when organizers create relationships among workers that tie workers' understandings of their self-interest—broadly conceived—to interests in a collective. Particularly when the benefits to collective action cannot be restricted to those who have acted, organizing is necessarily reliant on collective effervescence more than on the promise of individual payoffs. This is even more the case among low-wage service-sector workers, who are looking for interpersonal respect as much as or more than they are looking for raises. And yet existing labor unions are problematic vehicles for such transcendence.

Against this background, the problem for OUR Walmart is and remains one of scale. Faced with intensive opposition to organizing on the shop floor, the organization regrouped online and developed a large constituency of workers who discuss all aspects of their work and lives. We evaluate the possibilities and perils of the move online through a text analysis of the discussion board. Here, again, we argue that friendship and trust are two distinct forms of relationship. We see the potential of community and solidarity in the move online, but also the danger that, without intensive moderation, it becomes a place of friendship at the expense of help, advice, trust.

IDEAS THAT WORKED AND IDEAS THAT DIDN'T WORK

We started this project with three orienting ideas. First, we had the idea that 20 students could make a difference to a social movement to recruit and organize Walmart workers. Second, we had the idea that students could make that difference in part by conducting interviews. We imagined that the interviews could be a lever by which people, by virtue of thinking about their lives as they unfolded, the processes by which they became workers at Walmart, could start to develop sociological imaginations. Third, we thought that we might learn the answer to an important question about influence and selection with respect to social justice–oriented engagement. With respect to the students, that question was simply: Do the experiences that people have, such as participating in the Summer for Respect (or joining the Peace Corps, or something else), change people, or are they already different, and do those differences lead them to join in the first place? We thought we could get to the answer for this question in part by scanning the students' brains before and after the project. And we thought this was an important question, because it goes to the heart of organizing for change—do the experiences people have with others working collectively change them, and if so, how?

As it turned out, two of those initial ideas were wrong. First, 20 students cannot jumpstart the labor movement in any meaningful way. Second, interviewing does not seem to be able to trigger the emergence of sociological imagination. On the third question we made some progress: we cannot precisely say whether experience or selection matters in terms of the vague set of outcomes we had in mind when we started, but we have some new thoughts about why programs may influence people. And we have some evidence that our program influenced the pathways of many of our students.

We also learned something equally important. As shown in the appendix, we may be able to identify the neural bases of social solidarity as it arises in groups. And we think that this fact makes sense of a cluster of other things we—and others who have studied movement participation—have observed. The most important of these facts is that one does not get activist engagement from friendship. One gets it from trust and influence. That there is an overlap between friends and people you trust and people whose influence matters is certain, but the overlap is not complete. There are many people we trust who are not our friends, and all of us have friends that we know—deep down—can't be trusted. The limits of friendship for organizing for change have implications for the mechanisms that groups use to build community. This may be the most important lesson for the discussion board as a strategy to build online communities that can be harnessed to act in the tangible world. The translation from the routinized expression of friendship and ritual support to acting cohesively in the face of opposition is not an easy one to make.[17]

We also learned a bunch of things that we did not expect. Strangely, we had not really thought about the lived experiences of Walmart workers when we set out to help OUR Walmart organize them. And we had not really thought about what happens on the shop floor—what those workers are doing in the context of their work. In this regard, we were like stereotypical old-school union organizers, believing that class positions map easily and automatically onto worker dispositions.

Nor had we thought deeply about how retail work and other low-wage work like it makes organizing along traditional lines immensely difficult. We knew, of course, that scale issues were very challenging, but we had not thought about the absence of a production line, flex scheduling, customer surveillance, or the role of the easy exit. We knew from our own experience that community matters, but we hadn't abstracted from that to understand that it mattered at Walmart, thinking—like most people—that bread-and-butter issues predominate for low-income workers. Of course, bread-and-butter issues matter immensely; it is the absence of resources that creates the vicious cycles that make stability so difficult and reproduce the conditions for inequality. But behind those processes we hadn't really seen how important creativity, community, recognition and respect were at places like Walmart. At Walmart we rediscovered the importance of community. We learned something about why labor movements succeed and why they fail. We got some ideas for how to move the labor movement along in the context of the transformation of work of which Walmart represents the leading edge. We hope you did too.

AND ANTHONY AND HIS COWORKERS?

When we last met Anthony, the young man with whom we began this book, he had already left Walmart and was working at Enterprise Rent-A-Car. As of this writing, Anthony has left Enterprise and drives a city bus around the South Side of Chicago on the night shift. His starting pay with the Chicago Transportation Authority was $21.33 an hour, the equivalent of about $45,000 a year. He expects to make as much as $70,000 as he gains seniority in the organization over the next five years, and he is in line for a great pension. He has a union.

Anthony's involvement in our project, he tells us, has made him consider going to college, where he would like to study law. But he knows the job he has is hard to come by, that there are thousands of people in line for it, and that even with a college degree he might not make as much as he is making now. So he is conflicted. He would like his work to feel more meaningful than it does right now, but his situation is more stable now than it's ever been, and it's hard to give that up.

The Pico Mighty Strikers we met in chapter 4 are no longer working at Walmart. When the company reopened the store, they were not offered their previous positions. Sandra, sadly, passed away in the summer of 2016. Dora and Michelle continued their involvement in OUR Walmart for years after they stopped working for Walmart, but neither remains involved today.

Gerald, the "old head" worker leader in the photo shop in Franklin, still works at Walmart. In the fall of 2014, he played a key role in suppressing a potential labor action at his store. The local OUR Walmart organizer, Robert, had planned for a one-day strike at the store that November—part of a wave of coordinated actions. Robert had most of the women on board and ready to walk when Gerald began to argue that they would all get fired if they struck. Despite Robert's assurances that this was not going to happen, Gerald convinced the women to back down, and the strike did not take place.

Stacy continues to work on the staff of OUR Walmart, which—after having its support cut by the UFCW in 2014—has grown from a skeleton group of three volunteers to nearly 16 paid staff in the last three years. Since the summer of 2014 she had been "screaming Wendy's name," hoping to convince Wendy—one of our students—to move to Florida so that the site, "my baby," could be in good hands. Needless to say, she and Wendy remain close.

Finally, Ann Regnerus, the woman who thought that all her coworkers had Stockholm syndrome and who railed against the condescension of the welfare office, worked for Walmart for just over four years in total, where she served in a variety of different departments, created displays, filled shelves with merchandise, and learned how to operate pallet jacks and cardboard balers. She now works in a job placement and career development center where she provides clients with help in developing their resumes, navigating employment listings, and promoting their skills to employers.

Three years after we were in the field, the vast majority of associates at Walmart that we met and talked with and whose struggles and hopes and achievements motivated this book had left Walmart and moved on to something else. They have been replaced by others.

APPENDIX

THE NEURAL SIGNATURES
OF GROUP LIFE

Throughout chapter 5 we discussed the different roles played by friendship and trust in an organizing campaign. Many of the conclusions we reached, but not all, are familiar to organizers themselves, who have often had an inchoate sense that it mattered less that one was a friend of a potential member than if that potential member was able to trust one to have his or her interests at heart. While friendship often invokes such trust, it carries with it a range of other expectations that are difficult for an organizer to meet—perhaps the most obvious of which are demands for time spent, dining, hanging out, and so on. Organizers don't have this kind of time available, as a general rule. And yet, at the same time, they are trying to bring about and induce a communal experience defined by a shared focus and orientation to the project of social change. To achieve that shared experience, people have to come to see themselves in a new light, as active members of a self-conscious community of similarly situated people with similar aims. They have to see themselves as sharing a project. New selves emerge out of new interactions with others, out of new social structures.

Generations of sociologists have argued that there must be some set of processes by which social structure finds its way into our ways of seeing and acting. Social structures are not just things outside us that we must navigate; they become us, shaping us and shaping the ways we see and relate to others. The internalization of structures is expressed in lots of different ways. By Pierre Bourdieu it is described as "habitus," which gives rise to the kinds of embodiments that characterize his description of peasant men as men who cannot dance in *The Bachelors' Ball*; by Richard Sennett and Jonathan Cobb, in *The Hidden Injuries of Class*, it is the set of beliefs and feelings that underwrite a class society by leading to actions that voluntarily reproduce it—like the self-blame and resignation that accompany one's inability to advance in a nominally meritocratic job market. Michael Burawoy, in *Manufacturing Consent*, and Nancy Chodorow, in *The Reproduction of Mothering*, observe how microinteractions—on the shop floor and in the home—reproduce class and gender relations, respectively, by way of the embodied understandings that such interactions produce.[1] In all of these cases, larger social structures—divisions between rural and urban, rich and poor, men and women—are seen to be reinforced and reproduced through embodied dispositions, beliefs, and feelings that emerge from our membership in such structures.

The premise that structures get into us is one that many sociologists take for granted. It is clearly right. But at the same time it is mysterious. Perhaps the particular causal mechanism doesn't matter; the outcome—the reproduction of social structure—is what we care about. And yet reproduction is not the only outcome. Sometimes people have understandings of themselves and others that generate social change. Organizing is about inducing that kind of realignment of self and other. And this means that the mechanisms by which structure gets into us might also contain the foundations for how change takes place. Therefore, it may matter how social structure gets inside us.

There are some hints to the puzzle of how it happens in the microstructures that arise—seemingly naturally—when people get together. For example, we know that humans create and navigate social structures, and we know that we do so in somewhat predictable ways. Status hierarchies emerge among people across all human groups, even if people start off with the best of intentions (like commune adherents, or social activist–oriented millennials).[2] We also know that there are basic relational building blocks out of which social structures tend to emerge: like the fact that we tend to like people who like us (dyadic affective reciprocity), or the fact that we tend to dislike the enemies of our friends and like the friends of our friends (balance).[3] Our idea is that these processes are the foundations for both social change and social reproduction.

Despite much theorizing about the instantiation of social structure in our perceptions, we know very little about how it happens. Perception is something that happens in our bodies, and mostly in our brains, which makes it somewhat foreign for sociologists. Nevertheless, if we care about how social structures reproduce themselves through individuals' perceptions and the conditions under which such structures might be unsettled, then it makes sense to try to see what is happening in our brains when we see and respond to social structure. That is what we tried to do when we embarked on using fMRI scans to understand the formation of social structure among the OUR Walmart volunteer students. In this appendix we introduce the results of those studies; both because they motivate the conclusions in chapter 5 (as already indicated) and because they are intrinsically interesting.

SOCIALIZING SOCIAL COGNITIVE NEUROSCIENCE

Back in late May 2014, while the students were still getting to know one another, most had agreed to climb into an fMRI scanner so we could look at their brains while they looked at one another and looked at themselves.[4] In early August, they went back into the scanner so we could see if and how their reactions to themselves and one another had changed. This time, physically and emotionally exhausted from the field, many of them fell asleep in the machine— this in spite of the deafening racket and constant stimuli.

How the brain works is mysterious but not a complete mystery. We know from people who have suffered traumatic brain injuries— where some part of their brain is removed or damaged—that differ- ent areas of the brain are responsible for our different capacities. For example, from one famous patient, H.M, we know that if we remove the hippocampus, the amygdala, and the entorhinal cortex, it is completely impossible for a person to store memories.[5] We know that people who lose their left superior temporal gyrus can't understand any language. And that those who lose their left inferior temporal gyrus can't say anything, even if they understand what is being said to them. So, we know what parts of the brain are required for memories, language reception, and language expression.[6]

Neuroscientists have also begun to think about the neurological underpinnings of social life, although here there is much more work to be done. We can now identify, at least generally speaking, the parts of the brain that are associated with self-recognition and self-reflection, as well as those parts of the brain that link us to others. We are beginning to understand, at the neurological level, the ways in which we rely on conceptions of self to under- stand those close to us, and—reciprocally—how our understandings of ourselves are influenced by what we think others think about us. And we can see some evidence that there are the neural path- ways by which inequalities in the social world get internalized—for example, the amygdala seems to be a neural correlate of implicit negative bias; and the dorsal anterior cingulate cortex is activated during the experience of social exclusion or loss.[7]

Current social cognitive neuroscience is, however, starkly lim- ited with respect to understanding the ways that the complex social worlds in which we live are shaped by and shape our neural responses to others, mainly because its standard research para- digm is completely asocial. The usual fMRI study oriented toward understanding how people respond to others puts the research subjects in a scanner and then subjects them to a "treatment," typically a highly stylized stimulus on a single dimension that is interesting to the researcher—for example, gender, or race, or age.[8] So, for example, one might wonder: Do our brains respond differently to older people than younger people? Neuroscientists "test" this idea by showing pictures of an old person and then a young person to someone while he or she is in the scanner. It turns out that our brains do respond differently to these kinds of abstract stimuli, at least sometimes. And yet, these kinds of abstract stimuli may not have anything to do with actual social processes. The motivation behind these kinds of research designs is the idea that by putting research subjects into purified environments one can more precisely estimate the effect of the treatment. If people lived in vacuum tubes, this kind of research project would make sense. But we don't.

We are interested in the same problem that the social cognitive neuroscientists are interested in—Can we identify the neural signatures of relationships? Are there neural processes that lead inexorably to inequality? Are there neural bases to social solidarity, to mutual attraction or distaste for other? But rather than abstract away from people's lived experiences of specific social relationships to answer these questions, we wanted to make sense of this specificity. Could the fMRI data that we collected at the beginning of the program help us understand how a group of actual people with actual relationships evolves over time? Could it help us understand how people see themselves, and those with whom they are interacting, and how this changes as relationships deepen? Would it help us understand resilience in the face of opposition and hardship?

We believed that we could learn the answers, or at least preliminary answers, to these questions, although to do so we would have to model face-to-face social networks as they evolved over time in the minds of our students. That required building a platform to see how our students saw themselves, and everyone else in their group.[9] To see the activity in our students' brains when they saw images of themselves or other group members, we needed to get the students into scanners. That turned out to be a good idea, independent of the science. It built community, and it indicated to the students just how unusual the project they were engaged in was. After all, no other internships are designed to capture the experiences of the interns as they unfold. The fMRI scanning helped convince everyone that whatever was going to happen would be interesting.

The students were both the target stimuli presented during the scan and the perceivers that viewed other stimuli. In other words, each participant in the scanner looked at repeated images of the other participants in the project, images of themselves, images of us, and images of a morphed or "ghost face" (as a control). While inside the scanner, they performed a simple cover task to maintain alertness (which worked during the first wave better than the second wave, when several fell asleep)—they were instructed to press a button with their pointer fingers each time a group member's face was presented and a different button with their ring fingers each time a "ghost face" was presented. We complemented this neurological data with more standard social network techniques. We asked students—at the beginning of the project, in the middle of the summer, and a few months after the project ended—how they felt about one another, and how they thought others felt about them, on a number of different dimensions. This meant that we were able to see how patterns of neural activation were related to patterns of reported affiliation.

INSIDE OUR BRAINS

Now we need to take a little detour into neuroscience to understand what gets measured in the brain and why we bother to measure it. What we see in an MRI study is the trace of brain activity. When the neurons in our brain are activated, when they are firing, blood flow increases to the regions where they are located. The MRI measures this increase in blood flow and by association allows us to infer that nearby neurons are active. In an fMRI, everything about the mechanics of an MRI stays the same. The "f" stands for functional, and the idea behind the fMRI is that by giving the brain things to respond to—stimuli of different kinds—we can detect where the neurons dealing with that stimuli are activated. We can look at activation, captured by blood flow, at the voxel level. A voxel sounds like it describes an animal like a hamster or ferret, but it is actually a place in a three-dimensional grid, like a pixel on a bitmap, or a location in a house. Say you are reading this while sitting on your couch, in your living room, in your house or apartment. If your apartment is your brain, we capture you on the couch (well, actually, just elevated a bit off the floor) in the region of your apartment that is the living room. There are over 100 billion (100,000,000,000) neurons in our brains on average. We have resolution at 160,000 voxels, so from one perspective, our data are not very granular: each of our locations "holds" around 600,000 neurons.

Because voxels are in space, they naturally aggregate up to regions with names, and there is a lot of neuroscientific data about what kinds of mental processes these regions represent. When it comes to the question of reading social structure, previous research points us to two different regions of greatest interest. The first is the ventromedial prefrontal cortex, the amygdala, and the ventral striatum, henceforth discussed collectively as the "valuation system." These are parts of the brain that are consistently implicated in processing the affective value and motivational significance of various stimuli, including other people. The second comprises the dorsomedial prefrontal cortex, temporoparietal junction, and precuneus. These interconnected regions are consistently activated in neuroimaging studies involving judgments about others' psychological characteristics, mental states, and intentions or the passive viewing of social stimuli—such as familiar faces—for which we might spontaneously make such attributions. There are lots of good reasons to suspect that the set of activities involved in theory of mind are taking place in and at the intersection of these regions.

For all of our work, we study these regions specifically, and for the work that we will discuss here, we focus most on the valuation region. A lot of others have worked on this region as well, and we know from their work that this is an area that is activated (lights up, colloquially) when people are presented with opportunities to earn money, and when, for example, primates have a chance to earn juice or bananas.[10] We think prizes, money, juice, and bananas are important, but our guess is that this part of the human brain evolved to solve important real-world problems that confront members of social groups: Who likes me? Who is important in this group? Who do other people/primates treat as important? Who should I look up to? And if solving these kinds of social navigation problems are important, we would solve them with the same system that tells us that juice is good—that is, our neural response would help us orient attention and focus on people whose actions are potentially rewarding so that we could then call up to consciousness what they might be up to, what they might be thinking about us, and so on.

AT FIRST, POPULARITY MATTERED, BUT ONLY AT FIRST

We have done this kind of experiment with a variety of groups, and in other settings we have been able to trace the neural signature of social status. Simply put, when one looks at someone who is of high status in a group, the valuation system is activated, even after netting out how much one likes that high-status person. In these other contexts, we have shown that this valuation activity seems also to lead to increased activity in regions of the brain related to social cognition.[11] People see high-status others as having motivational significance for them (valuation), and so they work harder to try to understand those high-status others' emotional states (social cognition). At the beginning of the summer we saw a similar pattern among the OUR Walmart students—those students who were more popular among their peers, whether they liked them or not, elicited more reward region activation than did the less popular.

Popularity mattered for neural activation before the project really got underway, in those first few days when students were meeting one another, making speeches, describing their aspirations, and introducing their motivations for joining the project. What is fascinating is that by the end of the summer, popularity was no longer related to activation of the reward system. Something happened over the summer, and whatever that was, it changed the social structure. The neural mechanism undergirding inequality in the group—what seemed to us to be a basic human characteristic—gave way to a much more nuanced response to group members, and in its wake a more supple form of social solidarity.

RECIPROCITY IS A SUPPLE FORM OF SOCIAL SOLIDARITY

Relationships among the Summer for Respect students evolved over time. One thing we discovered, based on the social network surveys alone, was that sociometric status—or popularity—explained a declining percentage of people's individual liking over time. In other words, the amount of variation in people's liking that was explained by targets' overall popularity declined sharply over the course of the summer. Relationships became more idiosyncratic, more individuated, determined less by group status and more by the specifics of people's relationships with one another.

We also discovered something else. The valuation activity in a perceiver's brain, what we might call implicit liking, when he or she looked at a target at the beginning of the summer was statistically unrelated to how much that perceiver reported liking—what we call explicit liking—that target at the time. But implicit liking at the beginning of the project was significantly associated with how much the perceiver explicitly reported liking the target months after the end of the project, even when controlling for how much the perceiver explicitly liked the target earlier. In other words, we discovered that we can predict explicit liking in the future based on implicit neural activation in the valuation region months earlier. One's brain knows who one is going to like and who is going to like oneself in the future.

The simplest explanation for affective reciprocity at the end of the program is that people who like each other at the start of the program like each other at the end, and vice versa. But that is not what is going on. All of our findings control for the effect of initial liking on later liking. Equally interesting, the students really did change their opinions about their peers the more they got to know them. In some cases, they liked each other a lot more, and in some cases, they really came to dislike each other. Continuity in explicit liking is not the mechanism for the increase in reciprocity that we observe.

What does the emergence of dyadic affective reciprocity have to do with the broader issues with which we are concerned in this book? What we observed among the students over the course of the summer is a movement from a version of mechanical solidarity, a solidarity based on common beliefs, to one of organic solidarity, a solidarity based on complementary differences. At the beginning of the summer, our students' perceptions of one another were driven largely by others' perceptions—a person's valuation region was activated when he or she looked at those who were popular among others, regardless of how much that student liked those popular people. By the end of the summer, the relationships among the students had deepened and differentiated; people's orientations toward one another were driven less by group-level status and more by the complementarities of their experiences with one another.

Reciprocity is one of the most basic building blocks of human cooperation.[12] Dyadic reciprocity generates group-level cooperation and cohesion in experimental and nonexperimental settings, in some cases more so than explicit group identity.[13] And this tendency toward reciprocity, or symmetry, in affective exchange is a mechanism that often works against the emergence (or reproduction) of hierarchy in those exchanges. This is true on an intuitive level—reciprocity, doing unto others as they do unto you—seems a plausible basis for interpersonal equality. But it may also be true at a broader, more systemic level as well. Affective reciprocity—at least how it is defined here, as mutual liking (or disliking)—is in some sense the opposite of domination; and as a human inclination it seems to run just as deep.

At the beginning of the summer, the students' brains were attuned to one another in ways that seemed likely to reproduce inequality among them—they were rewarded most when they looked at those most sociometrically popular. But what predicted the students' ultimate feelings about one another were the unique (or idiosyncratic) signals they were giving and receiving, which allowed the emergence of a community built around reciprocal dyads.

Interestingly, we recall thinking during those last days in August that maybe what we were seeing in the sweltering basement offices of INCITE was not just emotional exhaustion and release (although there was plenty of that), but the emergence of a stronger collective identity among the students. It would take a few more months for us to collect the data that supported that idea, but it turns out to be the case.

TRUSTING AND LIKING AND OTHER RELATIONSHIPS

"Liking" isn't the only relationship we have with others. And what it means to like someone is not as fixed as one might think. We used "liking" as a measure of how people felt about one another because other scholars have used this measure too and because most people think they know what it means. They do, but they don't necessarily share the same beliefs about what kinds of characteristics undergird it. That is because liking is context specific.

Imagine asking undergraduates how they felt about one another along a number of different dimensions and then asking the same questions to students at an elite professional school, for example, a business school at an elite northeastern university. For social justice–oriented undergraduates, "liking" was highly correlated with thinking that the person they were asked about liked them. Liking for these students was most strongly negatively associated with considering someone "shallow" and "carefree." In contrast, within the professional school groups, liking was most strongly associated with thinking someone was competent; and it was most strongly negatively associated with considering someone needy. Liking can mean strikingly different things in different social contexts.

Here is another surprising thing we learned from scanning the brains of the Summer for Respect participants: the brain itself seems to organize our responses to others around this distinction. The brain regions that are activated when we look at someone that we trust are the same regions that light up when we look at someone we help or we think we influence. In turn, the regions that are activated when we look at someone with whom we gossip are the same that are engaged when we look at someone with whom we get along or hang out. Our instrumental and affective orientations to others seem to have distinct neural correlates. Our brains organize relations in such a way as to keep largely distinct those relations in which we engage to achieve an external (shared or unshared) goal, and those which are ends in themselves.[16] This discovery provided the useful clue for organizing, which we discuss in chapter 5—namely, that it is far less important for the organizer to be a friend of those he or she organizes than to be trusted by them.

The new idea here is that there is a neural foundation to the distinction between affective and instrumental relations. Organizers have long thought this, albeit in much less academic language. Why does it matter? Well, for the reasons we embarked on this project: to figure out how people might change the social circumstances in which they live. The distinction we've discovered at the neural level supports the organizer's intuition that friendship and cooperation are different kinds of relations. And it is cooperation, rather than friendship, that, under the right conditions, can lead to social change.

NOTES

INTRODUCTION: THE REAL, REAL WALMART

1. A note on quotation practice: Throughout this book, quoted matter from writings (discussion boards, forums, and the like) is in italics; quoted matter from oral communications (as in this note) is in quotation marks. Quotations from published sources are attributed in the notes.

2. Donald Soderquist, *The Wal-Mart Way: The Inside Story of the Success of the World's Largest Company* (Nashville, Tenn.: Nelson, 2005), 97.

3. A 2005 poll conducted by Pew found that while 81 percent of respondents considered Walmart a good place to shop, far fewer (56 percent) believed it was a good place to work (see Pew Research Center for the People and the Press, "Wal-Mart—A Good Place to Shop but Some Critics Too," December 15, 2005). Even among those who regularly shop at Walmart, many feel ambivalent about it. As Charles Fishman reports in his book *The Wal-Mart Effect*, the advertising firm Foote, Cone & Belding once created a typology of Walmart shoppers based on research in Oklahoma City. The agency found that 15 percent of shoppers were what they labeled *conflicted shoppers*. This group made regular shopping trips to Walmart—more than once a week—but felt guilty about it because of the company's corporate practices. Fishman, *The Wal-Mart Effect* (New York: Penguin, 2006), 219–220. For a thorough account of the moral-market struggle between advocates and the company, see Rebekah Peeples Massengill, *Wal-Mart Wars: Moral Populism in the Twenty-First Century* (New York: New York University Press, 2013).

4. Charles Payne, *I've Got the Light of Freedom: The Organizing Tradition and the Mississippi Freedom Struggle* (Berkeley: University of California Press, 1995), 104.

5. Payne, *I've Got the Light of Freedom*, 297–299.

6. Doug McAdam, *Freedom Summer* (New York: Oxford University Press, 1988), 33.

7. McAdam, *Freedom Summer*, 40.

8. McAdam, *Freedom Summer*, 116.

9. McAdam, *Freedom Summer*, 146.

10. McAdam, *Freedom Summer*, 117.

11. McAdam, *Freedom Summer*, 118–126.

12. David Stark, *The Sense of Dissonance: Accounts of Worth in Economic Life* (Princeton, N.J.: Princeton University Press, 2009).

13. Some of the most well-known "new" union leaders, like Andy Stern of the Service Employees International Union (SEIU) and John Wilhelm of the Hotel Employees and Restaurant Employees International Union (HERE), were Ivy League graduates themselves.

14. Doug McAdam discusses the important role of "biographical availability" in explaining students' involvement in social protest: "Students, especially those drawn from privileged classes, are simply free, to a unique degree, of constraints that tend to make activism too time consuming or risky for other groups to engage in. Often freed from the demands of family, marriage, and full-time employment, students are uniquely available to express their political values through action." McAdam, *Freedom Summer*, 44. Parenthetically, this freedom from relational constraints also seems to work pretty well as an explanation for young people's disproportionate involvement in crime.

15. Rick Fantasia and Kim Voss, *Hard Work: Remaking the American Labor Movement* (Berkeley: University of California Press, 2004), 132.

16. See also Daisy Rooks and Robert A. Penney, "Outsiders in the Union: Organizing, Consent and Union Recognition Campaigns," *Social Movement Studies* 15, no. 5 (2016): 498–514.

17. Nella Van Dyke, Marc Dixon, and Helen Carlon, "Manufacturing Dissent: Labor Revitalization, Union Summer and Student Protest," *Social Forces* 86, no. 1 (2007): 193–214.

18. Nelson Lichtenstein, "A Race Between Cynicism and Hope: Labor and Academia," *New Labor Forum* 10 (2002): 71–79.

19. "A Look Back: A Time of Change, Determination and Courage," Vanderbilt University, accessed August 1, 2016, www.vanderbilt.edu/celebrating blackhistory/look-back.

20. Michael K. Honey, *Going Down Jericho Road: The Memphis Strike, Martin Luther King's Last Campaign* (New York: Norton, 2007), 300.

21. This concept of freedom, about which we will say more, draws on the idea of "republican freedom" that has been articulated eloquently by political philosophers like Philip Pettit and Elizabeth Anderson. Philip Pettit, *Republicanism: A Theory of Freedom and Government* (New York: Oxford University Press, 1997); and Elizabeth Anderson, "What Is the Point of Equality?," *Ethics* 109, no. 2 (1999): 287–337.

22. "Our Locations," Wal-Mart Stores, accessed February 13, 2015, http://corporate.walmart.com/our-story/locations/united-states; Bureau of Labor Statistics, "The Employment Situation—January 2015," www.bls.gov/news.release/archives/empsit_02062015.pdf. [Accessed February 2, 2018].

23. Michael Burawoy, "The Extended Case Method," *Sociological Theory* 16, no. 1 (1998): 4–33, p. 14.

24. Bethany Moreton. *To Serve God and Wal-Mart: The Making of Christian Free Enterprise* (Cambridge: Harvard University Press, 2009), 42. See also Deane Simpson, "Nomadic Urbanism: The Senior Full-Time Recreational Vehicle Community," *Interstices* 34 (2009): 34–46. Simpson writes of the policy, "RVers have a free, relatively safe, accessible and reliable network of locations in which to stay overnight, with access to bathrooms and store supplies; and in return, Walmart maintains a large number of loyal customers who occupy parking lot space only during the overnight off-peak period" (41–42). Not insignificant to Walmart, the RVers also provide free security.

25. The threat of a Hilary Clinton presidency was very good for the gun industry, her loss a challenge for it. The share price of American Outdoor Brands (formerly Smith & Wesson) fell by approximately 25 percent immediately following the election of Donald Trump. See Lois Beckett, "US Gun Makers Battle 'Trump Slump' as Sales Fall Compared to 2016," *The Guardian*, September 8, 2017, www.theguardian.com/us-news/2017/sep/08/us-gun-makers-battle-trump-slump-as-sales-fall-by-100m-compared-to-2016.

26. The night before, we had parked the RV in the center of Binghamton, New York, looking for somewhere to eat. A middle-aged couple who said they had lived there for the previous 20 years, couldn't recommend a single place within walking distance, telling us that there used to be restaurants here, but that they have all moved to the malls on the outskirts of the city. (That said, we looked on Yelp and found the Lost Dog Café right downtown; it seemed hip to us and the food was delicious).

27. Michael Burawoy, *Manufacturing Consent: Changes in the Labor Process Under Monopoly Capitalism* (Chicago: University of Chicago Press, 1979).

28. C. Wright Mills, *The Sociological Imagination* (New York: Grove, 1959).

29. Having students interview each other served both as training for the oral histories we hoped they would collect and a way to build connections with one another.

30. Ignoring the inaccurate report title, according to a Pew study, 89 percent of Americans surveyed considered themselves some version of "middle class," "upper middle class," or "lower middle class" in 2012, relatively unchanged from the 91 percent who considered themselves a member of one of these categories in 2008. Rich Morin and Seth Motel, "A Third of Americans Now Say They Are in the Lower Classes," Pew Research Center (2012), www.pewsocialtrends.org/2012/09/10/a-third-of-americans-now -say-they-are-in-the-lower-classes.

31. "Noe Valley Real Estate Market Overview," Trulia, accessed December 30, 2015, www.trulia.com/real_estate/Noe_Valley-San_Francisco/1443; and "United States Home Prices & Values," Zillow, accessed December 31, 2015,www.zillow.com/home-values.

32. "Urban: About Us," The Urban School of San Francisco, accessed December 30, 2015, www.urbanschool.org/page.cfm?p=16.

33. "Urban: Admissions," The Urban School of San Francisco, accessed December 30, 2015,www.urbanschool.org/page.cfm?p=170.

34. In *Freedom Summer*, McAdam discusses the ways in which the booming economy of the 1960s helps to make sense of the volunteers' enthusiasm about the project. He quotes one volunteer: " 'There was this general feeling that you were invulnerable; there would always be a job for you. Jobs or material success—all that stuff—were sort of a given. So I never felt it was one or the other [a job or participation in Freedom Summer]' " (17).

35. Discussed in more detail later, employers are always confronted with the problem of turning purchased labor power—i.e., workers' time— into actual labor or productive work. Walmart draws on elements of many different management strategies, but the core of what we will call Walmartism still rests on the "simple control" structures prevalent in late nineteenth-century manufacturing, in which workers' investments are minimal. One downside for the company is that many workers have very low commitment to its success; but the upside is that disgruntled workers often leave rather than fight. See Richard Edwards, *Contested Terrain: The Transformation of the Workplace in the Twentieth Century* (New York: Basic, 1979).

36. Carole Cain, "Personal Stories: Identity Acquisition and Self-Understanding in Alcoholics Anonymous," *Ethos* 19, no. 2 (1991): 210–253.

37. Those who took our survey were fairly representative of Walmart workers by geography and race, though our sample had somewhat older respondents and more female respondents than the population of Walmart workers. We estimate the geographic distribution of Walmart workers based on the distribution of Walmarts nationwide (by square footage). We estimate the race and gender composition of Walmart's labor force using the Walmart *2016 Culture, Diversity & Inclusion Report*, accessed September 14, 2017, https://cdn.corporate.walmart.com/8c/08/6bc1b69f4a94a423957d4c2162db/wm-cdireport2016-v27-reader-pages.pdf. Walmart does not report the age of its workforce, but we approximate the age distribution of Walmart associates using the 2011–2015 American Community Survey five-year estimates, which allow us to estimate the age distribution of those working in the "department store" industry of which Walmart is a part.

38. John Creswell, *Designing and Conducting Mixed Methods Research* (Thousand Oaks, Calif.: Sage, 2007); and R. Burke Johnson, Anthony J. Onwuegbuzie, and Lisa A. Turner, "Toward a Definition of Mixed Methods Research," *Journal of Mixed Methods Research* 1, no. 2 (2007): 112–133.

39. The quote, often paraphrased, comes from Marcel Proust: "The only true voyage, the only bath in the Fountain of Youth, would be not to visit strange lands but to possess other eyes, to see the universe through the eyes of another, of a hundred others, to see the hundred universes that each of them sees, that each of them is." Proust, *The Captive: The Fugitive*, vol. 5 of *In Search of Lost Time*, trans. C. K. Scott Moncrieff and Terence Kilmartin (London: Chatto & Windus, 1993[1992]), 343.

40. Burawoy, "The Extended Case Method," 14.

41. Massengill, *Wal-Mart Wars*.

1. PATHWAYS

1. Richard McCormack, "A GM Factory with 2,100 Workers Closes, and 33,000 Other People Lose Their Jobs—Impacting 120,000," *Manufacturing and Technology News* 17:1, www.manufacturingnews.com/news/10/0112/GM.html; and Marian J. Krzyzowski and Lawrence A. Molnar, "Impacts of the Automotive Industry's Restructuring" (presentation before the Chicago Federal Reserve Bank, 2009).

2. Andrew R. L. Cayton, "The Significance of Ohio in the Early American Republic," in *The Center of a Great Empire: The Ohio Country in the Early Republic,*

ed. Andrew R. L. Cayton and Stuart D. Hobbs (Athens: Ohio University Press, 2005), 4; and Krissy Clark, "America's Forgotten Forerunner to Silicon Valley," *BBC News Marketplace*, March 20, 2015.

3. Hal R. Varian, "Computer Mediated Transactions," *American Economic Review* 100, no. 2 (2010): 1–10.

4. Peter L. Jakab, *Visions of a Flying Machine: The Wright Brothers and the Process of Invention* (Washington, D.C.: Smithsonian Institution, 1990).

5. Richard S. Rosenbloom, "Leadership, Capabilities, and Technological Change: The Transformation of NCR in the Electronic Era," *Strategic Management Journal* 21 (2000): 1083–1103, p. 1098.

6. Ben Rooney, "Ohio Reels as NCR Moves to Georgia," *CNN Money*, June 2, 2009, http://money.cnn.com/2009/06/02/news/companies/ncr _corporation_headquarters.

7. National Cash Register, "NCR to Install 10,000 Self-Checkout Devices at More Than 1,200 Walmart Locations," press release, October 31, 2012, www.ncr.com/news/news-releases/retail/ncr-to-install-10-000-self -checkout-devices-at-more-than-1-200-walmart-locations.

8. The Special Supplemental Nutrition Program for Women, Infants and Children (WIC) is a federal welfare program for low-income pregnant women, breastfeeding women, and children under the age of five. WIC benefits entitle participants to a specific "package" of food determined by the U.S. Department of Agriculture. https://www.fns.usda.gov/wic /wic-benefits-and-services, accessed February 5, 2018.

9. Pierre Bourdieu calls this "hysteresis," when people's dispositions are "confronted with conditions of actualization different from those in which they were produced. This is true in particular whenever agents perpetuate dispositions made obsolete by transformations of the objective conditions." Pierre Bourdieu, *Pascalian Meditations* (Stanford: Stanford University Press, 2000 [1997]).

10. Arlie R. Hochschild, *The Managed Heart: Commercialization of Human Feeling* (Berkeley: University of California Press, 1983).

11. Paul Willis, *Learning to Labor: How Working Class Kids Get Working Class Jobs* (New York: Columbia University Press, 1981).

12. Based on data Walmart reports to the Equal Employment Opportunity Commission, reported in Walmart's *2014 Diversity & Inclusion Report*, 24. http://bestpractices.diversityinc.com/medialib/uploads/2014/09 /Walmart-2014-Diversity-Inclusion-Report.pdf, accessed February 5, 2018.

13. Nelson Lichtenstein, *The Retail Revolution: How Wal-Mart Created a Brave New World of Business* (New York: Picador, 2010[2009]), p. 78. This strikes us as a weirdly idealized image of what farm women did, and it is not at

all clear to us that better roads made wage work more attractive or that agricultural reorganization made farming untenable, but whatever the motives, the point that retail work provided a supplement (rather than the core) to family income is correct.

14. Arlie R. Hochschild, *The Time Bind: When Work Becomes Home and Home Becomes Work* (New York: Metropolitan, 1997).

15. The trend had actually begun somewhat earlier. Women had begun to enter the paid workforce during World War II, when they had been actively recruited into wartime manufacturing. See Ruth Milkman, *Gender at Work: The Dynamics of Job Segregation by Sex During World War II* (Urbana: University of Illinois Press, 1987). Even after the war, when traditional family norms reasserted themselves, many working-class women sought part-time clerical and service work so their families might fully partake in modern consumer society. As Alice Kessler-Harris writes, "Homes and cars, refrigerators and washing machines, telephones and multiple televisions required higher incomes. . . . Higher real wages of male breadwinners could pay for some of these, but as the level of consumer aspiration rose, wives sought to aid husbands in the quest for the good life. The two-income family emerged." Alice Kessler-Harris, *Out to Work: A History of Wage-Earning Women in the United States* (New York: Oxford University Press, 1982), 302. In turn, women's increasing workforce participation may also have increased the U.S. labor supply in ways that reinforced the declining real wages of the working class overall. See Daron Acemoglu, David H. Autor, and David Lyle, "Women, War, and Wages: The Effect of Female Labor Supply on the Wage Structure at Midcentury," *Journal of Political Economy* 112, no. 3 (2004): 497–550.

16. Pew Research Center, "The Rise in Dual Income Households," June 18, 2015, www.pewresearch.org/ft_dual-income-households-1960-2012-2.

17. Lillian B. Rubin, *Families on the Fault Line: America's Working Class Speaks About the Family, the Economy, Race, and Ethnicity* (New York: HarperCollins, 1994), 81.

18. Claudia Goldin, "Richard T. Ely Lecture: The Quiet Revolution That Transformed Women's Employment, Education, and Family," *AEA Papers and Proceedings* 96, no. 2 (2006): 1–21. Goldin makes the compelling observation that the field of labor economics itself developed in reference to women's labor market participation: "It would not be much of an exaggeration to claim that women gave 'birth' to modern labor economics, especially labor supply. Economists need variance to analyze changes in behavioral responses, and women provided an abundance of that" (3).

19. Arlie Hochschild, *The Second Shift: Working Parents and the Revolution at Home* (New York: Viking, 1989).

20. Daniel Schneider, "Gender Deviance and Household Work: The Role of Occupation," *American Journal of Sociology* 117, no. 4 (2012): 1029–1072.

21. Milt Freudenheim, "More Help Wanted: Older Workers Please Apply," *New York Times*, March 23, 2005.

22. Michael A. Smyer and Marcie Pitt-Catsouphes, "The Meanings of Work for Older Workers," *Generations* 31, no. 1 (2007): 23–30.

23. Donald Soderquist, *The Wal-Mart Way: The Inside Story of the Success of the World's Largest Company* (Nashville, Tenn.: Nelson, 2005), 74–75.

24. Dan Kadlec, "The End of an Era: Iconic Greeters Reassigned at Walmart," *Time*, February 7, 2012, http://business.time.com/2012/02/07/end-of-an-era-iconic-greeters-reassigned-at-walmart.

25. Viviana Zelizer, "The Social Meaning of Money: 'Special Monies,'" *American Journal of Sociology* 95, no. 2 (1989): 342–377.

26. Video games for young men especially may provide a sense of community, and may also help to account for the exceptionally high unemployment rate (22 percent) of unskilled men age 20–30. Eric Hurst, "Video Killed the Radio Star: How Games, Phones, and Other Tech Innovations Are Changing the Labor Force," Chicago Booth Review, September 1, 2016, http://review.chicagobooth.edu/economics/2016/article/video-killed-radio-star.

27. Christopher Ingraham, "Wal-Mart Has a Lower Acceptance Rate Than Harvard," *Wonkblog* (blog), *Washington Post*, March 28, 2014, www.washingtonpost.com/blogs/wonkblog/wp/2014/03/28/wal-mart-has-a-lower-acceptance-rate-than-harvard.

28. In each case, this was true even after controlling for factors like pay, age, race, gender, how many years one had worked at Walmart, and how one rated Walmart as an employer. That said, this result could also be an outcome of an endogenous process.

29. Democratic staff of the U.S. House Committee on Education and the Workforce, *The Low-Wage Drag on Our Economy: Wal-Mart's Low Wages and Their Effect on Taxpayers and Economic Growth* (May 2013), http://democrats-edworkforce.house.gov/imo/media/doc/WalMartReport-May2013.pdf, accessed February 5, 2018.

30. Americans for Tax Fairness, "Walmart on Tax Day: How Taxpayers Subsidize America's Biggest Employer and Richest Family," April 2014, https://americansfortaxfairness.org/files/Walmart-on-Tax-Day-Americans-for-Tax-Fairness-11.pdf.

31. For instance, when work requirements were first proposed in Wisconsin as part of Wisconsin Works in 1995, a year before national welfare reform

(modeled on Wisconsin) was passed, representatives from the Restaurant Association and other low-wage employers spoke in favor. See Jane L. Collins and Victoria Mayer, *Both Hands Tied: Welfare Reform and the Race to the Bottom in the Low-Wage Labor Market* (Chicago: Chicago University Press, 2010), 56.

32. Jane Collins writes, "The connection between Wal-Mart's profits and poverty became clearer to me in 2004, when I was collecting the work histories of forty women who were losing access to welfare in Milwaukee and Racine, Wisconsin. Wal-Mart figured prominently in nearly every narrative. A large proportion of the women I spoke with had worked at Wal-Mart at one time or another and told stories about their experiences. . . . An even larger proportion of the women—virtually all of them—shopped at Walmart. What is more, they saw shopping at Wal-Mart as crucial to making ends meet—the only way they could afford to buy clothing and diapers for the children." Jane Collins, "The Opposite of Fordism: Wal-Mart Rolls Back a Regime of Accumulation" (paper prepared for What's Wrong with America? conference at MIT, Cambridge, Mass., May 26, 2006).

33. Was Walmart doing something different during this time? Certainly, the company was expanding during this period, but it was not expanding any more rapidly than it had been in the years previously. If anything, store openings slowed slightly during the second half of the 1990s.

34. Margaret R. Somers and Fred Block, "From Poverty to Perversity: Ideas, Markets, and Institutions over 200 Years of Welfare Debate," *American Sociological Review* 70 (2005): 260–287.

35. For a beautiful description of the loss of community that follows a Walmart closing, see Ed Pilkington, "What Happened When Walmart Left," *The Guardian*, July 9, 2017, www.theguardian.com/us-news/2017/jul/09/what-happened-when-walmart-left. Equally interesting, some aspects of welfare reform, especially the earned income tax credit (EITC), were perceived positively by beneficiaries. Jennifer Sykes and colleagues, for example, argue that EITC recipients see the credit "as a springboard for upward mobility. Thus, by conferring dignity and spurring dreams, the EITC enhances feelings of citizenship and social inclusion." Jennifer Sykes, Katrin Križ, Kathryn Edin, and Sarah Halpern-Meekin, "Dignity and Dreams," *American Sociological Review* 80, no. 2 (2014): 243–267.

36. Raj Chetty, David Grusky, Maximilian Hell, Nathaniel Hendren, Robert Manduca, and Jimmy Narang, "The Fading American Dream: Trends in Absolute Income Mobility Since 1940" (National Bureau of Economic Research Working Paper 22910, Cambridge Mass., 2016).

37. Walmart, https://corporate.walmart.com/our-story/working-at-walmart, accessed February 5, 2018.

38. All salary estimates below are based on reports from Glassdoor.com, accessed May 15, 2017.
39. Estimates made using the Current Population Survey. U.S. Census Bureau, Current Population Survey dataset (Washington, D.C.: Government Printing Office, 1984-2017).
40. Richard Fry, *For First Time in Modern Era, Living with Parents Edges Out Other Living Arrangements for 18-to 34-Year-Olds* (Washington, D.C.: Pew Research Center, May 2016).
41. Maurice Emsellem and Michelle Natividad Rodriguez, "Advancing a Federal Fair Chance Hiring Agenda" (National Employment Law Project, New York, January 2015).
42. Dylan Minor, Nicola Persico, and Deborah M. Weiss, "Criminal Background and Job Performance" (Working Paper, May 4, 2017), https://ssrn.com/abstract=2851951, accessed June 15, 2017. They conclude, "Our estimates suggest that the *average* customer service worker with a criminal record is a better deal for the employer than the average worker without a record" (19). See also Jennifer Lundquist, Devah Pager, and Eiko Strader, "Does a Criminal Past Predict Worker Performance? Evidence from America's Largest Employers," *Social Forces* 96, no. 3 (2018): 1039–1068. and Autumn Spanne, "Can Hiring Ex-offenders Make a Business More Profitable?," *The Guardian*, February 4, 2016, www.theguardian.com/sustainable-business/2016/feb/04/us-prison-system-ex-offenders-employment-walmart-target-civil-rights.
43. In an examination of military service among people with criminal records, Lundquist et al observe, "The scarcity of stable employment for felons is likely to generate greater commitment to an employer who is willing to take a chance on them" (Lundquist, Pager, and Strader, "Does a Criminal Past Predict Worker Performance?", 21). Those who had felonies (and who had received felony waivers to serve) were more likely to be promoted than those without records; they were also more likely to die in service. See also Gretchen Purser, "'Still Doin' Time': Clamoring for Work in the Day Labor Industry," *WorkingUSA: The Journal of Labor and Society* 15 (2012): 397–415.

2. THE SHOP FLOOR

1. Paco Underhill, *Why We Buy: The Science of Shopping* (New York: Simon & Schuster, 1999).
2. Michael Burawoy, *Manufacturing Consent: Changes in the Labor Process Under Monopoly Capitalism* (Chicago: University of Chicago Press, 1979); and

Richard Edwards, *Contested Terrain: The Transformation of the Workplace in the Twentieth Century* (New York: Basic Books, 1979).

3. Richard Thaler and Cass Sunstein, *Nudge: Improving Decisions About Health, Wealth, and Happiness* (New Haven: Yale University Press, 2008).

4. Taking such labor-surveillance technologies one step further, Amazon recently patented designs for a wristband that it may require its distribution center employees to wear. More than merely tracking the locations of workers bodies, the bands "would use ultrasonic tracking to identify the precise location of a worker's hands as they retrieve items" and would "vibrate against the wearer's skin to point their hand in the right direction." Olivia Solon, "Amazon Patents Wristband that Tracks Workers' Movements," *The Guardian*, January 31, 2018.

5. Our analysis extends the conclusions of Stuart Tannock, who rejects the conventional wisdom that large chain stores create routinized and standard experiences for employees. In an examination of three stores in one fast-food chain, he writes that workers "almost universally insist on the distinctiveness of the individual outlets in which they work." Stuart Tannock, *Youth at Work: The Unionized Fast Food and Grocery Workplace* (Philadelphia: Temple University Press, 2001), 61.

6. "Missed Connections: Seen But Not Spoken to: An Atlas of Where We're (Almost) Finding Love," *Missed Connections* (blog), *Psychology Today*, February 22, 2013, accessed January 11, 2017, www.psychologytoday.com /blog/brainstorm/201302/missed-connections.

7. Bethany Moreton, *To Serve God and Wal-Mart: The Making of Christian Free Enterprise* (Cambridge: Harvard University Press, 2009). Moreton writes, "Walton's biography of finance, inherited security, and public inputs was hardly the stuff of a convincing Horatio Alger tale, but a host of mythologizers relentlessly forced Walton's personal history into the threadbare rags-to-riches plot line" (45).

8. Moreton, *To Serve God and Wal-Mart*, 14–17.

9. Moreton, *To Serve God and Wal-Mart*, 37.

10. See Charles Fishman, *The Wal-Mart Effect* (New York: Penguin, 2006), 30. Thanks also to Dan Wang at Columbia Business School for his insights into the company's corporate culture and its diffusion.

11. In our survey, white workers report having more than seven friends at work, compared with fewer than five among non-white workers.

12. In the economics literature this is known as "monopsony." It operates like monopoly in reverse. Instead of raising prices and lowering product quality and quantity to increase profits, profits are increased by lowering wages and staffing levels, worker effort, and employee retention.

13. Joan Robinson, *Economic Philosophy* (Chicago: Aldine, 2006 [1962]).

14. The idea, developed by classical economists like David Ricardo and Adam Smith but popularized by Karl Marx, is that the value of a product derives from the amount of labor time (specifically, the amount of "socially necessary" labor time) it takes to produce it. See Karl Marx, *Capital: A Critique of Political Economy*, trans. Samuel Moore and Edward Aveling (Mineola, N.Y.: Dover, 2011 [1906]), 46.

15. See Moreton, *To Serve God and Wal-Mart*, 55–56.

16. Moreton, *To Serve God and Wal-Mart*, 49.

17. For some Walmart workers this feeling is a bit more literal. Walmart once had a habit of locking overnight employees in its stores—a practice it rationalized as necessary to keep criminals out, though one that was likely instituted to prevent employees from walking out with merchandise. Back in 1988, in a store in Savannah, Georgia, a worker collapsed and died on the floor of a Walmart after the paramedics were unable to get in. Steven Greenhouse, "Workers Assail Night Lock-Ins by Wal-Mart," *New York Times*, January 18, 2004.

18. Elizabeth Anderson, *Private Government: How Employers Rule Our Lives (and Why We Don't Talk About It)* (Princeton, N.J.: Princeton University Press, 2017), 63.

19. Alex Gourevitch, "Labor Republicanism and the Transformation of Work," *Political Theory* 41, no. 4 (2013): 591–617, p. 607.

20. Aldo Svaldi, "Injured Walmart Workers Win $8 Million Settlement," *Denver Post*, November 13, 2012, accessed August 16, 2016, www.denverpost.com /2012/11/13/injured-walmart-workers-win-8-million-settlement.

21. Dina Bakst, Elizabeth Gedmark, and Cara Suvall, "Pointing Out: How Walmart Unlawfully Punishes Workers for Medical Absences" (A Better Balance, New York, June 2017).

22. Amien Essif, "Walmart's Inhumane Policies for Pregnant Workers," *Working in These Times* (blog), November 6, 2014, http://inthesetimes.com /working/entry/17316/walmart_inhumane_pregnancy_policies.

23. One can imagine a whole study of the euphemistic language that Walmart popularized. Workers are "associates." Discipline is "coaching." One earns "points" for violations. "Flex scheduling" means part-time work. "Full-time" is 34 hours a week, almost a full day shorter than full-time work in the past.

24. These policies may violate the Family and Medical Leave Act and the Americans with Disabilities Act. A report prepared by the advocacy group A Better Balance, in coordination with OUR Walmart, alleges just this: "*Simply put:* Giving a worker a disciplinary 'point' for being absent due to

a disability or for taking care of themselves or a loved one with a serious medical condition is not only unfair, in many instances, it runs afoul of federal, state and local law." Bakst et al., "Pointing Out: How Walmart Unlawfully Punishes Workers for Medical Absences," 2. See also Rachel Abrams, "Walmart Is Accused of Punishing Workers," *New York Times*, June 1, 2017, www.nytimes.com/2017/06/01/business/walmart-workers -sick-days.html.

25. Olivera Perkins, "Is Walmart's Request of Associates to Help Provide Thanksgiving Dinner for Co-workers Proof of Low Wages?," *Cleveland.com*, November 18, 2013, www.cleveland.com/business/index.ssf/2013/11/is _walmarts_request_of_associa.html.

26. In turn, Walmart contributed approximately $3.6 million, the Walton Family Foundation contributed $4 million, and the Walmart Foundation contributed $2 million. Internal Revenue Service. 2013. Form 990. "Wal-Mart Associates in Critical Need Fund." A case was brought to the Federal Election Commission when it was discovered that Walmart was offering to "match" any dollar donation to Walmart's Political Action Committee with a *$2* contribution to the Associates in Critical Need Fund. The case was dismissed. See Craig Holman, Stephen Spaulding, Evelin Cruz, and Cynthia Murray. September 22, 2014. "Re: Complaint Against Wal-Mart Stores, Inc.," https://www.citizen.org/sites/default/files/fec-walmart -complaint.pdf.

3. THE STRUCTURE OF DOMINATION AND CONTROL

1. See, for instance, Thomas J. Holmes, "The Diffusion of Wal-Mart and Economies of Density," *Econometrica* 79, no. 1 (2011): 253–302.

2. See Charles Fishman, *The Wal-Mart Effect* (New York: Penguin, 2006), 75–76; and Nelson Lichtenstein, *The Retail Revolution: How Wal-Mart Created a Brave New World of Business* (New York: Picador, 2010[2009]), 68–69.

3. See Nelson Lichtenstein, "In the Age of Wal-Mart: Precarious Work and Authoritarian Management in the Global Supply Chain," in *Globalization and Precarious Forms of Production and Employment*, ed. Carole Thorney, Steve Jefferys, and Beatric Appay (Northampton, Mass.: Elgar, 2010), 10–22.

4. Markek Korczynski, "The Customer in the Sociology of Work: Different Ways of Going Beyond the Management-Worker Dyad," *Work, Employment & Society* 27, no. 6 (2013) NP1–NP7, https://doi.org/10.1177/0950017012464424; Robin Leidner, *Fast Food, Fast Talk: Service Work and the Routinization of*

Everyday Life (Berkeley: University of California Press, 1993); Steven Henry Lopez, "Workers, Managers, and Customers: Triangles of Power in Work Communities," *Work and Occupations* 37, no. 3 (2010): 251–271; and Holly J. McCammon and Larry J. Griffin, "Workers and Their Customers and Clients: An Editorial Introduction," *Work and Occupations* 27, no. 3 (2000): 278–293.

5. It is likely true that people try to find autonomy and community, and chafe against arbitrary authority, *wherever* they work, in which case these structural features of service work exacerbate and reinforce more general patterns of worker aspiration and irritation.

6. These examples are all drawn from the Walmart associates' discussion board.

7. Richard Edwards, *Contested Terrain: The Transformation of the Workplace in the Twentieth Century* (New York: Basic Books, 1979), 128. See also Michael Schwartz, *Radical Protest and Social Structure: The Southern Farmers' Alliance and Cotton Tenancy, 1880–1890* (New York: Academic, 1976).

8. In a rich comparative case study, Peter Ikeler compares work at Macy's, a traditional department store, with the big-box chain Target. He argues that Macy's relies on an "eroded craft" system of control, in which salespeople are responsible for having a deeper familiarity with a particular set of products and for engaging in more emotional depth with customers than their counterparts at Target. This department-specific knowledge presumably limits the extent to which workers at Macy's can be reallocated to different positions to match customer demand; it thus presumably also leads to slack time, because workers are anchored within slow departments. Peter Ikeler, *Hard Sell: Work and Resistance in Retail Chains* (Ithaca, N.Y.: Cornell University Press, 2016).

9. "New Market Force Information Study Finds Wegmans and Publix are America's Favorite Grocery Retailers," Market Force Information, April 16, 2016, www.marketforce.com/wegmans-and-publix-are-america%E2%80%99s -favorite-grocery-retailers-market-force-panel-research.

10. The closest analogy that comes to mind for those who don't go to Walmart is flying. The airlines have figured out that customers are willing to tolerate the most amazing forms of degradation to save the tiniest fraction of money. No one is even remotely happy about abysmal legroom, the absence of basic amenities, impossibly crowded overhead bins, limited food and drink, poorly paid and miserable staff, and surcharges for everything under the sun. Yet people really want to pay a few dollars less for their tickets, and so this is where the action is for the airlines. (In this case the temporal distance between buying a ticket and flying may have something to do with the reasons why customers fail to recognize the role they play in their own unhappiness.)

11. Jason Furman, "Wal-Mart: A Progressive Success Story," (Center for American Progress Working Paper, Washington, D.C., 2005), https://www.mackinac.org/archives/2006/walmart.pdf.

12. Jerry Hausman and Ephraim Leibtag, "CPI Bias from Supercenters: Does the BLS Know that Wal-Mart Exists?" (NBER Working Paper 10712, National Bureau of Economic Research, Cambridge, Mass., August 2004).

13. Daniel Gross, "The Wal-Mart Puzzle: The Economy's Tanking. So Why Is It Thriving?," *Slate*, February 6, 2008, www.slate.com/articles/business/moneybox/2008/02/the_walmart_puzzle.html.

14. Jared Cummans, "Is Wal-Mart's Stock Recession Proof? (WMT)," *Dividend .com*, January 30, 2015, www.dividend.com/how-to-invest/wal-mart-and-the-recession-factor-wmt.

15. Rebekah Peeples Massengil, *Wal-Mart Wars: Moral Populism in the Twenty-First Century* (New York: New York University Press, 2013).

16. For example, it assumes that worker productivity would not increase (and turnover would not decrease) in response to better wages and working conditions, contradicting ideas now widely accepted in economic theory. Carl Shapiro and Joseph E. Stiglitz, "Equilibrium Unemployment as a Worker Discipline Device," *American Economic Review* 74, no. 3 (1984): 433–444. It also assumes that the company's only option in the face of higher labor costs would be to pass them on to customers, rather than to suppliers, financiers, landlords, and shareholders. Finally, even if such costs were all passed on to customers, they would likely be quite small, "dispersed in small amounts among many consumers across the income spectrum," as one analysis put it. Ken Jacobs, Dave Graham-Squire, and Stephanie Luce, "Living Wage Policies and Big-Box Retail: How a Higher Wage Standard Would Impact Walmart Workers and Shoppers" (research brief, Center for Labor Research and Education, University of California, Berkeley, April 2011). Customers could still save a lot, even if workers were paid a living wage. One might also make the converse argument to see its absurdity: If low prices are more important than decent wages and benefits, why pay workers anything at all? Think of all the savings!

17. Leidner, *Fast Food, Fast Talk*.

18. Peter Bearman, *Doormen* (Chicago: University of Chicago Press, 2005).

19. Arlie R. Hochschild, *The Managed Heart: Commercialization of Human Feeling* (Berkeley: University of California Press, 1983); and Rachel Sherman, *Class Acts: Service and Inequality in Luxury Hotels* (Berkeley: University of California Press, 2007).

20. Joshua Sperber, "Yelp and Labor Discipline: How the Internet Works for Capitalism," *New Labor Forum* 23, no. 2 (2014): 68–74.

21. See, for example, Linda Fuller and Vicki Smith, "Consumers' Reports: Management by Customers in a Changing Economy," *Work, Employment & Society* 5, no. 1 (1991): 1–16; and Sperber, "Yelp and Labor Discipline."

22. Alex Gourevitch, "Labor Republicanism and the Transformation of Work," *Political Theory* 41, no. 4 (2013): 591–617.

23. Edwards, *Contested Terrain*, 29. This is, of course, one of those classic motifs about the "old days" that cannot possibly be entirely true.

24. Edwards, *Contested Terrain*, 33.

25. Edwards, *Contested Terrain*, 58–61. See also William Carwardine, *The Pullman Strike* (New York: Arno, 1969 [1894]).

26. Edwards, *Contested Terrain*.

27. Peter Ikeler (*Hard Sell*) describes the labor process at Target and other big-box stores as "service Toyotism," a model of post-Fordist flexible specialization that he contrasts with the "eroded craft" at Macy's. While this formulation captures aspects of work at Walmart, it seems to overstate the degree to which companies like Target actually invest in their workers and allow workers control over the labor process. For a good summary of post-Fordism in theory and practice, see Steven Vallas, "Rethinking Post-Fordism: The Meaning of Workplace Flexibility," *Sociological Theory* 17, no. 1 (1999): 68–101.

28. As a company that rose to power through the innovations it introduced in the logistics of retail, and as a key intermediary between manufacturers and consumers, Walmart may well embody post-Fordism: "a form of flexible accumulation where capital moves detached from the spatial confines of local labor forces and consumption patterns." David Karjanen, "The Wal-Mart Effect and the New Face of Capitalism: Labor Market and Community Impacts of the Megaretailer," in *Wal-Mart: The Face of Twenty-First-Century Capitalism*, ed. Nelson Lichtenstein (New York: New Press, 2006), 162. As a workplace, however, it does not.

29. See Stuart Tannock, *Youth at Work: The Unionized Fast Food and Grocery Workplace* (Philadelphia: Temple University Press, 2001), 53.

30. See Gregory Bateson, *Steps to an Ecology of Mind* (New York: Ballantine, 1972). Bateson develops the theory of the double bind as inducing schizophrenia and autism; here one realizes as well that unresolvable orders at work produce disengagement as a reaction.

31. Tannock calls this peer pressure "concertive control" (*Youth at Work*, 73).

32. Nelson Lichtenstein ("In the Age of Wal-Mart," 19) cites Michael Bergdahl, who describes the advantages of high turnover: "It's hard to believe, but turnover drops millions of dollars to the bottom line in cost savings for the company. When an experienced associate leaves the company he or she is replaced by an entry-level associate at a lower wage. Turnover of associates,

for this reason, actually appears, from an expense standpoint, to be a competitive advantage." Michael Bergdahl, *What I Learned from Sam Walton: How to Compete and Thrive in a Wal-Mart World* (Hoboken, N.J.: Wiley, 2004).

33. Barbara Ehrenreich beautifully describes the range of tests she was required to take in order to get hired by Walmart. Barbara Ehrenreich, *Nickel and Dimed: On (Not) Getting by in America* (New York: Holt, 2002).

34. "In a chilling reversal of Henry Ford's strategy, which was to pay his workers amply so they could buy Ford cars, Wal-Mart's stingy compensation policies . . . contribute to an economy in which, increasingly, workers can only afford to shop at Walmart." Liza Featherstone, "Down and Out in Discount America," *The Nation*, December 16, 2004, www.thenation.com/article/down-and-out-discount-america.

35. In a compelling theoretical article, Elizabeth Anderson asks, "What is the point of equality?" Elizabeth Anderson, "What Is the Point of Equality?," *Ethics* 109, no. 2 (1999): 287–337. She argues that recent egalitarian theorists have focused too heavily on equality of opportunity, in turn accepting "the justice of whatever inequalities result from adults' voluntary choices" (291). She continues that such a conception of equality, what she calls "luck egalitarianism," "underwrites a hybrid institutional scheme: free markets, to govern the distribution of goods attributable to factors for which individuals are responsible, and the welfare state, to govern the distribution of goods attributable to factors beyond the individual's control" (308). In other words, these theorists emphasize the importance of giving individuals equal chances to occupy certain social roles or positions in society, but—she argues—neglect that the "primary subject of justice is the institutional arrangements that generate people's opportunity over time" (309). For her, what matters is not just how people are allocated to places in a distribution, but the shape of the distribution itself and what this distribution implies about how people relate to one another. And so she proposes that egalitarians ought to focus on what she calls "democratic egalitarianism," or creating social conditions in which people are able to live without being dominated by others, a "collective self-determination by means of open discussion among equals, in accordance with rules acceptable to all" (313).

36. W. Lloyd Warner and John Low, *The Social System of the Modern Factory: The Strike: A Social Analysis* (New Haven, Conn.: Yale University Press, 1947). Warner and Low report an interaction in which a worker in a shoe factory, absent because of illness, returns and is put to work on another machine and asks "Where is my machine?" The foreman says, "Your machine? Did you buy it? Maybe you would like to. Maybe you could buy the factory, too. What do you mean, your machine?"

4. MAKING CONTACT

1. Eric Leifer, "Interaction Preludes to Role Setting: Exploratory Local Action," *American Sociological Review* 53, no. 6 (1988): 865–878.

2. Charles M. Payne, *I've Got the Light of Freedom: The Organizing Tradition and the Mississippi Freedom Struggle* (Berkeley: University of California Press, 1995).

3. Adrian Mayer, "The Significance of Quasi-groups in the Study of Complex Societies," in *The Social Anthropology of Complex Societies*, ed. Michael Banton (New York: Praeger, 1966), 97–122.

4. Richard B. Freeman, "What Can Labor Organizations Do for U.S. Workers when Unions Can't Do What Unions Used to Do?," in *What Works for Workers? Public Policies and Innovative Strategies for Low-Wage Workers*, ed. Stephanie Luce, Jennifer Luff, Joseph A. McCartin, and Ruth Milkman (New York: Russell Sage Foundation, 2014), 67–68.

5. See, for instance, Kate Bronfenbrenner and Robert Hickey, *Blueprint for Change: A National Assessment of Winning Union Organizing Strategies* (Ithaca, N.Y.: Cornell University, New York State School of Industrial and Labor Relations, 2003). Electronic version, https://digitalcommons.ilr.cornell .edu/monograph/5/, accessed February 6, 2018.

6. In their classic study *What Do Unions Do*, Richard Freeman and James Medoff find that unionized workers tend to be quite happy with the ways that unions enhance wages and benefits and handle grievances, but much less happy with the ways that unions give workers a say on the job or help to make the job more interesting. Richard Freeman and James Medoff, *What Do Unions Do* (New York: Basic Books, 1984), 144.

7. This is a particularly egregious example of the handling of a tension that is, in subtler ways, difficult to avoid in the relationships between paid union staffers and worker-leaders. Teresa Sharpe, "Democratic Spaces and Successful Campaigns: The Dynamics of Staff Authority and Worker Participation in an Organizing Union," in *Reorganizing Labor: Organizing and Organizers in the New Union Movement*, ed. Ruth Milkman and Kim Voss (Ithaca, N.Y.: Cornell University Press, 2004), 62–87.

8. Bruce Western, "A Comparative Study of Working-Class Disorganization: Union Decline in Eighteen Advanced Capitalist Countries," *American Sociological Review* 63, no. 2 (1995), 182–183.

9. Robert E. Baldwin, *The Decline of U.S. Labor Unions and the Role of Trade* (Washington, D.C.: Institute for International Economics, 2003); and Tali Kristal, "The Capitalist Machine: Computerization, Workers' Power, and the Decline in Labor's Share Within U.S. Industries," *American Sociological Review* 78, no. 3 (2013), 361–389. The current failure of the self-checkout

line provides some indication of the limits of worker replacement by machines, though it is possible that "smart stores" may eliminate most of the front-end workers within the next decade. Steven Lopez, *Reorganizing the Rust Belt: An Inside Study of the American Labor Movement* (Berkeley: University of California Press, 2004), 243n32.

10. Robert Michael Smith, *From Blackjacks to Briefcases: A History of Commercialized Strikebreaking and Unionbusting in the United States* (Athens: Ohio University Press, 2003); Kate Bronfenbrenner, "No Holds Barred—The Intensification of Employer Opposition to Organizing," Economic Policy Institute Briefing Paper #235 (2009); John Logan, "The Union Avoidance Industry in the United States," *British Journal of Industrial Relations* 44, no. 4 (2006), 651–675; Morris M. Kleiner, "Intensity of Management Resistance: Understanding the Decline of Unionization in the Private Sector," *Journal of Labor Research* 22, no. 3 (2001), 519–540; Richard B. Freeman and Morris M. Kleiner, "Employer Behavior in the Face of Union Organizing Drives," *Industrial and Labor Relations Review* 43, no. 4 (1990), 351–365.

11. Bronfenbrenner 2009, 3.

12. Bronfenbrenner 2009, 3.

13. See Kim Voss, *The Making of American Exceptionalism: The Knights of Labor and Class Formation in the Nineteenth Century* (Ithaca, N.Y.: Cornell University Press, 1993).

14. See Richard Schneirov, Shelton Stromquist, and Nick Salvatore, *The Pullman Strike and the Crisis of the 1890s: Essays on Labor and Politics* (Urbana: University of Illinois Press, 1999); and Rick Fantasia and Kim Voss, *Hard Work: Remaking the American Labor Movement* (Berkeley: University of California Press, 2004), 38.

15. Voss, *The Making of American Exceptionalism*; and Fantasia and Voss, *Hard Work*, 36–39. Fantasia and Voss cite Michael Mann, who reports that between 1871 and 1914, between 500 and 800 workers were killed in labor disputes in the United States, compared with 7 in England, 35 in France, and 16 in Germany. Michael Mann, *The Sources of Social Power*, vol. 2, *The Rise of Classes and Nation States, 1760–1914* (New York: Cambridge University Press, 1993).

16. Fantasia and Voss, *Hard Work*, 26; and Robert Zeiger, *American Workers, American Unions* (Baltimore, Md.: John Hopkins University Press, 1994).

17. Bruce Western, *Between Class and Market: Postwar Unionization in the Capitalist Democracies* (Princeton, N.J.: Princeton University Press, 1997); and Fantasia and Voss, *Hard Work*, 19–25.

18. Peter Bearman and Kevin Everett, "The Structure of Social Protest, 1961–1983," *Social Networks* 15 (1993): 171–200.

19. Penny Lewis (2013) complicates the stereotype of the working-class "hard hat," offering a sophisticated analysis of the roles of race, class, and party in the anti–Vietnam War movement. She upends the conventional wisdom by demonstrating the extent of working-class opposition to the war, yet supports the argument we make here by showing how this opposition tended not to find expression in the conservative mainstream of the American labor movement at the time. Nor did this working-class opposition, for that matter, make it into popular understandings of the anti-war movement then or ever since. Penny Lewis, *Hardhats, Hippies, and Hawks: The Vietnam Antiwar Movement as Myth and Memory* (Ithaca, N.Y.: Cornell University Press, 2013).

20. Stuart Tannock, *Youth at Work: The Unionized Fast Food and Grocery Workplace* (Philadelphia: Temple University Press, 2001), part 3.

21. Fantasia and Voss, *Hard Work*, 64; and Stanley Aronowitz, *The Death and Life of American Labor: Toward a New Workers' Movement* (New York: Verso, 2014).

22. Epitomizing this view was AFL-CIO president George Meany who, in 1972, responded to a reporter's question about declining union membership rates by answering, "Why should we worry about organizing groups of people who do not appear to want to be organized?" See Paul Buhle, *Taking Care of Business: Samuel Gompers, George Meany, Lane Kirkland, and the Tragedy of American Labor* (New York: Monthly Review Press, 1999), 196.

23. In a comprehensive review of the literature, Jake Rosenfeld makes a convincing argument that economic, institutional, and political changes explain the decline of traditional labor unions more than "the relative zeal with which contemporary unions are seeking to expand their memberships." Jake Rosenfeld, *What Unions No Longer Do* (Cambridge: Harvard University Press, 2014), 14. He observes that, since the mid-1990s, a few large unions have invested tremendous resources into increasing membership, with little effect. On the other hand, Jane McAlevey also makes a compelling case that organizational strategy matters, and that a failure to engage in strategic organizing "is the main reason why modern movements have not replicated the kinds of gains achieved by the earlier labor and civil rights movements." Jane McAlevey, *No Shortcuts: Organizing for Power in the New Gilded Age* (New York: Oxford University Press, 2016), 10.

24. Union membership rates in retail are estimated from the Current Population Survey. U.S. Census Bureau, Current Population Survey dataset (Washington D.C.: Government Printing Office, 1984–2017).

25. Kim Voss and Rachel Sherman, "Breaking the Iron Law of Oligarchy: Union Revitalization in the American Labor Movement," *American Journal of Sociology* 106, no. 2 (2000): 303–349, p. 331. Voss and Sherman divide

their cases into "fully revitalized" and "partially revitalized" union locals. Whereas 50 percent of the SEIU locals and 40 percent of the HERE locals were "fully revitalized," none of the UFCW locals were.

26. Kim Moody, *US Labor in Trouble and Transition: The Failure of Reform from Above, the Promise of Revival from Below* (New York: Verso, 2007), 233.

27. Ruth Milkman, "Win or Lose: Lessons from Two Contrasting Union Campaigns," *Social Policy* 35, no. 2 (2004–2005): 43–47.

28. Nelson Lichtenstein, "Wal-Mart: A Template for Twenty-First-Century Capitalism," in *Walmart: The Face of Twenty-First Century Capitalism*, ed. Nelson Lichtenstein (New York: New Press, 2006), 3–30. Lichtenstein writes that this collection of essays actually emerged as a result of the strike.

29. Voss and Sherman, "Breaking the Iron Law of Oligarchy."

30. See Milkman, "Win or Lose."

31. The Hotel Employees and Restaurant Employees Union, now part of UNITE HERE, may be the union that today gets closest to this evangelism.

32. Here it is worth noting that the most important union campaigns of the last decades have been in such sectors. That is not accidental: the structuring of employment is increasingly driving workers into settings (like home health care) where working to rule as a strategy for resistance is likely fruitless.

33. Alexis de Tocqueville, *Democracy in America*, translated by George Lawrence, edited by J. P. Mayer (New York: Harper & Row, 1969), p. 517.

34. Saul Alinsky, *Rules for Radicals: A Practical Primer for Realistic Radicals* (New York: Vintage, 1989 [1971]); Hahrie Han, *How Organizations Develop Activists: Civic Associations and Leadership in the 21st Century* (New York: Oxford University Press, 2014); and Jane McAlevey, *No Shortcuts: Organizing for Power in the New Gilded Age* (New York: Oxford University Press, 2016).

35. Steven Greenhouse, "Wal-Mart Plays Down Labor Protests at Its Stores," *New York Times*, November 23, 2012.

36. Josh Eidelson, "The Great Walmart Walkout," *The Nation*, December 19, 2012.

37. Susan Berfield, "How Walmart Keeps an Eye on Its Massive Workforce: The Retail Giant Is Always Watching," *Bloomberg Businessweek*, November 24, 2015, www.bloomberg.com/features/2015-walmart-union-surveillance.

38. Schuyler Velasco, "Walmart Legal Troubles Mount as Black Friday Walkout Looms," *Christian Science Monitor*, October 23, 2012, www .csmonitor.com/Business/2012/1023/Walmart-legal-troubles-mount -as-Black-Friday-walkout-looms.

39. Of course the encounter wasn't exactly serendipitous; the organizer was quite purposefully working through her existing networks to find possible recruits.

40. Albert Hirschman, *Exit, Voice, and Loyalty: Responses to Decline in Firms, Organizations, and States* (Cambridge: Harvard University Press, 1970).

41. Kelly Services, one of the oldest temp agencies in the country, was founded in Detroit in 1946, soon after the end of World War II, by William Russell Kelly, who paired a need among employers for "Kelly girls," a flexible workforce of young women who would provide secretarial services on demand, with a pool of young women, many of whom had been recruited into full-time work during the war and chafed at again being consigned to traditional prewar gender norms. See, e.g., Ruth Milkman, *Gender at Work: The Dynamics of Job Segregation by Sex During World War II* (Urbana: University of Illinois Press, 1987). According to Kelly's obituary in the *Times*, an early advertisement for the company exhorted, "The next time you get fed up with the household routine, join the Kelly Girl Service," and Kelly himself had discussed how "we had our employees view a filmstrip to help them explain to their husbands or fathers why it was all right for a woman to be working." Leslie Eaton, "William Kelly, 92, Founder of Temporary Jobs Company," *New York Times*, January 8, 1998, accessed October 16, 2015, www.nytimes.com/1998/01/08/business/william-kelly-92-founder-of-temporary-jobs-company.html.

42. Mancur Olson, *The Logic of Collective Action: Public Goods and the Theory of Groups* (Cambridge, MA: Harvard University Press, 1971).

43. Tannock, *Youth at Work*, 113.

44. In his *Domination and the Arts of Resistance*, James Scott discusses how his analysis of domination is complicated in situations in which there is some room for exit, and that the case of the contemporary working class shows "how essential the existence of some choice is in raising the possibility of hegemonic incorporation." Nevertheless, he points out, "Even in the case of the contemporary working class, it appears that slights to one's dignity and close surveillance and control of one's work loom at least as large in accounts of oppression as do narrower concerns of work and compensation." James C. Scott, *Domination and the Arts of Resistance: Hidden Transcripts* (New Haven: Yale University Press, 1990), 22–23.

45. Hirschman, *Exit, Voice, and Loyalty*, 27–29.

46. Hirschman, *Exit, Voice, and Loyalty*, 77.

47. What did it mean to sign up? Workers who signed up as members committed to paying $5 per month to OUR Walmart. Members were not necessarily public about their membership, but signing brought one into the network of others who were known to Walmart management as OUR Walmart members. Members were also expected to participate in regular meetings and to plan and execute local actions. And signing put one at risk of being identified as anti-Walmart by supervisors who were hypersensitive to any signs of potential resistance.

48. Miller McPherson, Lynn Smith-Lovin, and James M. Cook, "Birds of a Feather: Homophily in Social Networks," *Annual Review of Sociology* 27 (2001): 415–444.

49. The one clear deviation from the trend was between the fifth and sixth signing, which has a much higher marginal signing time than those on either side of it. (This may very well be coincidental, given the small number of stores with 50 signers, but is consistent with classic research on small groups that suggests an optimal size of five. J. Richard Hackman and Neil Vidmar, "Effects of Size and Task Type on Group Performance and Member Reactions," *Sociometry* 33, no. 1 (1970): 37–54.

50. See, for instance, Mark Granovetter, "Threshold Models of Collective Behavior," *American Journal of Sociology* 83, no. 6 (1978): 1420–1443; and Pamela Oliver, Gerald Marwell, and Ruy Teixeira, "A Theory of the Critical Mass. I. Interdependence, Group Heterogeneity, and the Production of Collective Action," *American Journal of Sociology* 91, no. 3 (1985): 522–556.

51. The relationship between one's support for joining a labor organization and being in a customer-facing role is not always positive, as it is at Walmart. In hotels, for example, front desk workers tend to be the hardest to organize, because they tend to be on a different, management track. Conversation with Teresa Sharpe.

52. Selection on personality (broadly construed) could influence their role in the campaign. Fitting-room associates, while likely to sign up for the organization, were relatively unlikely to be a "first signer" in a store—only one out of 26 fitting-room associates (3.8 percent) was a first signer. In contrast, 17 of the 124 cart pushers (13.7 percent) were first signers. Organizers might reach cart pushers first, or cart pushers might be more independent-minded than other employees. A mix of both processes is probably in play, and either way, cart pushers are more likely to be the first movers. Walmart workers don't precisely select their jobs, of course, but they do have opportunities to put themselves in different settings. While not all cart pushers, for example, want to be cart pushers, those who want to be will have no trouble being assigned to work outdoors, as the job is generally undesirable.

53. For a more detailed exploration of this relationship, see Suresh Naidu and Adam Reich, "Collective Action and Customer Service in Retail," *Industrial and Labor Relations Review* (2017), https://doi.org/10.1177/0019793917748601.

54. Several economists have used "distance from Bentonville" in combination with year fixed effects to instrument the presence of Walmart in a region. See, for instance, David Neumark, Junfu Zhang, and Stephen Ciccarella, "The Effects of Wal-Mart on Local Labor Markets," *Journal of Urban Economics* 63 (2008): 405–430.

55. Admittedly, such hot shop organizing—organizing where there is the most expressed worker interest—has to be integrated with the overall aims of a movement. One can jump from hot shop to hot shop willy-nilly and find that the movement is weaker because effort is scattered across space and unable to fuel itself.

5. SOCIAL TIES AND SOCIAL CHANGE

1. Bruce Nissen, "Alternative Strategic Directions for the U.S. Labor Movement," *Labor Studies Journal* 28, no. 1 (2003): 133–155; and Kim Moody, *US Labor in Trouble and Transition: The Failure of Reform from Above, the Promise of Revival from Below* (New York: Verso, 2007).

2. Richard A. Peterson and Roger M. Kern, "Changing Highbrow Taste: From Snob to Omnivore," *American Sociological Review* 61 (1996): 900–907; and Shamus Khan, *Privilege: The Making of An Adolescent Elite at St. Paul's School* (Princeton, N.J.: Princeton University Press, 2011). In case there is any doubt, they also still sequester themselves in privileged hamlets.

3. As we have suggested, this outcome was not preordained. OUR Walmart had succeeded in pushing Walmart to a breaking point on the eve of the 2012 Black Friday strikes. By the summer of 2014, however, this momentum had largely dissipated.

4. Nelson Lichtenstein, *The Retail Revolution: How Wal-Mart Created a Brave New World of Business* (New York: Picador, 2010[2009]), 182.

5. Randall Palmer and Allison Martell, "Canada Court Rules Against Wal-Mart Over Quebec Store Closure," Reuters, June 27, 2014, http://ca.reuters .com/article/domesticNews/idCAKBN0F21HM20140627.

6. Michael Schwartz, *Radical Protest and Social Structure: The Southern Farmers' Alliance and Cotton Tenancy, 1880-1890* (New York: Academic, 1976). See also E. E. Schattschneider, *The Semi-Sovereign People: A Realist's View of Democracy in America* (Hinsdale, Ill.: Dryden, 1960).

7. Lichtenstein (2010[2009]), 184–196.

8. In addition to accounts of being terminated on the basis of video capture, associates report, for example, that store managers watch the tape, observe who is talking to whom, and then ask about the content of those conversations.

9. Steven Greenhouse, "How Walmart Persuades Its Workers Not to Unionize," *The Atlantic*, June 8, 2015, www.theatlantic.com/business/archive/2015/06 /how-walmart-convinces-its-employees-not-to-unionize/395051.

10. www.youtube.com/watch?v=ZD2Nt4LS5yg [Accessed September 9, 2016].

11. Hyojoung Kim and Peter Bearman, "The Structure and Dynamics of Movement Participation," *American Sociological Review* 62, no. 1 (1997): 70–93.
12. That feels like the all too common academic experience of spending all day writing and discovering the next morning that you added a single comma.
13. There are roughly 147 million workers in nonfarm occupations in the United States. Walmart employs 1.4 million workers, or 1 percent. Central Florida has many retired people, and they live in houses. It follows that the chance that someone working at Walmart was behind one of the closed doors that the students knocked on was absurdly low, about 1 in 150, just about the same as winning $5 in the Florida Gold Rush Double scratch-off lottery.
14. The idea that class overlies and is consolidated with other social cleavages rather than crosscutting them. See Patricia Hill Collins, "It's All in the Family: Intersections of Gender, Race, and Nation," *Hypatia* 13, no. 3 (1998): 62–82; Leslie McCall, *Complex Inequality: Gender, Class, and Race in the New Economy* (New York: Routledge, 2001); and Leslie McCall, "The Complexity of Intersectionality," *Signs* 30, no. 3 (2005): 1771–1800.
15. The difference in how sites were organized may reflect whether or not the lead staffers were OUR Walmart hires or UFCW assignees. When the latter were running the show, as in Chicago and Los Angeles, creativity in developing new organizing strategies, care for inclusiveness, and sensitivity to feelings seemed less prevalent.
16. Stanley Milgram, *Obedience to Authority: An Experimental View* (New York: Harper & Row, 1974); for a useful summary, see Barrington Moore, *Injustice: The Social Bases of Obedience and Revolt* (Stamford, Conn.: Ray Freiman, 1978), 94–100.
17. William A. Gamson, Bruce Fireman, and Steven Rytina, *Encounters with Unjust Authority* (Homewood, Ill.: Dorsey, 1982).

6. OUR WALMART ON THE LINE

1. Nelson Lichtenstein, ed., *Wal-Mart: The Face of Twenty-First-Century Capitalism*, (New York: New Press, 2006).
2. "In Letter to Associates, Walmart CEO Doug McMillon Announces Higher Pay," Walmart Today (blog), February 19, 2015, http://blog.walmart.com/opportunity/20150219/in-letter-to-associates-walmart-ceo-doug-mcmillon-announces-higher-pay.
3. Paul Krugman, "Walmart's Visible Hand," *New York Times*, March 2, 2015, www.nytimes.com/2015/03/02/opinion/paul-krugman-walmarts-visible-hand.html.

4. Benn Steil and Dinah Walker, "Why Did Walmart Raise Its Wages?," *Forbes*, April 2, 2015, www.forbes.com/sites/realspin/2015/04/02/why-did -walmart-raises-its-wages/#691ea41c2a9e.

5. Neil Irwin, "How Did Walmart Get Cleaner Stores and Higher Sales? It Paid Its People More," *New York Times*, October 15, 2016, www.nytimes .com/2016/10/16/upshot/how-did-walmart-get-cleaner-stores-and -higher-sales-it-paid-its-people-more.html?_r=0.

6. Lydia DePillis, "A Key Union Appears to Be Backing Away from One of Labor's Most Prominent Campaigns," *Wonkblog* (blog), *Washington Post*, April 15, 2015, www.washingtonpost.com/news/wonk/wp/2015/04/15 /one-union-appears-to-be-backing-away-from-labors-most-prominent -campaign.

 The article documented support for campaigns like OUR Walmart and the Fight for Fifteen, and then asked: "What if it never turns protestors into dues-paying members? Actually winning elections at giant employers like Wal-Mart and McDonald's, which have gone to great lengths to deter unionization, appears nearly impossible. What if the unions' return on that organizing investment, besides the satisfaction of having helped workers more broadly, is essentially zero?"

7. Cora Lewis, "Union Fires Walmart Campaigners as Focus Shifts to Media," *Buzzfeed News*, June 30, 2015, www.buzzfeed.com/coralewis/union-fires -walmart-campaigners-as-focus-shifts-to-media?utm_term= .vhDpnrkyZB#.vyN4Av1lgB.

8. Chris Isadore, "Walmart Ups Pay Well Above Minimum Wage," *CNN Money*, February 19, 2015, http://money.cnn.com/2015/02/19/news/companies /walmart-wages.

9. Meghan DeMaria, "Walmart Is Raising Its Minimum Wage for More Than 100,000 U.S. Workers," *The Week*, June 2, 2015, http://theweek.com/speed reads/558414/walmart-raising-minimum-wage-more-than-100000 -workers.

10. Steven Greenhouse, "Wal-Mart Plays Down Labor Protests at Its Stores," *New York Times*, November 23, 2012.

11. Robert H. Zieger, *The CIO 1935–1955* (Chapel Hill: University of North Carolina Press, 1995); Sidney Fine, *Sit-Down: The General Motors Strike of 1936–1937* (Ann Arbor: University of Michigan Press, 1969); and Irving Bernstein, *Turbulent Years: A History of the American Worker, 1933–1941* (Boston: Houghton Mifflin, 1970 [1969]).

12. Saul Alinsky, *Rules for Radicals: A Practical Primer for Realistic Radicals* (New York: Vintage, 1989 [1971]), 105.

13. Jane McAlevey, *No Shortcuts: Organizing for Power* (New York: Oxford University Press, 2016), 201.

14. This is Louis Althusser's exposition on the religious teachings of Blaise Pascal. Louis Althusser, "Ideology and Ideological State Apparatuses," in *Media and Cultural Studies: Keyworks*, edited by Meenakshi Gigi Durham and Douglas M. Kellner (Malden, Mass.: Blackwell, 2006[2001]), 83.

15. Kim Voss and Rachel Sherman, "Breaking the Iron Law of Oligarchy: Union Revitalization in the American Labor Movement," *American Journal of Sociology* 106, no. 2 (2000): 303–349.

16. Alinsky, *Rules for Radicals*, 93.

17. David Brody, *Labor Embattled: History, Power, Rights* (Champaign, Ill.: University of Illinois Press, 2005).

18. Kate E. Andrias, "A Robust Public Debate: Realizing Free Speech in Workplace Representation Elections," *The Yale Law Journal* 112, no. 8 (2003), 2415–2416; and Nelson Lichtenstein, *The Retail Revolution: How Wal-Mart Created a Brave New World of Business* (New York: Picador, 2010[2009]), 159.

19. For example, in both *N.L.R.B. v. Babcock & Wilcox, Co.* (1956) and *Lechmere, Inc. v. N.L.R.B.* (1992), the Court reasoned that workers' organization rights needed to be balanced against a company's property rights, and so it was within an employer's right to ban nonemployee organizers from "trespassing" by handing out literature in or around a company parking lot. Scholars have suggested that such redefinitions contributed to a decline in union election victories in the years after *Babcock*. Sarah Korn, "Property Rights and Job Security: Workplace Solicitation by Nonemployee Union Organizers," *The Yale Law Journal*, 94, no. 2 (1984), 383; see also Paul Weiler, "Promises to Keep: Securing Workers' Rights to Self-Organization Under the NLRA," *Harvard Law Review* 96, no. 8 (1983), 1796–1827.

20. Voss and Rachel Sherman, "Breaking the Iron Law of Oligarchy"; and Ruth Milkman, *L.A. Story: Immigrant Workers and the Future of the U.S. Labor Movement* (New York: Russell Sage Foundation, 2006).

21. Granted, even this sort of interactive freedom is not guaranteed. Employers can try to limit the types of interactions that organizers (and others) have with employees—primarily through the enactment and enforcement of "no solicitation" policies. Such policies are technically legal, so long as they do not enforce the policy discriminately against unions, and provided that employers do not establish them for the "sole purpose" of thwarting an organizing drive (Andrias [2003], 2441; *N.L.R.B. v. St. Francis Healthcare Centre* [2000]; G. Harrison Darby and Margaret Bryant, "When Unions Knock, How Should Employers Answer?," *HR Magazine* 42, no. 7 (1997), 124–129. Current law tends to uphold bans on the distribution of literature and requests for signatures at the workplace. In a 2003 decision, the National Labor Relations Board (NLRB) wrote that the presentation of a card for a worker to sign crossed the line into solicitation, because

it "prompts an immediate response from the individual or individuals being solicited and therefore presents a greater potential for interference with employer productivity if the employees are supposed to be working" (*Wal-Mart Stores*, 340 NLRB 639). But it seems to leave open *other* kinds of conversation about worker organization—those that do not involve explicit appeals for support and do not "disrupt" worker productivity.

22. Erik Forman, "Let's Get to Work: 'Salting' Built the Early American Labor Movement—and It Can Revive It Today," *Jacobin*, February 7, 2017, www.jacobinmag.com/2017/02/labor-unions-workers-salts-students-organizing; and Carey Dall and Jonathan Cohen, "Salting the Earth: Organizing for the Long Haul," *New Labor Forum* 10 (2002): 36–41.

23. Brett Caraway, "OUR Walmart: A Case Study of Connective Action," *Information, Communication & Society* 19, no. 7 (2015): 1–14.

24. Na Sun, Patrick Pei-Luen Raw, and Liang Ma, "Understanding Lurkers in Online Communities: A Literature Review," *Computers in Human Behavior* 38 (2014): 110–117.

25. Peter Bearman, *Doormen* (Chicago: University of Chicago Press, 2005).

26. Alix Rule, Jean-Philippe Cointet, and Peter S. Bearman, "Lexical Shifts, Substantive Changes, and Continuity in State of the Union Discourse," *Proceedings of the National Academy of Sciences* 112, no. 35 (2015), 10837–10844; Mark Hoffman, Jean-Philippe Cointet, Philipp Brandt, Newton Key, and Peter Bearman. "The (Protestant) Bible, the (Printed) Sermon, and the Word(s): The Semantic Structure of the Conformist and Dissenting Bible, 1660–1780." *Poetics* (Forthcoming), https://doi.org/10.1016/j.poetic.2017.11.002.

27. Pamela Oliver, Gerald Marwell, and Ruy Teixeira, "A Theory of the Critical Mass. I. Interdependence, Group Heterogeneity, and the Production of Collective Action," *American Journal of Sociology* 91, no. 3 (1985): 522–556.

28. Zeynep Tufekci, *Twitter and Tear Gas: The Power and Fragility of Networked Protest* (New Haven: Yale University Press, 2017), 154–156.

29. Marshall Ganz discusses how the United Farm Workers incorporated principles of mutual aid into its organizing before it became a powerful collective movement. See Marshall Ganz, *Why David Sometimes Wins: Leadership, Organization, and Strategy in the California Farm Worker Movement* (New York: Oxford University Press, 2009).

30. Think Kickstarter or GoFundMe, but organized around collective action, e.g., "I agree to strike if and only if 60 percent of my coworkers also agree to strike."

31. In 2012, the ACLU released an app, MobileJustice, that allows citizens to record interactions with law enforcement. One might imagine a similar function to record cases of unfair discipline or harassment within

the workplace. "MobileJustice," ACLU, accessed October 10, 2017, www
.aclu.org/issues/criminal-law-reform/reforming-police-practices
/aclu-apps-record-police-conduct.

32. See, for instance, Mai-Ly N. Steers, Robert E. Wickham, and Linda K.
Acitelli, "Seeing Everyone Else's Highlight Reels: How Facebook Usage Is
Linked to Depressive Symptoms," *Journal of Social and Clinical Psychology*
33, no. 8 (2014): 701–731. The findings here could also quite easily be an
artifact of a more complex selection process; people with nothing else to
do spend more time on Facebook than those with alternatives, and the
absence of alternatives is depressing. Or it could be because on Facebook,
as in real life, one's friends have more friends than one does, on average,
and this might make one feel less desirable. Or it may be that Facebook
encourages a certain kind of vacuity simply because the expectation is for
a short post, and it is hard not to be vacuous in just a few sentences, and
prolonged exposure to vacuous content is ultimately quite depressing.

33. Erving Goffman, *The Presentation of Self in Everyday Life* (New York: Doubleday, 1959). Thanks to Chris Muller and Sammy Zahran for discussions about
this idea.

7. OUR WALMART

1. Richard D. Kahlenberg and Moshe Z. Marvit, *Why Labor Organizing Should
Be a Civil Right: Rebuilding a Middle-Class Democracy by Enhancing Worker Voice*
(New York: Century Foundation, 2012).

2. Alexandra Bradbury, "Generation Temp: Auto Workers March for Civil Rights
Again," *Labor Notes*, July 22, 2014. www.labornotes.org/blogs/2014/07
/generation-temp-auto-workers-march-civil-rights-again?language=es.

3. Mike Elk, "Pro-union Rally in Mississippi Unites Workers with Community:
'We Are Ready,'" *The Guardian*, March 5, 2017, www.theguardian.com/us
-news/2017/mar/05/union-rally-mississippi-nissan-bernie-sanders.

4. Nick Carey, "Nissan Mississippi Workers Vote Heavily Against Unionization,"
Reuters, August 5, 2017, www.reuters.com/article/us-uaw-mississippi
-nissan/nissan-mississippi-workers-vote-heavily-against-unionization
-idUSKBN1AL02O.

5. We cannot say definitively that the reunion deepened students' commitment; it may be selection, in that the groups that felt most committed
to the project sent delegations because of their commitment. That said,
distance from Tougaloo is probably a better explanation for variation in
attendance, since it was the longest drive from Chicago and Los Angeles.

6. Jana Kasperkevic, "Struggling Workers Take Wage Protest to Upscale Doorstep of Walmart Heiress Alice Walton," *The Guardian*, October 17, 2014, www.theguardian.com/money/us-money-blog/2014/oct/17 /walmart-workers-protest-arrests-alice-walton-home.

7. Noam Scheiber, "Nissan Workers in Mississippi Reject Union Bid by U.A.W.," *New York Times*, August 5, 2017, www.nytimes.com/2017/08/05 /business/nissan-united-auto-workers-union.html.

8. Justin Miller, "Nissan Union Loss Underscores Labor's Big Dilemma," *American Prospect*, August 8, 2017, http://prospect.org/article/nissan -union-loss-underscores-labor-big-dilemma.

9. Scheiber, "Nissan Workers in Mississippi Reject Union Bid by U.A.W."

10. Chris Brooks, "Why Did Nissan Workers Vote No?" *Labor Notes*, August 11, 2017, www.labornotes.org/2017/08/why-did-nissan-workers-vote-no.

11. Joe Allen, "A Crushing Blow," *Jacobin*, August 7, 2017, accessed October 1, 2017, www.jacobinmag.com/2017/08/uaw-mississippi-nissan-union-labor -election-autoworkers.

12. Scheiber, "Nissan Workers in Mississippi Reject Union Bid by U.A.W."

13. Steven Greenhouse, "Volkswagen Vote Is Defeat for Labor in South," *New York Times*, February 14, 2014, www.nytimes.com/2014/02/15/business /volkswagen-workers-reject-forming-a-union.html.

14. Scheiber, "Nissan Workers in Mississippi Reject Union Bid by U.A.W."

15. Bureau of Labor Statistics, "Union Members–2010," https://www.bls.gov /news.release/archives/union2_01212011.pdf, accessed February 8, 2018; Bureau of Labor Statistics, "Union Members–2017" https://www.bls.gov /news.release/pdf/union2.pdf, accessed February 8, 2018.

16. Harold Meyerson, "A Post-Election Numbers Game," *Washington Post*, November 5, 2010, www.washingtonpost.com/wp-dyn/content/article /2010/11/04/AR2010110406639.html?nav=hcmodule.

17. This may be one of the reasons, as an aside, for the failed outcomes of a wide array of Facebook mobilization revolutions. It is often observed that a key difference between the relative success of the Tunisian incarnation of the Arab Spring and the Egyptian incarnation, for example, reflects the fact that while for both movements Facebook was critical for getting people into the streets, the capacity to resist the resurgence of dictatorial control in Tunisia uniquely arose from the fact that the ties that bound individuals together were deeply associational, linked to secondary associations far more robust than those of their Egyptian counterparts.

APPENDIX: THE NEURAL SIGNATURES OF GROUP LIFE

1. Pierre Bourdieu, *The Bachelor's Ball: Crisis of Peasant Society in Béarn* (Chicago: University of Chicago Press, 2008); Richard Sennett and Jonathan Cobb, *The Hidden Injuries of Class* (New York: Vintage, 1972); Michael Burawoy, *Manufacturing Consent: Changes in the Labor Process Under Monopoly Capitalism* (Chicago: University of Chicago Press, 1979); and Nancy Chodorow, *The Reproduction of Mothering: Psychoanalysis and the Sociology of Gender* (Berkeley: University of California Press, 1978).

2. Jo Freeman, "The Tyranny of Structurelessness," *Berkeley Journal of Sociology* 17 (1972): 151–164; John Levi Martin, "Power, Authority, and the Constraint of Belief Systems," *American Journal of Sociology* 107, no. 4 (2002): 861–904; and James A. Davis, "Clustering and Hierarchy in Interpersonal Relations: Testing Two Graph Theoretical Models on 742 Sociomatrices," *American Sociological Review* 35, no. 5 (1970): 843–851.

3. Peter Bearman, "Generalized Exchange," *American Journal of Sociology* 102, no. 5 (1997): 1383–1415; Alvin W. Gouldner, "The Norm of Reciprocity: A Preliminary Statement," *American Sociological Review* 25, no. 2 (1960): 161–178; and Georg Simmel, *The Sociology of Georg Simmel* (Glencoe, Ill.: Free Press, 1950).

4. Luke Dittrich, *Patient H.M.: A Story of Memory, Madness, and Family Secrets* (New York: Random House, 2016).

5. Hal Blumenfeld, *Neuroanatomy Through Clinical Cases* (Sunderland, Mass.: Sinauer, 2010).

6. For a review, see Matthew D. Lieberman, "Social Cognitive Neuroscience: A Review of Core Processes," *Annual Review of Psychology* 58 (2007): 259–289.

7. Noam Zerubavel, Peter S. Bearman, Jochen Weber, and Kevin N. Ochsner, "Neural Mechanisms Tracking Popularity in Real-World Social Networks," *Proceedings of the National Academy of Sciences USA* 112, no. 49 (2015): 15072–15077.

8. Zerubavel et al., "Neural Mechanisms Tracking Popularity in Real-World Social Networks."

9. Suzanne N. Haber and Brian Knutson, "The Reward Circuit: Linking Primate Anatomy and Human Imaging," *Neuropsychopharmacology* 35, no. 1 (2010): 4–26.

10. Zerubavel et al., "Neural Mechanisms Tracking Popularity in Real-World Social Networks."

11. Martin A. Nowak, "Five Rules for the Evolution of Cooperation," *Science* 314 (2006): 1560–1563; and Peter Bearman, "Generalized Exchange," *American Journal of Sociology* 102, no. 5 (1997): 1383–1415.

12. Denise Anthony, "Cooperation in Microcredit Borrowing Groups: Identity, Sanctions, and Reciprocity in the Production of Collective Goods," *American Sociological Review* 70 (2005): 496–515.

13. Stanley Milgram, *Obedience to Authority: An Experimental View* (New York: Harper & Row, 1974); for a useful summary, see Barrington Moore, *Injustice: The Social Bases of Obedience and Revolt* (Stamford, Conn.: Freiman, 1978), 94–100.

14. William A. Gamson, Bruce Fireman, and Steven Rytina, *Encounters with Unjust Authority* (Homewood, Ill.: Dorsey, 1982).

15. As an aside, this may be one of the reasons that having kids (sharing an instrumental project) does not save marriages that have gone awry with respect to reciprocal affect.

BIBLIOGRAPHY

Acemoglu, Daron, David H. Autor, and David Lyle. "Women, War, and Wages: The Effect of Female Labor Supply on the Wage Structure at Midcentury." *Journal of Political Economy* 112, no. 3 (2004): 497–550.

Acitelli, Linda K., Mai-Ly N. Steers, and Robert E. Wickham. "Seeing Everyone Else's Highlight Reels: How Facebook Usage Is Linked to Depressive Symptoms." *Journal of Social and Clinical Psychology* 33, no. 8 (2014): 701–731.

Alinsky, Saul. *Rules for Radicals: A Practical Primer for Realistic Radicals.* New York: Vintage, 1989 [1971].

Anderson, Elizabeth and Philip Pettit. *Republicanism: A Theory of Freedom and Government.* New York: Oxford University Press, 1997.

Anderson, Elizabeth. *Private Government: How Employers Rule Our Lives (and Why We Don't Talk About It).* Princeton, N.J.: Princeton University Press, 2017.

——. "What Is the Point of Equality?" *Ethics* 109, no. 2 (1999): 287–337.

Andrias, Kate E. "A Robust Public Debate: Realizing Free Speech in Workplace Representation Elections." *The Yale Law Journal* 112, no. 8 (2003): 2415–2416.

Anthony, Denise. "Cooperation in Microcredit Borrowing Groups: Identity, Sanctions, and Reciprocity in the Production of Collective Goods." *American Sociological Review* 70, no. 3 (2005): 496–515.

Aronowitz, Stanley, *The Death and Life of American Labor: Toward a New Workers' Movement.* New York: Verso, 2014.

Bakst, Dina, Elizabeth Gedmark, and Cara Suvall. "Pointing Out: How Walmart Unlawfully Punishes Workers for Medical Absences." A Better Balance,

New York, June 2017. https://www.abetterbalance.org/wp-content/uploads/2017/05/Pointing-Out-Walmart-Report-FINAL.pdf

Baldwin, Robert E. *The Decline of U.S. Labor Unions and the Role of Trade*. Washington, D.C.: Institute for International Economics, 2003.

Bateson, Gregory. *Steps to an Ecology of Mind*. New York: Ballantine, 1972.

Bearman, Peter. "Generalized Exchange." *American Journal of Sociology* 102, no. 5 (1997): 1383–1415.

——. *Doormen*. Chicago: University of Chicago Press, 2005.

Bearman, Peter and Kevin Everett. "The Structure of Social Protest, 1961–1983." *Social Networks* 15, no. 2 (1993): 171–200.

Bearman, Peter and Hyojoung Kim. "The Structure and Dynamics of Movement Participation." *American Sociological Review* 62, no. 1 (1997): 70–93.

Bearman, Peter S., Kevin N. Ochsner, Jochen Weber, and Noam Zerubavel. "Neural Mechanisms Tracking Popularity in Real-World Social Networks." *Proceedings of the National Academy of Sciences USA* 112, no. 49 (2015): 15072–15077.

Bergdahl, Michael. *What I Learned from Sam Walton: How to Compete and Thrive in a Wal-Mart World*. Hoboken, N.J.: Wiley, 2004.

Bernstein, Irving. *Turbulent Years: A History of the American Worker, 1933–1941*. Boston: Houghton Mifflin, 1970 [1969].

Block, Fred and Margaret R. Somers. "From Poverty to Perversity: Ideas, Markets, and Institutions over 200 Years of Welfare Debate." *American Sociological Review* 70, no. 2 (2005): 260–287.

Blumenfeld, Hal. *Neuroanatomy Through Clinical Cases*. Sunderland, Mass.: Sinauer, 2010.

Bourdieu, Pierre. *The Bachelor's Ball: Crisis of Peasant Society in Béarn*. Chicago: University of Chicago Press, 2008.

——. *Pascalian Meditations*. Stanford: Stanford University Press, 2000[1997].

Brody, David. *Labor Embattled: History, Power, Rights*. Champaign: University of Illinois Press, 2005.

Bronfenbrenner, Kate. "No Holds Barred—The Intensification of Employer Opposition to Organizing." Economic Policy Institute Briefing Paper #235, 2009.

Bronfenbrenner, Kate and Robert Hickey. *Blueprint for Change: A National Assessment of Winning Union Organizing Strategies*. Ithaca, N.Y.: Cornell University, New York State School of Industrial and Labor Relations, 2003.

Buhle, Paul. *Taking Care of Business: Samuel Gompers, George Meany, Lane Kirkland, and the Tragedy of American Labor*. New York: Monthly Review Press, 1999.

Burawoy, Michael. "The Extended Case Method." *Sociological Theory* 16, no. 1 (1998): 4–33.

——. *Manufacturing Consent: Changes in the Labor Process Under Monopoly Capitalism*. Chicago: University of Chicago Press, 1979.

Cain, Carole. "Personal Stories: Identity Acquisition and Self-Understanding in Alcoholics Anonymous." *Ethos* 19, no. 2 (1991): 210–253.

Caraway, Brett. "OUR Walmart: A Case Study of Connective Action." *Information, Communication & Society* 19, no. 7 (2015): 1–14.

Carlon, Helen, Marc Dixon, and Nella Van Dyke. "Manufacturing Dissent: Labor Revitalization, Union Summer and Student Protest." *Social Forces* 86, no. 1 (2007): 193–214.

Carwardine, William. *The Pullman Strike.* New York: Arno, 1969 [1894].

Cayton, Andrew R. L. "The Significance of Ohio in the Early American Republic." In *The Center of a Great Empire: The Ohio Country in the Early Republic*, edited by Andrew R. L. Cayton and Stuart D. Hobbs, 1–10. Athens: Ohio University Press, 2005.

Chetty, Raj, David Grusky, Maximilian Hell, Nathaniel Hendren, Robert Manduca, and Jimmy Narang. "The Fading American Dream: Trends in Absolute Income Mobility Since 1940." National Bureau of Economic Research Working Paper 22910, Cambridge Mass., 2016.

Chodorow, Nancy. *The Reproduction of Mothering: Psychoanalysis and the Sociology of Gender.* Berkeley: University of California Press, 1978.

Ciccarella, Stephen, David Neumark, and Junfu Zhang. "The Effects of Wal-Mart on Local Labor Markets." *Journal of Urban Economics* 63 (2008): 405–430.

Cobb, Jonathan and Richard Sennett. *The Hidden Injuries of Class.* New York: Vintage, 1972.

Cohen, Jonathan and Carey Dall. "Salting the Earth: Organizing for the Long Haul." *New Labor Forum* 10 (2002): 36–41.

Collins, Jane. "The Opposite of Fordism: Wal-Mart Rolls Back a Regime of Accumulation." Paper prepared for What's Wrong with America? conference at MIT, Cambridge, Mass., May 26, 2006.

Collins, Jane L. and Victoria Mayer. *Both Hands Tied: Welfare Reform and the Race to the Bottom in the Low-Wage Labor Market.* Chicago: University of Chicago Press, 2010.

Collins, Patricia Hill. "It's All in the Family: Intersections of Gender, Race, and Nation." *Hypatia* 13, no. 3 (1998): 62–82.

Cook, James M., Miller McPherson, and Lynn Smith-Lovin. "Birds of a Feather: Homophily in Social Networks." *Annual Review of Sociology* 27 (2001): 415–444.

Creswell, John. *Designing and Conducting Mixed Methods Research.* Thousand Oaks, Calif.: Sage, 2007.

Darby, G. Harrison and Margaret Bryant. "When Unions Knock, How Should Employers Answer?" *HR Magazine* 42, no. 7 (1997): 124–129.

Davis, James A. "Clustering and Hierarchy in Interpersonal Relations: Testing Two Graph Theoretical Models on 742 Sociomatrices." *American Sociological Review* 35, no. 5 (1970): 843–851.

Dittrich, Luke. *Patient H. M.: A Story of Memory, Madness, and Family Secrets.* New York: Random House, 2016.

Edwards, Richard. *Contested Terrain: The Transformation of the Workplace in the Twentieth Century.* New York: Basic Books, 1979.

Ehrenreich, Barbara. *Nickel and Dimed: On (Not) Getting by in America.* New York: Holt, 2002.

Emsellem, Maurice and Michelle Natividad Rodriguez, "Advancing a Federal Fair Chance Hiring Agenda." National Employment Law Project, New York, January 2015.

Fantasia, Rick and Kim Voss. *Hard Work: Remaking the American Labor Movement* Berkeley: University of California Press, 2004.

Fine, Sidney. *Sit-Down: The General Motors Strike of 1936-1937.* Ann Arbor: University of Michigan Press, 1969.

Fireman, Bruce, William A. Gamson, and Steven Rytina. *Encounters with Unjust Authority* Homewood, Ill.: Dorsey, 1982.

Fishman, Charles. *The Wal-Mart Effect.* New York: Penguin, 2006.

Freeman, Jo. "The Tyranny of Structurelessness." *Berkeley Journal of Sociology* 17 (1972): 151–164.

Freeman, Richard B. "What Can Labor Organizations Do for U.S. Workers when Unions Can't Do What Unions Used to Do?" In *What Works for Workers? Public Policies and Innovative Strategies for Low-Wage Workers,* edited by Stephanie Luce, Jennifer Luff, Joseph A. McCartin, and Ruth Milkman, 50–78. New York: Russell Sage Foundation, 2014.

Freeman, Richard B. and Morris M. Kleiner. "Employer Behavior in the Face of Union Organizing Drives." *Industrial and Labor Relations Review* 43, no. 4 (1990): 351–365.

Freeman, Richard and James Medoff. *What Do Unions Do?* New York: Basic Books, 1984.

Fry, Richard. *For First Time in Modern Era, Living with Parents Edges Out Other Living Arrangements for 18- to 34-Year-Olds.* Washington, D.C.: Pew Research Center, May 2016.

Fuller, Linda and Vicki Smith. "Consumers' Reports: Management by Customers in a Changing Economy." *Work, Employment & Society* 5, no. 1 (1991): 1–16.

Ganz, Marshall. *Why David Sometimes Wins: Leadership, Organization, and Strategy in the California Farm Worker Movement.* New York: Oxford University Press, 2009.

Goffman, Erving. *The Presentation of Self in Everyday Life.* New York: Doubleday, 1959.

Goldin, Claudia. "Richard T. Ely Lecture: The Quiet Revolution That Transformed Women's Employment, Education, and Family." *AEA Papers and Proceedings* 96, no. 2 (2006): 1–21

Gouldner, Alvin W. "The Norm of Reciprocity: A Preliminary Statement." *American Sociological Review* 25, no. 2 (1960): 161–178.

Gourevitch, Alex. "Labor Republicanism and the Transformation of Work." *Political Theory* 41, no. 4 (2013): 591–617.

Granovetter, Mark. "Threshold Models of Collective Behavior." *American Journal of Sociology* 83, no. 6 (1978): 1420–1443.

Haber, Suzanne N. and Brian Knutson. "The Reward Circuit: Linking Primate Anatomy and Human Imaging." *Neuropsychopharmacology* 35, no. 1 (2010): 4–26.

Hackman, J. Richard and Neil Vidmar. "Effects of Size and Task Type on Group Performance and Member Reactions." *Sociometry* 33, no. 1 (1970): 37–54.

Hausman, Jerry and Ephraim Leibtag. "CPI Bias from Supercenters: Does the BLS Know that Wal-Mart Exists?" *NBER Working Paper 10712,* National Bureau of Economic Research, Cambridge, Mass., August 2004.

Hirschman, Albert. *Exit, Voice, and Loyalty: Responses to Decline in Firms, Organizations, and States.* Cambridge: Harvard University Press, 1970.

Hochschild, Arlie R. *The Managed Heart: Commercialization of Human Feeling.* Berkeley: University of California Press, 1983.

——. *The Second Shift: Working Parents and the Revolution at Home.* New York: Viking, 1989.

——. *The Time Bind: When Work Becomes Home and Home Becomes Work.* New York: Metropolitan, 1997.

Hoffman, Mark, Jean-Philippe Cointet, Philipp Brandt, Newton Key, and Peter Bearman. "The (Protestant) Bible, the (Printed) Sermon, and the Word(s): The Semantic Structure of the Conformist and Dissenting Bible, 1660–1780." *Poetics* (Forthcoming), https://doi.org/10.1016/j.poetic.2017.11.002.

Holmes, Thomas J. "The Diffusion of Wal-Mart and Economies of Density." *Econometrica* 79, no. 1 (2011): 253–302.

Honey, Michael K. *Going Down Jericho Road: The Memphis Strike, Martin Luther King's Last Campaign.* New York: Norton, 2007.

Han, Hahrie. *How Organizations Develop Activists: Civic Associations and Leadership in the 21st Century.* New York: Oxford University Press, 2014.

Ikeler, Peter. *Hard Sell: Work and Resistance in Retail Chains.* Ithaca, N.Y.: Cornell University Press, 2016.

Jacobs, Ken, Dave Graham-Squire, and Stephanie Luce. "Living Wage Policies and Big-Box Retail: How a Higher Wage Standard Would Impact Walmart Workers and Shoppers." *Center for Labor Research and Education, University of California*, Berkeley, April 2011.

Jakab, Peter L. *Visions of a Flying Machine: The Wright Brothers and the Process of Invention.* Washington, D.C.: Smithsonian Institution, 1990.

Johnson, R. Burke, Anthony J. Onwuegbuzie, and Lisa A., Turner. "Toward a Definition of Mixed Methods Research." *Journal of Mixed Methods Research* 1, no. 2 (2007): 112–133.

Kahlenberg, Richard D. and Moshe Z. Marvit. *Why Labor Organizing Should Be a Civil Right: Rebuilding a Middle-Class Democracy by Enhancing Worker Voice*. New York: Century Foundation, 2012.

Karjanen, David. "The Wal-Mart Effect and the New Face of Capitalism: Labor Market and Community Impacts of the Megaretailer." In *Wal-Mart: The Face of Twenty-First-Century Capitalism*, edited by Nelson Lichtenstein, 143–162. New York: New Press, 2006.

Kern, Roger M. and Richard A. Peterson. "Changing Highbrow Taste: From Snob to Omnivore." *American Sociological Review* 61 (1996): 900–907.

Kessler-Harris, Alice. *Out to Work: A History of Wage-Earning Women in the United States*. New York: Oxford University Press, 1982.

Khan, Shamus. *Privilege: The Making of An Adolescent Elite at St. Paul's School*. Princeton, N.J.: Princeton University Press, 2011.

Kleiner, Morris M. "Intensity of Management Resistance: Understanding the Decline of Unionization in the Private Sector." *Journal of Labor Research* 22, no. 3 (2001): 519–540.

Korczynski, Markek. "The Customer in the Sociology of Work: Different Ways of Going Beyond the Management-Worker Dyad." *Work, Employment & Society* 27, no. 6 (2013): NP1–NP7.

Korn, Sarah. "Property Rights and Job Security: Workplace Solicitation by Non-employee Union Organizers." *The Yale Law Journal*, 94, no. 2 (1984): 374–393.

Kristal, Tali. "The Capitalist Machine: Computerization, Workers' Power, and the Decline in Labor's Share Within U.S. Industries." *American Sociological Review* 78, no. 3 (2013): 361–389.

Leidner, Robin. *Fast Food, Fast Talk: Service Work and the Routinization of Everyday Life*. Berkeley: University of California Press, 1993.

Leifer, Eric. "Interaction Preludes to Role Setting: Exploratory Local Action." *American Sociological Review* 53, no. 6 (1988): 865–878.

Lewis, Penny. *Hardhats, Hippies, and Hawks: The Vietnam Antiwar Movement as Myth and Memory*. Ithaca, N.Y.: Cornell University Press, 2013.

Lichtenstein, Nelson. "In the Age of Wal-Mart: Precarious Work and Authoritarian Management in the Global Supply Chain." In *Globalization and Precarious Forms of Production and Employment*, edited by Carole Thorney, Steve Jefferys, and Beatric Appay, 10–22. Northampton, Mass.: Elgar, 2010.

——. "A Race Between Cynicism and Hope: Labor and Academia." *New Labor Forum* 10 (2002): 71–79.

——. *The Retail Revolution: How Wal-Mart Created a Brave New World of Business*. New York: Picador, 2010 [2009].

——. "Wal-Mart: A Template for Twenty-First-Century Capitalism." In *Walmart: The Face of Twenty-First Century Capitalism*, edited by Nelson Lichtenstein, 3–30. New York: New Press, 2006.

Lieberman, Matthew D. "Social Cognitive Neuroscience: A Review of Core Processes." *Annual Review of Psychology* 58 (2007): 259–289.

Logan, John. "The Union Avoidance Industry in the United States." *British Journal of Industrial Relations* 44, no. 4 (2006): 651–675.

Lopez, Steven Henry. "Workers, Managers, and Customers: Triangles of Power in Work Communities." *Work and Occupations* 37, no. 3 (2010): 251–271.

Lopez, Steven. *Reorganizing the Rust Belt: An Inside Study of the American Labor Movement*. Berkeley: University of California Press, 2004.

Low, John and W. Lloyd Warner. *The Social System of the Modern Factory: The Strike: A Social Analysis*. New Haven, Conn.: Yale University Press, 1947.

Lundquist, Jennifer, Devah Pager, and Eiko Strader. "Does a Criminal Past Predict Worker Performance? Evidence from America's Largest Employer." *Social Forces* 96, no. 3 (2018): 1039–1068.

Ma, Liang, Pei-Luen Patrick Rau, and Na Sun. "Understanding Lurkers in Online Communities: A Literature Review." *Computers in Human Behavior* 38 (2014): 110–117.

Mann, Michael. *The Sources of Social Power, vol. 2, The Rise of Classes and Nation States, 1760–1914*. New York: Cambridge University Press, 1993.

Martin, John Levi. "Power, Authority, and the Constraint of Belief Systems." *American Journal of Sociology* 107, no. 4 (2002): 861–904.

Marwell, Gerald, Pamela Oliver, and Ruy Teixeira. "A Theory of the Critical Mass. I. Interdependence, Group Heterogeneity, and the Production of Collective Action." *American Journal of Sociology* 91, no. 3 (1985): 522–556.

Marx, Karl. *Capital: A Critique of Political Economy*. Translated by Samuel Moore and Edward Aveling. Mineola, N.Y.: Dover, 2011 [1906].

Massengill, Rebekah Peeples. *Wal-Mart Wars: Moral Populism in the Twenty-First Century*. New York: New York University Press, 2013.

Mayer, Adrian. "The Significance of Quasi-groups in the Study of Complex Societies." In *The Social Anthropology of Complex Societies*, edited by Michael Banton, 97–122. New York: Praeger, 1966.

McAdam, Doug. *Freedom Summer*. New York: Oxford University Press, 1988.

McAlevey, Jane. *No Shortcuts: Organizing for Power in the New Gilded Age*. New York: Oxford University Press, 2016.

McCall, Leslie. *Complex Inequality: Gender, Class, and Race in the New Economy*. New York: Routledge, 2001.

——. "The Complexity of Intersectionality." *Signs* 30, no. 3 (2005): 1771–1800.

McCammon, Holly J. and Larry J. Griffin. "Workers and Their Customers and Clients: An Editorial Introduction." *Work and Occupations* 27, no. 3 (2000): 278–293.

Milgram, Stanley. *Obedience to Authority: An Experimental View*. New York: Harper & Row, 1974.

Milkman, Ruth. "Win or Lose: Lessons from Two Contrasting Union Campaigns." *Social Policy* 35, no. 2 (2004–2005): 43–47.

——. *Gender at Work: The Dynamics of Job Segregation by Sex During World War II*. Urbana: University of Illinois Press, 1987.

Mills, C. Wright. *The Sociological Imagination*. New York: Grove, 1959.

Minor, Dylan, Nicola Persico, and Deborah M., Weiss. "Criminal Background and Job Performance" (Working Paper, May 4, 2017), *https://ssrn.com/abstract=2851951*.

Moody, Kim. *US Labor in Trouble and Transition: The Failure of Reform from Above, the Promise of Revival from Below*. New York: Verso, 2007.

Moore, Barrington. *Injustice: The Social Bases of Obedience and Revolt*. Stamford, Conn.: Ray Freiman & Company, 1978.

Moreton, Bethany. *To Serve God and Wal-Mart: The Making of Christian Free Enterprise*. Cambridge: Harvard University Press, 2009.

Naidu, Suresh and Adam Reich. "Collective Action and Customer Service in Retail." *Industrial and Labor Relations Review (2017)*. https://doi.org/10.1177/0019793917748601.

Newman, Katherine S. *No Shame in My Game: The Working Poor in the Inner City*. New York: Russell Sage Foundation, 1999.

Nissen, Bruce. "Alternative Strategic Directions for the U.S. Labor Movement." *Labor Studies Journal* 28, no. 1 (2003): 133–155.

Nowak, Martin A. "Five Rules for the Evolution of Cooperation." *Science* 314 (2006): 1560–1563.

Payne, Charles. *I've Got the Light of Freedom: The Organizing Tradition and the Mississippi Freedom Struggle*. Berkeley: University of California Press, 1995.

Penny, Robert A. and Daisy Rooks. "Outsiders in the Union: Organizing, Consent and Union Recognition Campaigns." *Social Movement Studies* 15, no. 5 (2016): 498–514.

Pitt-Catsouphes, Marcie and Michael A. Smyer. "The Meanings of Work for Older Workers." *Generations* 31, no. 1 (2007): 23–30.

Proust, Marcel. *The Captive: The Fugitive, vol. 5 of In Search of Lost Time*. Translated by C. K. Scott Moncrieff and Terence Kilmartin. London: Chatto & Windus, 1993 [1992].

Purser, Gretchen. "'Still Doin' Time': Clamoring for Work in the Day Labor Industry." *WorkingUSA: The Journal of Labor and Society* 15, no. 3 (2012): 397–415.

Putnam, Robert. *Bowling Alone: The Collapse and Revival of American Community*. New York: Simon & Schuster, 2000.

Robinson, Joan. *Economic Philosophy*. Chicago: Aldine, 2006 [1962].

Rosenbloom, Richard S. "Leadership, Capabilities, and Technological Change: The Transformation of NCR in the Electronic Era." *Strategic Management Journal* 21 (2000): 1083–1103.

Rosenfeld, Jake. *What Unions No Longer Do.* Cambridge: Harvard University Press, 2014.

Rubin, Lillian B. *Families on the Fault Line: America's Working Class Speaks About the Family, the Economy, Race, and Ethnicity.* New York: HarperCollins, 1994.

Rule, Alix, Jean-Philippe Cointet, and Peter S. Bearman. "Lexical Shifts, Substantive Changes, and Continuity in State of the Union Discourse." *Proceedings of the National Academy of Sciences* 112, no. 35 (2015).

Salvatore, Nick, Richard Schneirov, and Shelton Stromquist. *The Pullman Strike and the Crisis of the 1890s: Essays on Labor and Politics.* Urbana: University of Illinois Press, 1999.

Schattschneider, E. E. *The Semi-Sovereign People: A Realist's View of Democracy in America.* Hinsdale, Ill.: Dryden, 1960.

Schneider, Daniel. "Gender Deviance and Household Work: The Role of Occupation." *American Journal of Sociology* 117, no. 4 (2012): 1029–1072.

Schwartz, Michael. *Radical Protest and Social Structure: The Southern Farmers' Alliance and Cotton Tenancy, 1880–1890.* New York: Academic, 1976.

Scott, James C. *Domination and the Arts of Resistance: Hidden Transcripts.* New Haven: Yale University Press, 1990.

Shapiro, Carl and Joseph E. Stiglitz. "Equilibrium Unemployment as a Worker Discipline Device." *American Economic Review* 74, no. 3 (1984): 433–444.

Sharpe, Teresa. "Democratic Spaces and Successful Campaigns: The Dynamics of Staff Authority and Worker Participation in an Organizing Union." In *Reorganizing Labor: Organizing and Organizers in the New Union Movement*, edited by Ruth Milkman and Kim Voss, 62–87. Ithaca, N.Y.: Cornell University Press, 2004.

Sherman, Rachel. *Class Acts: Service and Inequality in Luxury Hotels.* Berkeley: University of California Press, 2007.

Sherman, Rachel and Kim Voss. "Breaking the Iron Law of Oligarchy: Union Revitalization in the American Labor Movement." *American Journal of Sociology* 106, no. 2 (2000): 303–349.

Simmel, Georg. *The Sociology of Georg Simmel.* Glencoe, Ill.: Free Press, 1950.

Simpson, Deane. "Nomadic Urbanism: The Senior Full-Time Recreational Vehicle Community." *Interstices* 34 (2009): 41–46.

Smith, Robert Michael. *From Blackjacks to Briefcases: A History of Commercialized Strikebreaking and Unionbusting in the United States.* Athens: Ohio University Press, 2003.

Soderquist, Donald. *The Wal-Mart Way: The Inside Story of the Success of the World's Company.* Nashville, Tenn.: Nelson, 2005.

Sperber, Joshua, "Yelp and Labor Discipline: How the Internet Works for Capitalism," *New Labor Forum* 23, no. 2 (2014): 68–74.

Stark, David. *The Sense of Dissonance: Accounts of Worth in Economic Life*. Princeton, N.J.: Princeton University Press, 2009.

Sunstein, Cass and Richard Thaler. *Nudge: Improving Decisions About Health, Wealth, and Happiness*. New Haven: Yale University Press, 2008.

Sykes, Jennifer, Katrin Križ, Kathryn Edin, and Sarah Halpern-Meekin. "Dignity and Dreams." *American Sociological Review* 80, no. 2 (2014): 243–267.

Tannock, Stuart. *Youth at Work: The Unionized Fast Food and Grocery Workplace*. Philadelphia: Temple University Press, 2001.

Tufekci, Zeynep. *Twitter and Tear Gas: The Power and Fragility of Networked Protest*. New Haven: Yale University Press, 2017.

Underhill, Paco. *Why We Buy: The Science of Shopping*. New York: Simon & Schuster, 1999.

Vallas, Steven. "Rethinking Post-Fordism: The Meaning of Workplace Flexibility." *Sociological Theory* 17, no. 1 (1999): 68–101.

Varian, Hal R. "Computer Mediated Transactions." *American Economic Review* 100, no. 2 (2010): 1–10.

Voss, Kim. *The Making of American Exceptionalism: The Knights of Labor and Class Formation in the Nineteenth Century*. Ithaca, N.Y.: Cornell University Press, 1993.

Weiler, Paul. "Promises to Keep: Securing Workers' Rights to Self-Organization Under the NLRA," *Harvard Law Review* 96, no. 8 (1983): 1796–1827.

Western, Bruce. *Between Class and Market: Postwar Unionization in the Capitalist Democracies*. Princeton, N.J.: Princeton University Press, 1997.

——. "A Comparative Study of Working-Class Disorganization: Union Decline in Eighteen Advanced Capitalist Countries." *American Sociological Review* 63, no. 2 (1995), 182–183.

Willis, Paul. *Learning to Labor: How Working Class Kids Get Working Class Jobs*. New York: Columbia University Press, 1981.

Withington, Phil. "Company and Sociability in Early Modern England." *Social History* 32, no. 3 (2007): 291–307.

Zelizer, Viviana. "The Social Meaning of Money: 'Special Monies.'" *American Journal of Sociology* 95, no. 2 (1989): 342–377.

Zieger, Robert. *American Workers, American Unions*. Baltimore, Md.: John Hopkins University Press, 1994.

——. *The CIO 1935-1955*. Chapel Hill: University of North Carolina Press, 1995.

INDEX

Page numbers in italics indicate figures or tables

Milton Keynes UK
Ingram Content Group UK Ltd.
UKHW011809201023
431041UK00005B/224